Without Keys:

My 15 Weeks
With the Street People

BY PAT MCDONOUGH

Without Keys:
My 15 Weeks
With the Street People

BY PAT MCDONOUGH

Art by R. Padre Johnson

TERRA SANCTA PRESS, INC.
Hopkins, MN 55343-0576

Printed in the United States of America using New Baskerville TT and Helvetica. The paper used in this publication meets the minimum requirements of American National Standard for Information Services— Permanence of Paper for Printed Library Materials, ANSI Z39.48-1984. The hardbound version of this book meets the minimum requirements for library use.

FIRST EDITION 1996
First Printing October, 1996

Publishers Cataloging in Publication Data: August 1, 1996.
McDonough, Patricia Ann 1943-
    Without Keys: My 15 Weeks With the Street People/Pat McDonough

ISBN 0-9653467-1-4 (cloth), ISBN 0-9653467-0-6 (paper)

Without Keys: My 15 Weeks With the Street People is the most comprehensive personal book on homelessness available. Readers participate with her as this middle-class mother of two is suddenly on the streets in Minneapolis in the winter of '83-'84, struggling to access social services for basic needs and to gain insights into what The System's provision of goods and services to The Homeless is really like. She encounters unmet needs in those who serve, carrying her reader into fascinating stories and varying perspectives: participants', service workers' and volunteers', and the "non-involved." Through vignettes, stories told by Street People, entries from her journal, and drawings of emotions of Street People, readers experience a slice of life becoming familiar with the freedom and frustrations— the surprising daily life of people in pursuit of basic necessities for personal survival. The book deals with comraderie, difficult people, avoiding burn-out in social workers, training volunteers and contemporary issues of housing/homelessness. *Without Keys* is also a spiritual journey from dejection and dismay to hope and trust through attention to inner process, prayer, and personal development. While geographically set in downtown Minneapolis where people call themselves Street People, not The Homeless, this is a book of nationally applicable value in discussion of public policy, and as a teaching tool. It is also an easy, entertaining read.

1. Anthropology - General - Special. 2. Sociology - Homelessness. 3. Sociology - Homeless. 4. Art. 5. Peace and Justice. 6. Public Policy Issues - Housing. 7. Public Policy Issues - Social Services. 8. Social Work. 9. Economics - Work Force. 10. Medical - Nutritional Deficiencies. 11. MN - Hennepin Co. - Minneapolis. 12. Psychology. 13. Psychiatry - Mental Health. 14. Religion - Prayer.
    Extensive Table of Contents. Supplemental Items. Figure List. Update. Appendix. Bibliography. Index. Cover oil painting and pencil/charcoal drawings of Street People by R. Padre Johnson. 30 + 396 pgs.

GN320.M

Published by:

TERRA SANCTA PRESS, INC.
P. O. Box 576
Hopkins, MN 55343-0576

PROLOGUE

The word "homeless" has a sting to it. I never thought I would be part of "the homeless." I am a mother of two sons, an educated working middle-class person, and a business owner earning a living. Yet for about three months in the brutal winter of 1983-84, I was on the street in Minneapolis, Minnesota, out of economic necessity resulting from an interstate court order concerning my children. The court order was a surprise in timing and recommendation: it was not based on the geographic situation, needs identified, nor legal remedies originally proposed. The court order caused a surprise repercussion for me: it required me to stay in Minnesota, where I had no income and no housing options because I resided in Pennsylvania. Since I had no other viable temporary housing alternative in the Twin Cities area, I therefore accepted the opportunity to live in a shelter, among a segment of the homeless who choose to refer to themselves as the Street People. Some of this is a story of wasted lives and broken spirits, of the miserable aggravations that the homeless endure daily, of the ponderous uncoordinated multi-layered bureaucracies that attempt to help but often end up creating chaos. Yet even more, the story is of the unexpected camaraderie of the streets, of the resiliency of the human spirit, and the sustaining power of hope.

Two years earlier I had had a husband, two children, and a five-bedroom house in the country. Although it was my choice to get a divorce, I did not realize how difficult it would be, economically, because there were complications including judicial improprieties, attorneys' conflicts of interest, parental abduction, and multi-state jurisdictions. The previous year, the divorce settlement caused the house and property to be sold and the proceeds divided. My share paid lawyers, and bought me a business suit and a Kaypro CP/M computer (to learn on).

What possessions I did keep from the divorce (far less than what I brought into the marriage) I eventually sold to cover legal expenses when my children were not returned after a parental visita-

tion out-of-state. I sold oak, cherry and walnut furniture that I had
personally restored; family antiques and collectibles; three collections of Depression glass from my mother; a sword from the Civil
War found on my maternal great-grandparents' property near
Antietam MD; first-edition books; a Moroccan brass from my aunt
and uncle; sixteen place-settings of Flow Blue china that had been
in my family for 200 years (and that my grandmother had given me
when I was four.) After a time, I had nothing left to sell. I didn't
realize then that selling things also meant selling family ties, past
and present, selling family history, selling out family memories and
traditions. But it couldn't fit through the eye of the needle where
I had to pass. Looking back, I know that the seven years in court
was a time of testing and intense spiritual growth— a time I would
prefer never to re-live, but a time that has left me wiser, humbler,
more compassionate, and what seems permanently indebted to
lawyers.

*

The setting in which most of the events described here took
place in downtown Minneapolis where Street People congregate,
such as in the Crystal Court, the City Center (a downtown enclosed
three-story shopping mall and fast-food center), the Harvest House
Cafeteria in Woolworth's, the public library, the bus station, and
certain social service distribution points such as the House of
Charity (also known as Brother DePaul's), the Hennepin County
Government Center, Hennepin County Medical Center, store-front
clinics, various offices for social services, and the Skyway. "The
Skyway" is a series of elevated (second or third story), enclosed,
heated passageways which connect most of the office buildings and
commercial spaces of downtown Minneapolis. The sides of the
Skyway are lined with offices, banks, restaurants, and stores, so that
it is possible to walk several miles in a controlled environment in
the downtown on a weekday without having to go outside—
especially in brutal weather. The Skyway has some major terminals
which open up: at the Crystal Court, the City Center, and the
Government Center. These areas are the hubs for spokes of the
Skyway.   The independent social service agencies were not
connected to the Skyway. To reach those, Street People and others
must walk outside, regardless of the weather.

Although the media refer to people who are in the shelter system or sleeping on the street as "The Homeless," the people I encountered referred to themselves as "Street People." To them, "The Homeless" was a term that included not only Street People but also "hobos," "railroad transients," some of the "river-bank dwellers," "bums," "panhandlers," "people under the highway bridges," "people who live in vehicles," and "young people who live in squats." In keeping with their right to be identified as they prefer, I will use the term "Street People" when referring to homeless street people in Minneapolis, and "The Homeless" when speaking of homeless people, in general, as that term applies to the national issue of homelessness.

Every person who lands on the street has a unique story to tell, and in my case, the events that led me there had to do primarily with a nightmare of complex court cases. At the time this story took place, my sons were living in Minnesota under the custody of their father, who had refused to provide certain necessary care after failing to bring them back to me after a visitation. Because of a "gag order" placed by the court, I cannot discuss the court and related details of my story in this book— The reader will have to accept on faith that I had important motivation to be where I was at that time; and reasons, beyond my every effort to provide remedies, concerning why I could not prevent being penniless in that situation. What I can say is that I had commuted between the East Coast and Minnesota to see my children and to appear in court for a number of years. The reason for pursuing the course of action that I did, on behalf of my children, was extremely serious and in order to facilitate seeking remedies for my children, I was unexpectedly ordered by the court to remain in Minnesota for the period of time when this story took place.

*

Between the depressed housing economy of Pennsylvania then and the demands of being on-call to appear in court in Minnesota on one hour's notice, there was no job as an employee that could provide me that much flexibility. Ironically, at the time I found myself "homeless" in Minneapolis, I had a home in Pennsylvania.

I had just completed a one-year contract on Long Island (NY), as housing specialist. When my contract expired, I chose not to renew it and return to my home base in Central Pennsylvania.

In general, my work has been to set up and carry out specific project(s), on contract, for a specific duration (usually years). For a time, I also tried my hand at real estate sales. I had managed housing rehabilitation programs. When absolutely necessary and appropriate between contracts, I drew unemployment compensation. During the period when in Minneapolis, I was not on home ground, and the Minnesota court cases demanded substantial commitments of time and energy. In addition, I had not yet established contacts necessary to procure contracts in the Twin Cities. Therefore I worked as a "temp" during this "homeless" period—clerical, accounting, and data-entry jobs.

*

When the Minnesota court finished one such hearing, at four o'clock on a December afternoon, the court order me to remain in Hennepin County (Minneapolis MN) for what was suggested would be a two-week stay. I could have gotten on a plane and gone home to Pennsylvania, but that would have been letting my sons down and also would have put me in contempt of court. I needed to stay. Two weeks was the initial estimate of how long it would last, but I found the time stretching out, again and again, until two weeks had become nearly three months.

Initially I rented a room at a residential YMCA within walking distance of the court building. When the cheese, crackers, fruit, juice, and trail-snacks I had brought with me ran out, my cash was running out. It was only a few days until Christmas, and I was faced with the alarming certainty that I was about to be on the street. I still had rent and utilities to pay, back home.

To keep occupied and give me a chance to think, I went to the church (St. Olaf's Catholic Church) to sit in the quiet of the sanctuary. I felt a nudge to walk around. I noticed the placard: "Church Office." I found myself rapping on the door. When a mature woman (a nun in civvies) answered, I found myself offering to do volunteer work for a day. She used me three days, to do posting and envelope-stuffing. On the third day, when she asked, I briefly shared my situation with her. She gave me a referral to Catholic Social Services (CSS) nearby on 8th Street. At CSS I was told they might know of something; I should give them time to make a few phone calls and come back the next day. I knew nothing of the shelter system. In a scene that seems ridiculous in retrospect, I arrived at the House of Charity with my flight bag, luggage, folding luggage-carrier, and my executive briefcase— seeing all this baggage, a "guest" announced facetiously, "Well, if it ain't Miss Mary Tyler Moore moving into the House of Charity." I was now a temporary resident at a shelter for the homeless. This was to be my home for the next three months.

✻

THE PEOPLE

While nationally we refer to The Homeless, they are not in any way a homogeneous group. "The Street People" I met included the mentally ill, developmentally handicapped, economically dislocated, under-skilled; couples (consisting of a caregiver and a care-recipient); entire families with small children, dislocated homemakers, battered women, displaced minors, youth who lacked even minimal literacy skills, post-operative patients in recovery, dislocated victims of the family court system and/or administrative law courts, undercover cops, the elderly, the unemployable, the voluntarily retired, the disabled, the disgruntled, and the people I called the "ex's" (a term many people think identifies all Street People); here the ex's included paroled ex-convicts, those recovering from chemical dependency (drug addicts and/or alcoholics), and those others who have not yet become "ex"-anything— the robbers, the killers, and the chemical abusers (drug addicts and/or alcoholics). The majority of Street People I met were displaced by the economic system, in some way, or were mentally ill.

✻

In this book, I also wanted to "label" working professionals— middle managers, secretaries, social service workers— as the People in the Middle. But most readers who might remotely be thought of as the People in the Middle objected so strenuously to being labeled anything that, for the most part, I have tempered those references. Moreover, the people in the middle and the people at the top have the political power to implement some remedies. The disparity between the rich, the middle class, the somewhat disadvantaged, and those completely below the safety net, was very apparent in the Skyway, at the Crystal Court, and at the Government Center, where differences could easily be spotted because of the glaring contrasts. For example, above the Skyway level in the Crystal Court were several lounges for wealthy investors (e.g., doctors, owners of Fortune 500 companies, and the like.)

I often thought of the people privileged to use these lounges as "the women in mink coats and men in the camelhair coats," meaning women and men privileged enough to afford and flaunt ownership of coats made with authentic fur. An item so expensive to purchase that such purchase was beyond the ability of most. But, since then, animal rights issues have displaced fur coats and fur wear has taken on a different political meaning so that such coats now sometimes show up in Free Stores.

Nevertheless, those "at the top of the food chain" have a disproportionate cumulative advantage: wealth, privilege, networks, perks, and incentives. The system works with equal vigor to provide cumulative disadvantages against the working poor and people in all phases of poverty (i.e., working poor, welfare recipients, single-parent heads of households, street persons, underemployed). It is as if this were one more "family secret" of our nation.

In draft form this book had a working title *Falling Through the Safety Net*. In the draft that was circulated, such labels made readers uncomfortable. Interestingly, it was the persons of most wealth who insisted on being part of the middle class. Since the book was first written, however, what has occurred is that more formerly middle class persons have accumulated the wealth and power at the top but their self-identifying labels have not caught up with the realization. In the intervening years, the rich have gotten richer and the poor

have gotten poorer, and the middle class seems to be evaporating.[1]
It seems that the top now wants to be called "the middle," the
middle has slipped toward, and into the net, and the bottom is
below the safety net.

*

APPLICATION

Although I was in Minneapolis when I experienced the situations
related in this book, the circumstances are similar throughout the
United States. Homeless people are not only in cities but also in
the suburbs and in rural areas all across America. Most people
prefer not to see them, but to see past them. With each economic
recession or cut in social programs, the outlook is that more people
will be displaced and become homeless.

According newspaper accounts and reports to the Minneapolis
City Council, as of July 6, 1995, in the previous ten years those
depending on the shelter system in the Minneapolis/Hennepin
County area increased in number by 1,000%. The most current
census data of Homeless in Minneapolis did not survey House of
Charity or the Drake.

*

THE SYSTEM

I use the term "The System" in the broad sense to mean any
agency or organization with which a Street Person must interact in
order to obtain a minimum of basic necessities such as food,
shelter, clothing, mail, check-cashing, medical and dental care,
employment opportunities, legal assistance, and access to bathrooms, places to sit, and telephones. All people need basic necessities, supplies, and support for survival. Street People generally
have exhausted the usual resources and networks to fill these needs.
Many were willing to work; many were in fact working or checking
in daily with work placement services. The vast majority, however,

---

[1]   "An income of $200,000 isn't all that much," Rep. Sonny Bono (R -CA).
    "Making anywhere from $300,000 to $750,000 a year, that's middle class,"
Rep. Frederick Heineman (R - NC)

were unable to work at traditional employment because of mental illness and the restrictions placed on them by their disability income.

Street People lack resources for their basic necessities so The System (as a last resort) is supposed to assist them to obtain the basic necessities, supplies, and support for survival, and (ideally) to enable them to become self-supporting and self-sufficient. Therefore I believe the people who deliver these services, resources, and referrals must be considered alongside the homeless, because The System and those who administer it are inadvertently interdependent with the homeless. To present a realistic picture, the discussion must be about life of both the people who deliver the social services and the street people as well.

*

ATTITUDE

Most Street People I met lived in an "Attitude of Hope" that living on the street and being dependent on The System was not the way it would always be. Those who had such hope seemed to tolerate even the intolerable with endurance, good humor, and fortitude. Those without hope were often immersed in despair or deep-seated rage. Even with hope, it was hard not to be outraged at the absurdities that The System established and the ways it worked to perpetuate dependence. While I was with the Street People, we shared a common bond, that we were all in the same sinking lifeboat, but we were working only as individuals at plugging the holes. The unity was in our expectations that life could and should somehow be different.

*

METHODOLOGY

When I collected these stories, I usually mentioned that at some point I might write a book about my experience and might include their stories. Since I was in the same situation they were in, and I was not there to exploit them or their stories, they seemed flattered that I cared enough about what they said. No one objected. Their stories are written as nearly as possible word-for-word, just as they related them to me. The things that happened to me are also authentic. The places mentioned are real.

I could not tell everyone's story, but I did have a goal to present a sample of most of the kinds of people I encountered on the street. I also wanted to protect the privacy of those about whom I wrote. Therefore, I have taken real stories and real people and blended some of their physical characteristics to create characters in composite. For example, for a story of a person who was mentally ill, I might describe the physical appearance and mannerisms of several persons suffering from a similar mental illness, to create one composite character to represent all the persons in this group. I did not, however, alter the examples, dialogues, or situations; they are from real life. I have also created fictitious names, because I did not learn most actual names. The method I used was to store in my memory the words, manner of expression, and cadence of what people said until I could write it completely each evening. I had been trained in journalism and in interviewing techniques and had used this method for research that I had previously conducted (e.g., books I co-authored for the U.S. Public Health Service.) I also made frequent, brief journal-entries throughout each day, as sort of miniature reality-checks.

In Minneapolis, I had a temporary night job in a bank that required my presence, but required my attention only when the computer's Automated Teller Machines (ATM) jammed at banks in remote locations. It was only really busy at 8 p.m., around midnight, and on Fridays. When a machine jammed, based on a typed trouble-shooting guide, I would instruct the computer to tell the ATM how to fix itself. If this didn't work, I phoned the programmer, who would relay instructions to me on the telephone to type into the main computer to relay to the ATM to threaten it, "Shape up or be replaced with an Instant Cash machine. Machine, you will no longer have humans staying up all night in a bank to give you emotional and technical support." It was during the evening shift, three nights a week, when the computer was functioning properly, that I was free to read or write. The journaling cleared my mind, grounded me, and freed my spirit. I was able to write the first draft of this book and to enter the dialogues of the day's conversations and happenings into my journal. Maintaining my sense of humor and my sense of the ridiculous seemed important, as a way to deal with the frustrations of my own situation.

For methodology of the artwork, see the last paragraph of the Acknowledgements section.

*

ORGANIZATION

The book is subdivided into Parts, each with somewhat different tone and perspective. Part I: The House of Charity plunges the reader into life in a shelter and typical days. Part II: Who Are Street People?, through vignettes and narratives, introduces the variety of circumstances that brought the people I met to street life. Part III: Delivery of Social Services moves the reader through parts of the social services delivery system as a recipient and begins the journey into how this changed me on a deep interior level. Part IV: Necessities and Survival assesses the complex of basic human needs that must be met. The chapter is loosely based on the Corporal and Spiritual Works of Mercy (see Appendix). Part V: Different Needs, Perspectives, and Expectations continues to assess needs. Here the viewpoint purposely shifts among the perspectives of recipient, social worker, and worker-observer, as I did each day, and looks at some of the needs of front-line social workers. Part VI: Public Policy presents a brief assessment of housing and economic policy. Part VII: Feelings, Frustration, Fatigue, and Distress was written in response to questions from cross-cultural (and co-cultural) trainers, psychologists, ministers, sociologists and others who asked for inclusion of information about what skills I brought into this experience that were relevant, and information about changes I experienced within. Part VIII: In God's Refinery is about hope, faith, and changes of attitude. Part IX: Disengaging plunges the reader into the absurdities and incongruities of the last two days of my experience, as I was abruptly psychologically detaching from street and shelter living. Part X: Repercussions and Values is also in response to suggestions of professionals who asked for a statement of what personal priorities came into focus during this experience. Part XI: That Was Then, This Is Now moves the reader into present time, with recent information from other sources. In this chapter, observations and recommendations for change are presented. The Appendix presents useful information that seemed important but fit less well in the text.

✼

THE STYLE

Some early readers have had problems with my verb tenses and shifts in time and perspective. The key is that a *journal entry* is written in present tense. *Reflections,* written later, use past tense. The *narrative episodes* are written in dialogue as they happened. Within a narrative, an *update or a comment* about something which clearly occurred after March 31, 1984, is in brackets or as a footnote. *Interior monologue* appears in italics. *Useful or statistical information* which is not necessarily part of a narrative appears separated by a border or is shaded as well. Journal entries are not always in the exact chronology that they appeared in original journal so that commentaries on a particular subject can be placed more closely together. The sequence is true to the changing tone of my journal as the time progressed.

✼

STATISTICS

Accurate statistical data on The Homeless is almost nonexistent. There have been some attempts at counting The Homeless by making a one night count or one week count. However, on the selected nights, many of the winter-only shelters had already closed. The most recent studies, which attempted a comprehensive approach in the Twin Cities, are now eight years old and suffered from a number of weaknesses in the survey design. For example, the statistical information counts as "coming from out of state" persons who in fact are returning to Minnesota even when it has always been their home base. Some reports do not make a distinction between persons coming to the Twin Cities from other parts of Minnesota as opposed to coming from other parts of the United States. Some do not make a distinction if a person is coming to Minneapolis from St. Paul or going to St. Paul from Minneapolis (both are part of the same metropolitan area.) The 1990 Census data for Hennepin County is also a poor indicator as it lists 1,069 Homeless Persons countywide when shelter workers reported a count in the 3,000 range in Minneapolis alone.[2] Therefore I have not relied heavily on statistical evidence but instead on experiential reporting of my own story, and focused primarily on the window of December 19, 1983, through March 31, 1984, and shall leave it to others to assess current numbers. Since Minneapolis here is used as a microcosm, it is recommended that the reader use this work as a springboard to evaluate the situation of The Homeless, and delivery of social services to them, in the reader's own area.

✳

WHY DIDN'T YOU? WHY COULDN'T YOU?

I have already mentioned that I had sold all the possessions I could. But I am usually asked, "Why didn't you borrow from someone?" While my mother, a senior, sent me money from time to time, when I asked for a loan (at above market-rate interest), she turned me down because she needed it. There were no savings left to fall back on; years of legal battles had cost me more than $42,000, and I was in debt. The losses eventually went much higher. As for friends, some stuck by me, some chose not to "take sides" in the divorce, and a few ended up abandoning me; for the number who abandoned me, I made many more new, more genuine friends. At that point, those to whom I could turn, I had already tapped out. One friend loaned me $400 but it was short term— and I made sure to pay it back on time.[3]

---

[2] Minneapolis is within the confines of Hennepin County, MN.

[3] My journal entry 10/29/83: How wonderful friends have been through all this! I thought I would lose friends by getting a divorce, but I have gained and gained. My old friendships are enriched. The spiritual part of my life, the friendship part of my life, and my writing have taken on wonderful new depth.

I had left no legitimate and honorable stone unturned. I am resourceful and hard-working. Although this is about street people, many ordinary men and women are only one pay check away from being on the street themselves, and many things that happen to street people will also ring true for these readers. Vignettes may be funny, heart-warming, outrageous, distressing, or horrendous. I invite you to stand at this window to view the life of street people to experience it as I did that winter, through my eyes, ears, nose, feet, back, teeth, and other senses— and to experience from the recipient's vantage the front-line workers for the delivery system of social services as well. Join me in walking through that winter from the interior of my spirit and my heart.

✳

DEDICATION

As in my real life, this book is dedicated to my proudest treasures, the delights of my heart: my gold-plated kids, now grown, only for whom all this was worth it.

ACKNOWLEDGMENTS

I express my gratitude and deep appreciation to Catholic Social Services and Brother DePaul's House of Charity and their staffs (including Liz Follsum) for allowing me to stay at the House of Charity; for the social services I received during the brief "homeless" period described in this work; and for certain persons who listened with compassion and served with professionalism during that time, especially my Minneapolis Legal Aid lawyer Jean Farrand and her competent staff; Mrs. Pollack at First Bank System; Cherie Andresen the (good) Guardian Ad Litem; Public Defender Karen Nasby; for two kindly ladies in the Pennsylvania Unemployment Office at Bloomsburg and Milton, PA; the many friends who stuck by me and my children; and five years later to Linda Ojala, (an aggressive and effective attorney my children affectionately called "Our Doberman"), and especially to Judge Gary Larson, a judge of justice, fairness as well as mercy, who eventually made the difference.

My deep appreciation also goes to the following friends for editing and proofreading: Ginny Hansen (The Pen Doctor), Carolyn Hamilton (The Organizer), Dave Garland (studio700), Barbara Pirie (Cross-Cultural/Co-Cultural Expert), Mary Ellen Mueller (MTM, Inc.), Marjorie Kelly (*Business Ethics* magazine). Special thanks goes to Permissions Editor Joan Gordon (Joan Gordon etc., Inc.) and to all the loyal and persistent nudgers, exhorters, encouragers, friends and promoters in my prayer and study groups who would not let me give up on getting the manuscript into print and into the public eye, among them: D. Smith, J. Davenport, and R. Morris.

I want to express my special thanks to R. Padre Johnson for his generosity and sacrifice in creating the original art for this book. He "walked miles in my moccasins" to recreate my journey. For this research in 1996, Padre spent time hanging out with Street People so that he would absorb the emotions, the appearance, and the spirit of street people. From that experience, he has created composite figures to show the range of feelings we all share in the human family, feelings which so clearly come across in the faces and stances of those under the weight, and sometimes freedom, of homelessness. The drawings are portrayals of the essential spirit of characters in the book, as well as of the spirit we saw in the people we met in 1996— their depth and life history expressed in a look, posture, attitude, and appearance.

Join me on this journey of the spirit.

TABLE OF CONTENTS

SUPPLEMENTAL ITEMS

FIGURE LIST

PART I: THE HOUSE OF CHARITY

When I stepped into the lobby of Brother DePaul's House of Charity, a blue fog of cigarette smoke was hanging from the ceiling to about waist level. People were sitting on old plastic chairs, on the window sills, on the radiators. People were standing shoulder to shoulder. Others were sleeping on the floor in parkas. To enter the room, you had to step over these sleeping giants. I wondered how anyone could sleep like that with so much commotion.

It was only 9 a.m. Today "Intake" would not open for another hour. The social workers usually began Intake at 11 a.m., but because of the severe cold, this day they started at 10 a.m. I edged my way in and across the room, and found a small area to sit on the filthy floor behind the TV. I could still remember the Dick Van Dyke public-service TV-announcement advising children to crawl along the floor in case of fire. He was right. The air did seem cleaner closer to the floor.

A heavy-set man was lying on his side, asleep on the dirty carpet. His beltless trousers had slipped down, exposing his behind. I wondered if he had been on the floor like that all night? As he dreamed, his legs jerked and moved the way a dog chases a rabbit in a dream. In the long cold day of waiting, others stretched out on the floor drifting into sleep–sleep like death. They looked so sickly. I felt so sad: People flopped down like dogs on the floor to have a place to lie down. I didn't want to belong here.

I got my turn to meet with the social worker 3½ hours later. She was young, pretty, open-faced, with an auburn permed hairstyle, trim, earnest and compassionate. She really listened carefully. This social worker must have heard about 50 cases before I had my turn.

✳

Dear Journal,

By some confusion, my luggage got locked in the office of the social worker so I just have to make do with what I'm wearing until the office is unlocked tomorrow. This morning, when I walked to breakfast (the breakfast table was in another building two blocks away), the temperature was 26 degrees below zero, the windchill temperature was 66 degrees below zero. Many of the old guys jog the distance. I couldn't. My eye watered and the droplet froze on my eyelashes. My clean clothes were locked in the heated office, but I was locked out in the cold.

*

Dear Journal,

Last night my room was too cold. I slept in my clothes and put my coat over the blankets. I was so exhausted I could have slept anywhere. The wind blew all night.

As I put my socks on the radiator to dry, I discovered the radiator had been turned off. The other part of why it was so cold in here last night was that, at the top, the six-foot window was open over an inch. The opening had been concealed by the window shade, but when the shade fell on my head, I noticed the top sash of the window was open. No wonder I needed to sleep in my coat.

*

Dear Journal,

I feel isolated amid these strangers. I am feeling culture shock. I am thankful to have a place to stay. I especially need to be close to and with my children.

Minnesota is giving me a strong dose of cold weather— that I dislike. The windchill is 61 degrees below zero and I walked outside to a lot of places today.

I just ate a brown bag dinner— a sandwich (expiration date of two weeks ago), an orange with spots, and a wrapped sweet roll which I'll save for later.

Yesterday when I went to Catholic Charities for the first time, I was very hungry. I had a free cup of coffee and a jelly-filled donut there. The carpet mat by the door had puddles of road salt and sand. I tripped on my shoelace, and the donut flew onto that filthy mat. The grape jelly spurted out when it landed. A salty donut— now sort of a roadkill. I stared at it for a moment or two, then snatched it up and ate the donut anyway— that's how hungry I was.

*

Dear Journal,

We have to "LEAVE YOUR ROOM BY 7:30 a.m.   ROOMS REMAIN LOCKED UNTIL 4 p.m."[4]

At 64 degrees below zero windchill, it was extremely painful to walk more than three blocks without getting indoors somewhere, anywhere, to warm up and be out of the wind.   It is vitally important to know where you are going and what's open.   Not that the distances are all that great, but I have such trouble keeping warm even in summer.   I walked about two miles outside in that weather, and about 1½ miles inside the Skyway today.

During the first hours of waiting in lines, a lot of information was traded on what's open what time and where, so you can get inside. Coordinating all the schedules was a real hassle.   I couldn't keep them all in my head.   There were also three centers called "The Branches" where a Street Person could get free coffee and warm up, but they were only open a few hours a day.   At that time, each one had a different schedule each day.   Weekend schedules were weather-dependent.

Breakfast was something else.   It was oatmeal on a tray.   Right on the tray.   The portion was about a quart.   The oatmeal had no salt and tasted like hot nothing.   I poured blue milk on it to cool it off. The Native American across from me said, "Tray milk is always sour— must cover taste with sugar."   People passed me packets of sugar and I made sweet-and-sour oatmeal.   We had a choice of a fruit— prunes, pears, or applesauce.   And a choice of beverage: water, reconstituted skim milk, or coffee, and sometimes grapefruit juice.   I was so afraid I wouldn't get another meal that I ate every bit of it and pocketed the sweet roll to save for lunch.

---

[4]   See Appendix I for complete text.

Then I was out on the street on my feet for the day. Yesterday the social worker advised me to report to the United Way office building this morning at 9:30 a.m. to enter my name on a food list. I waited in line 1½ hours in a hallway. Unfortunately, last night's sandwich was a problem and I had to find a bathroom. When I got back I had lost my place in line, and had to wait for an hour or more again.

Inside the room, I was amazed. I had been told to stand in this line for food. But the room was also being used as a Santa's workshop of sorts— a room full of new toys sorted for gender and age donated by the people of the Twin Cities. I was given a voucher to select Christmas toys for my children. I selected two Matchbox toys, two remote-control cars, a kaleidoscope, and a puzzle. Still didn't know if I would be able to see my kids on Christmas but it was a relief to know that if I did, I would not be empty-handed. That was important to me. Tears trickled down my cheeks.

Under this program, I was entitled to: three toys for each child; and a choice of a Christmas dinner voucher, groceries for a Christmas dinner, or a check for the amount the groceries would have been if I had opted for groceries. The grocery bag had a choice of a big turkey or a ham. Since I had no place to cook here, I took the cash option, but a social worker had put me down for groceries. I waited another 1½ to get that straightened out, but then I got $14 cash in an envelope— That made my Christmas!

Next I went to Catholic Charities to ask for a "Jet Pass," a one month pass for an unemployed person to ride the local metropolitan transit commission ("MTC") bus for 25¢ at certain non-peak hours "for the expressed purpose of going to job interviews. Not good on weekends." Wait-in-line time one hour. By this time I had missed the free lunch at the soup kitchen, so I got a free cup of coffee at the place where I had been in line for the toys and ate the McGlynn's Danish I had saved from last night's dinner bag. There was no place to sit down. I stuffed the toys into my knapsack and headed for the unemployment office about a mile away.

I needed to file a Courtesy Claim today, to preserve my out-of-state unemployment claim rights, since I was not present in Pennsylvania to report in. I stood in that line forty-five minutes to get a number to let me stand in the real line. When I got to the front of that line, this is what happened:

"I can't give you a number because you have an out-of-state claim. Go stand in Line A."

After a twenty-minute wait in Line A: "You shouldn't be in Line A if you don't have a number. It's not polite to force your way ahead. You must stand in line to get a number like everyone else."

"I already stood in line for a number, and they sent me to you because it is an out-of-state Courtesy Claim."

"That's right. I don't handle them. Stand in Line B."

I waited in Line B for a long time because there was no clerk— late lunch hour, I guess. When Line B reopened, "Do you want Pennsylvania to hold your checks or transfer your claim to Minnesota?"

"How long will it take to transfer the claim, before I receive a check here?"

"Hard to say. It would take a while."

"What's a while?" I asked.

"Three months or so."

"I only plan to be here about two weeks. When I transferred it from New York to Pennsylvania, it took three months to get it transferred."

"If you are only here two weeks and I know it will take three months to get it to here, then it could take another three months to transfer it back from Minnesota— you'd probably be waiting six months for your next check. I'll just notify them to hold your checks until you get back. You check in here every two weeks. Now go check the Microfiche Job List, then report upstairs to register for work. You have to do that, or I can't give you credit on your Interstate Courtesy Claim for checking in with our office. You have to complete that."

Inside the Microfiche room I was given an excellent orientation to the job classification numbering system and how the machine worked. While I was searching for jobs, the shift changed and the orientation lady left. Going through the list, I found three jobs interesting. The new lady advised me, "You must go upstairs to get the details on the three jobs."

Upstairs I waited in a short line to get permission to wait in the long line to register for work. When I reached the front of the short line, "I'm sorry. You must go downstairs to the Microfiche Room. You need to have them complete the Tan Card for you, not the White Card."

I went back downstairs where eventually an Unemployment official rescued me. "You're better off going to a Temporary Employment Agency because the Microfiche is at least two weeks to a month out of date, and the competition is rough. Jobs in this city are usually filled within two weeks, before we ever get them posted to Microfiche. Besides you are over-qualified and 40 years old." He stamped my card to show that I'd made the effort with the Microfiche. I didn't get much information on the three jobs I'd found on the list. I didn't feel encouraged. I just wanted to get out of there before I really got down in the dumps.

Then I realized it was 4:30 p.m. I was going to miss visitation. "*My son would be disappointed in me for that,*" I thought. I was disappointed too. After all, to see my kids and to see to their interests was my whole purpose for being out here. To make matters worse, whenever I was late or missed an appointment it was noted in a book for court as evidence of "an uncaring mother."

I took a quarter and called him to explain. It sounded lame even as I said the truth, "I couldn't get there today because everything took longer than I ever realized it could. I had to check in with the Unemployment Office to see whether I could get any money to live on while I'm out here and to keep my Pennsylvania claim up-to-date or it would be terminated. I can't see you tomorrow because that is your dad's turn, so I will see you in two days for the whole afternoon." It was now a "peak hour" so I couldn't use the Jet Pass for the bus. I walked to Brother DePaul's to wait in line for a dinner bag and to get unlocked into a room. That was my day.

At 8 p.m. I sat down for the first time in twelve hours.

*

At the time I assumed that walking, standing, and waiting in line for so many hours was only necessary in the beginning, to get organized so I could get on with real life. I soon learned that walking, standing, and waiting were to take up six days a week every week. On the seventh day there were few lines, but endless walking to avoid being arrested for loitering and vagrancy.

*

Dear Journal,

I think I like my room; at least, it is sort of My Room. It has a brown iron bedstead, an old four-drawer dresser, a closet with a shelf, a radiator, a sink with hot and cold water, and a six-foot tall window. But what bothers me about the bed is that the bed-sheets are thinner than gauze and cover a mattress splattered with dried blood. I can see the blood stains clearly through the sheet. The blanket is full of cigarette holes. The bedspread is ragged and stained.

I decided to wash my clothes in the bedroom sink. It occurred to me that a sink in an almost exclusively male shelter probably had been used for more than washing, but the rules posted on the door stated that all sinks were sterilized weekly (I hoped not weakly) by the staff (sounds like staph). It looked clean. Germs have the decency or indecency to be invisible to the naked eye. The sink stopper didn't fit at all. A plastic bag wouldn't stay put. Finally I used an orange peel from my dinner bag and that worked pretty well.

In the ladies room, the one bathtub had no plumbing for a showerhead. Only the first to bathe got a clean tub. For the rest, the tub looked like a compost pile. For the time being, I resorted to taking Japanese bucket baths— very difficult when the only "bucket" was a styrofoam coffee cup. "*Oh, well. It will only be for two weeks,*" I told myself.

*

Dear Journal,

I have always wanted to master the short story, but I was afraid to tackle dialogue. I just figured out that I can use real dialogue to learn how to do dialogue. I always thought that writers had to make up everything fresh in their imagination that they put down on paper. Now I realize that to help me learn, I can capture dialogue rather than make it up. So journal, you're it. Let's see where it takes us.

*

Dear Journal,

There's an evening curfew. I have to be in the building by 8:30 p.m. and in my room by 9:30 p.m. At that time, a staff member beats on your door to see if you're asleep. It's called "Bed Check."

I look forward now to the curfew check— a staff member knocks on each door and wishes the occupant "Good night." It is pleasant and reassuring to hear "Good night" echoed personally thirty to forty times as he moves down the hall.

If you failed to answer Bed Check, however, your bed would be reassigned. There is a great demand for beds and shelter. Any violation of the rules and you're out on the street.

Even the lobby was full of men sleeping on the floor, packed like sardines. "*I guess it's better to be inside on a floor. Better, perhaps, to sleep like a sardine, than sleep like a horse, standing up,*" I thought. [The following week, it was so crowded I saw men asleep standing up, too.]

This is Christmas week. Who would want to be sleeping outdoors with the windchill 100 degrees below freezing?

At 6:30 a.m. a staff person pounded vigorously on each bedroom door to awaken everyone. (Those who had day labor jobs had gone out earlier.) If you planned on having coffee or breakfast, the next step was to wait in line for 30 minutes for a breakfast ticket distributed at the shelter's front desk to be used at the Food Service 2½ blocks away.

We had to be out of the shelter by 7:30 a.m.— that meant if you were still in the building at 8:00 a.m. you were kicked out of the building for a week. They were merciless about rules— so many more homeless people needed shelter. The good old supply-and-demand theory in action. Or, survival of the most compliant.

*

Dear Journal,

Pages and pages of rules are taped to the bedroom door and closet. The rules have things like:

"Please keep your body clean."

"If you need a change of clothes, tell the desk and they will arrange a token for you to go to the free store."

Another sign read: "We strongly encourage you to wash your clothing in the washers provided during the hours of 7 p.m. and 8 p.m. Anyone caught starting to wash clothes after 8:30 p.m. will be reprimanded." How can 85 or more people get all their clothes washed and dried in three washers and two dryers in 1½ hours or even in one week, with such restricted access to use them!

Tonight I am glad I decided to stay in my room and journal. I needed something to do in the evenings when I don't have to be somewhere else. I'm certainly not ready spend time in the reception room as the only woman with, on the average, 85 seedy men. Lately, because of the extreme cold, there have been 125 men admitted, but only 85 single beds in the building. The remaining 40 can sleep in the reception room: on the floor, on chairs, under chairs, under tables, as well as to sleep standing up.

✳

Dear Journal,

I am surviving but I am still uncomfortable with this arrangement.

The "guests" at the House of Charity often reek of body odor, stale tobacco smoke, unwashed clothes, and unclean coats. The population was never the same. Sometimes the preponderance was mentally ill women, other times young women. At Christmas it was mostly men. Then the men got disposable razors, little samples of after-shave lotions, and men's colognes. The aroma on Christmas day of all the different aftershaves and colognes on more than 100 faces was an olfactory shock. [This lasted for the Twelve Days of Christmas until the razors and samples were depleted.]

Thanks to the free barber, a monk from the Jesus People Church [then located on Hennepin Avenue], most of the men had reasonably neat hair, for a while. But as time passed, and also as different people arrived, most went back to having overgrown

manes sticking out in points from beneath ski caps. I think the
"sticking out in points" is a phenomenon of malnutrition. I have
seen hair like that on Caucasian poor people in Michigan, New
York, Pennsylvania and West Virginia, as well as Minnesota, so I
believe malnutrition must make hair brittle.

*

Dear Journal,
    If I could renovate the House of Charity, I would move some
walls and change the traffic flow. Arrival is through a vestibule.
The front desk is there, enclosed in glass, but it is the same front
desk where 85 to 125 people stand in line at the same time for a
dinner bag, to get room keys, to return room keys, and to get
certain passes.   One would think that these things could be
distributed to an individual all at the same time, but frequently it
required having to stand in line again for each item— and so the
passageway is generally clogged.
    The room to the right is the large room with chairs, TV, and
unmitigated cigarette smoke.   At minimum, it needs a strong
exhaust system and a ventilation system with HEPA (high efficiency
particulate accumulator) filters.   At the end is a desk which is the
TV-stand at night, and where the elderly receptionist guards the
sign-up sheets where you sign up for the right to stand in line for
whatever is being distributed on that particular day.   Her desk is in
the shadow of the Sacred Heart of Jesus, a statue about ten feet
high on a pedestal about four feet high, making Jesus' halo nearly
touch the ceiling.   Some say this Jesus statue was made homeless
after a Catholic church redecorated in response to Vatican II.
Regardless of how it got there, the Jesus statue spends its time
looking out the window, so everyone in the room is behind this
Jesus' back.   I felt some remote comfort to know it was there even
if it was only a gigantic good ol' plaster Jesus ("I don't care if it
rains or it freezes, long as I have my plastic Jesus glued on the dash
board of my car . . . ").
    One has to squeeze between this Jesus and the receptionist to
get to the book-shelf, which had only about 20 old books.   I mean
some had a date of 1890 on them.   Since there were no other
books, these books were well-read: a Gideon's Bible, some classic
fundamentalist texts, Corrie ten Boom's *The Hiding Place*, two copies

of *The Cross and the Switch Blade* by David Wilkerson, a set of Zane Gray's westerns, several journals of Anne Morrow Lindbergh, and a few mysteries.

Behind the receptionist's desk was a door. Inside the door were two desks, four chairs, and one light. The room was about the size of a bathroom. Here, at two intake desks, Catholic Social Services' social workers met with Street People one after another, hour after hour, day after day. Rumor had it that some of the social workers went crazy in this room. During my stay, one had a nervous breakdown. In addition to the stress of the stories, I thought the layout also left the staff in a vulnerable set-up. The desks were at each end of the room, one facing the wall. The room lacked a back way out. The only exit was to go through the door back into the room where 100 or so individuals, some clearly deranged, some angry, were waiting to have a turn. The social workers should have an escape route.

✳

I learned today that a chapel is at the back of the House of Charity. Only on Wednesday nights, Alcoholics Anonymous ("AA") meetings are held in the Chapel. No one else is allowed to use the chapel for any purpose at any time. I asked a staff person, "Why is the Chapel locked except for the once-a-week AA meeting?"

He said, "Every time it has been left open, it has been trashed. I guess some Street People are pissed off with God!"

"Most other AA groups meet every night, not just Wednesday nights," one man said. The AA attendees get to know one another more closely and so are able to be more supportive of one another, than the non-12-steppers here.

"What about a prayer meeting? Would that be a good idea?" I asked.

"Depends. If its one more being preached at, forget it. We get that 'bout everywhere. On the other hand, if we could sing some upbeat spirituals and pray with one another, it might be good fellowship."

✳

Dear Journal,

I am surprised to learn that the Street People do not like to be called "Hobos." They tell me the Hobo class lives on and around trains. Street People live on, around, and near streets, bridges, and the shelter system. They tell me there are also Boat People, here, and in St. Paul, who live along the river year round— but that some of them are even Yuppies. Street People do not like to be called "Bums," either. I got the impression that bums are either drunks or panhandlers. The distinctions are important to them. Later I consulted the dictionary definition, which indicated a bum is one who avoids work and seeks to live off others.

✳

Dear Journal,

It was late at night. I heard a clanging and clanking and talking outside my window. I looked out. The dumpster was just beneath my window. The ice on the parking lot reflected the moonlight in an eerie half-light. Three people were out there doing some kind of a dance in the moonlight, and two other people were in the dumpster. I watched to see what was making the noise. The people in the dumpster were throwing aluminum cans onto the parking lot. The gyrating people were stomping the cans flat. When they were done, they threw all the cans into the back of a pickup truck and drove away. I was moved to realize that this noisy business meant that even from the dumpster of the poorest of Minneapolis' poor, there was still something of economic value to salvage, and people needy enough to want to be salvaging it on such a cold night.

✳

The Crystal Court of the IDS Tower office building had become a gathering place in Minneapolis. The street level of The Crystal Court was a pavilion covered with an expansive skylight system shielding sidewalk cafes, Ticketron booth, flower vendors' stalls, and [at that time] a substantial arrangement of potted plants in about 100 one-cubic-yard plastic planters, interspersed with sand-filled containers of the same size for cigarette butts. Since there were only two or three public benches in all of downtown Minneapolis and the climate is brutal in the winter, the planters in

The Crystal Court were a gathering place for Street People to sit and to wait for the day to pass. The Street People would sit on the plastic planters among the spindly palm trees. Sometimes I saw as many as fifty Street People sitting in the palms during these long days. A few who were unable to obtain a bed-assignment at a shelter would also sleep against these little trees at night.

The unofficial rule in the Crystal Court was that a Street Person could be standing up, sitting in the planter or leaning against a little potted palm tree, but to lie down while sleeping would result in getting arrested for vagrancy. On the other hand, if a person got arrested early in the evening, there would be the whole night in the warm jail, and a few days to a few weeks in the warm work-house—that solved the proverbial need for "three hots and a cot" as well as for clothing and recreation for an entire two weeks. Not a bad reward for taking a nap.

That part of the Minneapolis Skyway System at the Crystal Court was cantilevered around the interior perimeter of the second level (similar to a balcony) on three sides; it overlooked the Crystal Court pavilion [see Fig. 3, p. 37]. At the second level and higher, the general public can look down on the courtyard where the Street People sat.

On the third level was [then] the Marquis Restaurant, with an open balcony that features the Mary Tyler Moore table, made famous in an opening scene of the TV series. A meal in the Marquis restaurant can cost $50 for one baby carrot, one small edible peapod, and two inch square of beef. From this elevated position, while dining, those who could afford the meal could look down on the destitute nibbling stale cake-donut crumbs while sitting in on the palm tree planter-stands. Even higher than this, there are glass enclosed bank offices, where office workers can look down on the Crystal Court pavilion. And higher yet, there is a lounge for the most prestigious "high-level guests" of the then First Federal Savings and Loan, who could munch complimentary fruit, veggies, soft bread-sticks, and refreshments while looking down on The Street People below.

✳

Excerpt from *Search for Shelter*[5]

To state only the obvious, to understand homelessness today one must understand not only why people are poor but why this poverty takes the distinctive form of having no place to live. Homelessness must be approached as one manifestation of the housing crisis at large.

Critical Perspectives on Housing
K. Hopper and J. Hamberg

The Problem

This year 23 million citizens of the richest nation in the world are on food stamps. This means that fully ten percent of our population are unable to afford the normal cost of one of the essentials to life, feeding themselves and their families. This is only one indicator of the sorry state of 'social justice' in our great country. Shelter, the other critical necessity of life, is in a similar state of crisis.

A survey conducted by the Metro Council report done in 1986 stated that: "On any night in the Twin Cities metro area, an estimated 1,100 people are homeless, staying in emergency shelters . . . "

It goes on to say: "The St. Paul Shelter Board reported that in one year 9,939 persons in St. Paul; 23,357 in Minneapolis; and 3,248 in the suburbs; for a total of 36,544 persons in one year were homeless. Another estimate based on interviews with shelter users who reported they had never stayed in a shelter before, revealed the 53,655 individuals used the shelter system in one year."

Who are the homeless?

The same Metro Council report listed three categories of homeless. To this list we have added another group who, although not actually homeless, are either housed inadequately or on the verge of being homeless.

---

[5] Kulman, Jonee, McCormack, Teresa, Grebner, Dennis, and VanDyne, Judith: *Search for Shelter: Architects and the Community Working Together to House the Homeless, Design Charrettes 1990-1991.* Minneapolis: Minneapolis Chapter of the American Institute of Architects, 1991, pp. 1- 2.

Chronically Homeless "People who primarily live on the street, mostly male (70-80%), minorities (50-60%), transient (up to 32%). Because they look homeless, they are often considered the real homeless . . . "

Intermittently Homeless "People who sometimes have permanent housing but often do not. This population if more diverse than the chronically homeless group and may share many of the same problems (mental illness, chemical dependence and poor health), but they are not as severely affected by them. Though they can live on their own with some help, they occasionally become homeless."

Situationally Homeless "People who become homeless as a result of situational stress or crisis. Emotional problems, natural disasters, or changes in the family, the housing market, public assistance programs or the economy are often the cause . . . This segment of the shelter population is increasingly represented by women and children, young and families."

Inadequately Housed Although not homeless, this very substantial group of people puts a 'downward pressure' on those who are homeless by being an increasingly larger group that is occupying a dwindling supply of low cost housing. These people occupy that portion of our housing supply that is old, in sub-standard condition and generally in violation of one or more codes. In 1980, the U.S. Census indicated that nearly 30% of the Minneapolis stock of low cost rental units located in or near the downtown were lost to demolition (urban renewal) or 'gentrification.' It also reported that approximately 2% (41,000 individuals) were living in overcrowded housing. Since that time, it has grown worse rather than better.

Figure 1. Fr. Blue philosopher, astronomer, retired educator.

PART II: WHO ARE STREET PEOPLE?

It was just after Christmas. I was walking toward the Food Service to get breakfast. The cold air cut like steel knives. Each breath stung like a million paper cuts. Toothless Max said something about this being the shortest day of the year. Leroy said, "Yeah, unless you is on the streets; den every day is the longest day of the year." An icy glare hung around the early morning sun. The sky was bright but gray.

THE ELDERLY: "THE CALL"

An old man in a blue parka, blue slacks, blue tennis shoes walked up beside me. Blue said softly, "You know, it isn't really the shortest day if you measure it celestially— the Perihelion— because we are nearing the end of the Century, and until the calendar gets re-adjusted in the year 2000, our Winter Solstice date will not be in synchronization with the heavens. The discrepancy is about four days' difference. It's our calendar that is off— not the heavens." He went on talking about it, becoming increasingly technical. He seemed to know his stuff.

Street people surprised me. Most knew more current events than a newscaster, because they got to read the world's newspapers in the library each day. Access to the world press news and time to read it thoughtfully and thoroughly is open to every literate street person. But the information on astronomy that Blue was sharing took more scholarship. It sparked my curiosity to ask this old man more.

We were in a queue outside the Food Service, when I asked him whether he had gone to college. It was bitter cold but we were somewhat out of the wind. He said, "I not only went to college, I taught college. I have several Ph.D.'s, one in astronomy."

"How did you get on the street?" I asked, making conversation.

Blue leaned toward me and whispered, "I was a Catholic priest. Sometimes a parish priest, sometimes I taught at a university."

"Well, how did you get here? Is this a ministry?"

"No, it is a misery!"

"Well, what are you doing here?"

"It's a long story, but then this is a long line. I was born in Minnesota and went to school here. I went into the seminary when I was a little boy— before I knew what it was. When my friends answered the 'Altar Call' at a retreat, I did too— I wanted to be with my chums. I was really too young to make such a decision. I entered the order and was ordained. With the decline in young men entering the priesthood, it became an order which did not expand. As I grew older, fewer and fewer men entered the order— they wouldn't dare recruit now like they did then."

"Anyway, after 50 years of service, when it was my turn to retire, the Provincial General told me, 'The order is bankrupt. There is no other source of funds. We didn't withhold social security for anyone because we had enough retirement fund before. I'm sorry but you will have to manage on your own'."

"Well, I just couldn't. So here I am. I am an old man, too old to work, and I'm not too well. I think I must be about 80. I rue the day I answered the call. It was not for me."

After that morning, whenever I wrote about him in my journal I referred to him as Father Blue, not just Blue.

✳

VULNERABILITY TO THEFT AND ETHICS OF STEALING NECESSITIES

Conversation this morning began with the topic of clothing— for example, where to get free clothes? What gloves are the warmest? How to secure a plastic bag under your coat to provide protection from the wind, and where to get the clean large plastic bag. How to stuff newspaper down your pant legs. Warm clothing was very much on our minds. The Free Store was cleaned out (high demand) and many guys needed shoes. Most especially needed socks and underwear, not just long underwear. These items weren't likely to be donated. There's probably a law against underwear.

"Them Free Stores never gots underwear," said Dennis, the pudgy guy with a young face and thinning hair. He was talking to the stocky lumberjack, Jack, next to him.

A "Free Store" is a place where you can receive donated used clothing, free. To be admitted to the Free Store requires an authorization voucher. Therefore there was yet another line to stand in to prove Need-and-Eligibility before you could stand in another line at another place to get access to the clothing. I hoped they took a person's word when they said they needed undergarments.

Another man joined in and contributed his solution for obtaining underwear, "Go to the Hennepin County Medical Center linen supply closet. Just walk by there real smooth, and reach your right hand on the pile as you go. The scrub suits are one size fits all." He showed us the blue ones he was wearing under his pantleg.

The lumberjack was wearing a homemade leather cap like a yarmulke, and a hand-stitched leather vest. He said, "My logging camp in the North woods upstate shut down because of the severe cold. Won't reopen 'til the weather is ready to stay above zero. I stayed in my cabin as long as I could, but the wind was fierce, and it was impossible to stay warm, so I finally gave in and came into town." He looked down past his beer belly and pointed to his feet— "These boots I got from the Free store is too small, but I had to have something. My duffel bag was stolen yesterday. Everything I owned was in it, even my coat."

A lot of talk was about the ethics of stealing necessities. This discussion continued to center on clothing. "Yeah, a lot of us had clothes stolen this week. It's cold. People gets desperate," said Duluth, the tall man, about 40, with wavy hair and freckles.

Ed, a scrawny toothless man, commented "Yeah, coats is important. Last week, I was let out of the Florida State Pen with only the summer stuff I had on when I was incarcerated. I was released on parole with no coat or nothing. Just my summer clothes, my watch, and a bus ticket home to Minneapolis and an order to report to a Parole Officer here within 36 hours. I grew up in the Twin Cities."

No one interrupted his story, so the thin man in the sheepskin jacket continued, "In Hagerstown, Maryland, I had to wait outside for a change of buses, and the wind was blowing fierce, that damp

Atlantic cold. My fingers was numb, my arms ached, my feet were freezing. I was shivering bad. All I could think of was, 'I gotta get a coat, 'cause if it's this cold in Maryland, what's it going to be like in Minnesota'."

"I was pacing up and down the sidewalk and stomping my feet," Ed continued. "I looked up. There in the store window across the street was a wool-fleece-lined leather coat. I was so cold, I didn't even think. I just went into that store, took the coat off the mannequin and put it on. It fit good."

The waiting line inched forward as he continued: "Then I seen my bus pull up. I rushed across the street and onto the bus. It wasn't 'til an hour later I noticed I still had the hang tags dangling. Everybody could see that I hadn't paid for the coat. It didn't even cross my mind this was a violation of parole," he said, shaking his head.

An older man replied, "I been cold before. And I been let out of prison before, just like you. But I don't steal nothin'. The only thing I owns is my self respect. Stealin' eats away that self respect. I don't do nothin' now to lessen my self respect 'cause that's all I have left. And it's valuable. So I don't mess with stealing— cold or no."

I was so fascinated by that conversation, that it was several hours later before I realized that I had been standing in line with 2 ex-cons. The men didn't seem like the purse-snatcher type, but I wondered what they had done. As a precaution, that was the last day I carried a purse on the street (I preferred to use a kid's type of rucksack anyway.) Moreover, it seemed silly to carry a purse when I had no money to put into it. It seemed even more ridiculous to carry a purse just to pretend I had money in it, when the people I was with had so little of anything, especially money. Conventional wisdom would say I ought to be afraid, but since I didn't have anything worth stealing, I supposed I didn't have a reason to be afraid. Janice Joplin's hit recording *Me and Bobby*

McGee popped into my head: "Freedom's just another word for nothin' left to lose."[6]

*

PERSONAL SAFETY: "OLD-FASHIONED CHRISTMAS DINNER"

The whole time I was on the street, the only time I think I might have gotten mugged was on Christmas Day. My younger son was with me on a pass, and we were discussing computer software and games and wearing the best of our limited wardrobes. We were walking along a narrow path through the snow past the Grain Exchange Building. I didn't exactly know where we were going, but I had heard that a family-owned restaurant, The Flour Kitchen, offered free Christmas dinners annually as thanksgiving to God for the restaurant's prosperity during the year.

A huge man, over 6 feet tall and about 300 pounds of muscle, was making his way along the narrow path in front of us. He was wearing beads, a leather jacket, and a black felt hat with a large feather in it. He seemed to be listening to what we were saying. Suddenly he backed into a space between 2 buildings and raised his arms over his head and leered down at us. I looked up into his black hardened eyes and wondered if this was it. Quickly I improvised, "Hey, man, is this the way to the free food?"

His whole face crumbled before my eyes. I've never seen anyone so disappointed. "Oh, come on," he said. "Follow me. You broke too? This way to Christmas Dinner"

"Yeah, it's hard times this year."

That was as close as I came to an "incident." We enjoyed the meal at the Flour Kitchen. As we stood in the cafeteria line, we exchanged a few pleasantries with our former would-be attacker as the volunteers loaded turkey dinner with all the trimmings on real plates with stainless steel flatware. We said a private Thanksgiving for this wonderful meal. Accepting it was a humbling experience. I remembered other Christmas dinners with friends and family in our big country kitchen. This was a far cry

---

[6]Lyrics and music by Kris Kristopherson, Combine Music Corp., EMI Music Publishing, 810 7th Ave., NY, NY 10019.

from home. We didn't linger because the line waiting to get in was so long.

Figure 2. "This way to Christmas dinner."

RELATIVE SAFETY [7]

Since I had prayed for a place to stay when I could no longer afford a motel or the YMCA, I accept that the House of Charity was an adequate answer to this prayer.

During this period I had certain knowledge that my life was in danger. My children's father (my former husband) had vowed, repeatedly and publicly to kill me, so at that time I knew my true danger was the risk my ex-husband presented. In comparison, being with the Street People felt pretty safe. In fact, some legal professionals felt it was a great cover.

I even pictured a cartoon— Frame 1: I am on the street. Frame 2: My ex-husband shows up. Frame 3: He is inundated by bums and bag ladies flailing him with all manner of bags and bedrolls. Frame 4: Intimidated, he flees in terror.

＊

THE MARGINALLY EMPLOYED: "DEFENSIBLE SPACE"

The following morning a long-haired man in a shabby, gray business suit carrying a leather brief case was in the breakfast queue. His stringy white hair had been touched up with gummy Grecian gold formula. He didn't talk much but in conversation I overheard him say, "I'm in Insurance. A licensed salesman. I make sales calls every day." Behind him in the line were two Black men [I named Mike and John], then Father Blue, then me.

We went inside in the same order, receiving toast and creamed corned beef slopped right onto our trays. The rule was to sit in the

---

[7] I later related this to the Jess Lair comment:

> You go most safely when you don't know where you go because then you are so fully conscious that you don't know where you are going that you pay careful attention to all clues and signs. You walk in a meditative way, conscious of the present moment, so then you are safe.

And I also related strongly with the title of his book.

Jesse K. Lair, "*I Don't Know Where I'm Going, But I Sure Ain't Lost*". New York: Ballentine Books, 1981. p. 20.

first available chair at the first available table. An unkempt insurance man sat down and plopped his leather brief case on the chair next to him. Mike followed him to the table and gently picked up the briefcase to set it on the floor so he could sit on the chair. The Insurance man rose abruptly and pulled a switch-blade. "I've claimed that chair. You touch it or my things, you're dead."

"Man, what you so uptight about? You don't own this chair. You know the rule. We come here to sit and eat and hit the street."

"You get away from this chair or I'll kill you."

Mike, John, Fr. Blue and I made an about-face to a table far in the back, rules or not. The insurance man won one chair for his body and four chairs for his brief case. Either the briefcase contained contraband, or this man was willing to kill for an empty chair that he didn't own.

I was constantly amazed at the turf wars among those who had nothing. I think when a Street Person gets a little smidgen of opportunity to establish a physical space boundary, it can take on an inflated value. In the evenings in the House of Charity, there were occasional altercations about how large a boundary a person could create around their person— no easy task when 85 or more people are sharing a crowded, smoke-filled room around one 13-inch television.

I know my social distance is usually three feet, more if I'm with strangers. Standing in crowded lines during the day doesn't allow any such niceties. When the House of Charity reception room became the TV room in the evening, I still felt too uncomfortable in such crowding to enjoy watching TV. I generally went into that room when I had a purpose to be there, to wait in line for some necessity like a tiny box of Tide, distributed once a week. I seldom sat out there in the evening.

✳

THE ALCOHOLIC: DULUTH'S STORY OF UNCLE JAKE

During a severe blizzard one Saturday, the House of Charity gave special permission to let us sit in the lobby for the day, even though we remained locked out of the other rooms. Without exception, TV viewing was only permitted in the evening. We were locked out of the sleeping rooms until 4 p.m. Card playing and games were prohibited (apparently in the past tempers had flared and fights had ensued when these pastimes were permitted.) To pass the time, we swapped stories.

Sitting in the chair next to mine was the tall lean man with freckles. He was well-groomed, had horn-rimmed glasses framing expressive hazel eyes. He spoke well, looked clean, new to street life. His hair was thick, dark, softly wavy. Had he had upper teeth, he could have been handsome. He said, "I've just got outta alcohol treatment in Duluth a couple a days ago," so I referred to him as "Duluth."

He told me the following story about his Uncle Jake, an incredible alcoholic. Duluth said, "My uncle Jake had the habit pretty bad, and it was putting his family in a bad way. Never enough money for bare necessities, because his drinking inconvenienced his being employed, and he loved his drink so much. His concerned wife, known as Aunt Alice, became a master spy, sleuthing out his hiding places in the medicine cabinet, the back of the toilet, in his shoes in the closet, and behind the paint cans in the garage. It became harder and harder for him to hide his supply, but he was a resourceful man, and he intended to continue to cultivate his taste despite his wife's determination to enforce temperance by "pouring every last bottle down the drain."

"Because of their financial condition, more and more things around the house were breaking down, especially the car. Uncle Jake's car seemed to be going downhill as fast as he was. He spent more and more time working under the hood. Since it became inconvenient to pass Aunt Alice whenever he went inside to get a little nip, he adapted the car windshield washer system to hold his supply. He put cups in the glove compartment and dispensed gin or vodka via a diverter tap."

"Since Aunt Alice was finding fewer and fewer bottles in the house, but Jake continued to be in a decline, Alice increased her surveillance. When she found the cups in the glove compartment, she knew there was a supply in the car but she could never pin down the hiding place. She even removed the seats but never found the hidden bottle. Every search proved fruitless— until the car had to go in for the annual state vehicle inspection. The windshield washers were inoperable. The inspecting mechanic discovered the hose leading to the glove compartment. When he disconnected it, he got splashed with vodka. You can imagine Aunt Alice confronting Jake on that one, and Jake's promises to reform."

Duluth smiled. We leaned forward to urge Duluth to continue the story. He went on: "For some time after, Alice found no more bottles, but as spring came Jake spent most of his time working the garden. It wasn't until us kids took a drink of water from the garden hose that my cousins and I discovered the gin in the hose."

Duluth led as he remembered the details. "One day we, that was my father Bill, my stepmother and I, went to visit Aunt Alice and Uncle Jake. Alice confided in Bill her concern over Jake's drinking and health. The next day, the family made plans to go to town for an all-day shopping trip. Since the car would only hold four, Jake was more than willing to stay home."

"Two miles out of town, Aunt Alice was so fretful, obsessing about the probability of Jake tying one on, that she insisted, 'Bill, take me back home. I know Jake has a bottle somewhere in the house and if he drinks all day, he will be dead before we get home.' Bill could take no more of Alice's carrying on, so to pacify her (and escape) Bill offered, 'Alice, we will go back, but let me out at the corner and I'll walk to the house and stay with Jake to be sure he doesn't drink all day. I promise. You all can enjoy the shopping trip.' The plan seemed to satisfy Alice."

"When Bill walked through the kitchen doorway, Uncle Jake had just reached deep into the flour bin, pulled out his bottle of Echo Spring and was gulping it, oblivious to the flour covering his sleeve, down the front of his flannel shirt, and all over the floor. 'There'll be all day to clean up and hide the clues,' Jake rationalized."

"'Put that away and get this cleaned up so Alice doesn't find out. I promised Alice I'd keep you sober today,' Bill said."

"'Aw, shucks, Bill. I'm just beginning to enjoy the day. You aren't going to ruin it for me, are you? Let me pour you a little taste.'"

"Just then Aunt Alice's booming voice filled the kitchen, 'Ruin it for you? You betcha I am! Gimme that bottle! You're going to AA right now or you're going to get out for good. And clean up that flour, too!'"

✳

The Alcoholic: Duluth's Own Story

Duluth went on to say, "My uncle Jake chose AA and we took him there. To our surprise, it worked for him. But I will never forget how much imagination Uncle Jake used. As a kid, I admired his hiding places," Duluth reminisced.

"I guess I admired Uncle Jake too much because I sorta followed in his footsteps. I just got out of treatment last month, upstate. I never want to have to go through Detox again. They put formaldehyde in me like I was being embalmed."

"I used to be in big business. I owned a shipping corporation based in Duluth, but my clientele covered the world. My income was in the six figures. My assets were in the millions. My first wife was a dream. I know that now. I was too busy then with my business to spend much time with her. We never even had any children. My second wife gave me back all the hell I had put my first wife through. I started to drink, socially I thought."

"When we had both had enough of the marriage, she got a top-notched lawyer. He was good too. He advised her to move to a certain county in California that was known for giving corporate wives high divorce settlements. She got the kids, took the company, and everything I owned. I guess I could have prolonged the fight but I wanted out of the marriage and I didn't want to have two alimony payments and child support. I gave her the company in lieu of monthly payments so she wouldn't be on my neck all the time," Duluth said.

"After she left, I know my drinking got out of hand. I didn't want to be another Uncle Jake, so finally I went into AA. I made that corporation from scratch after the war, and I can do it again. As long as I stay with AA I'll be all right."

He went on, "When I was drinking, I lost my visitation rights with my kids. I miss them so much. I really need to be a father to them. It's a big part of my life. She doesn't understand that. She thinks only mothers have parental feelings."

"I tried for a month to get a job up on the North Shore and over to Chicago, but they all said I was over-qualified. I've been trying to get work here too. Even day labor. Anything. I only have $1.15 left. I gotta get work. I can't leave town just now because the weather is too bad to hitchhike, and I can't afford a bus ticket." He ended his story, stood up, took a stretch and strolled out of the room.

Later that day, he spent his last money on a pack of cigarettes, and Dennis told him how to go about applying to get a free bus ticket out of town. A week later when the weather cleared, he left for California. He said his daughters lived there, and he hoped to find more job opportunities for someone with experience in the shipping business. He seems a determined, optimistic man. I hope he becomes one of AA's success stories.

*

CHEMICALLY DEPENDENT STUDENT: "TOGBA'S CAR"

Conversation then turned from alcohol to drugs. An African exchange student, Togba, joined the discussion.

"I'm living here because I got into trouble at the University. When I got suspended I had nowhere else to go. They are letting me stay here until I get something worked out with the University."

The student continued, "When I came to this city, I trusted everyone and made friends easily. My new friends took me to parties. We had good times. But they were false friends. They got me into trouble, and then I did not understand the consequences. That also got me into trouble with the University. My friends did not warn me about anything. 'Just try this, you'll like it.' Now I have this big trouble, and I never have any money either."

"My car broke down, too. While I was trying to get parts, it was ticketed for being on the wrong side of the street— something about snow plow rules. I moved it to the other side but that became wrong too because it was then on the other side of the street overnight and past 8 a.m. the following morning, so I got another ticket. I still couldn't get the part I needed right away because it is a very old car. The part was back ordered. I pushed it to another street that didn't have an 8 a.m. rule. It was most heavy. Then while I slept that night it snowed, and that made the snow emergency law occur on that street during the early hours of the snowfall. The snow removal crews had it towed away. I did not know of such snow-falling rules before my car was ticketed and towed away. The first ticket I owed about $15, then $85, now it must be $120 to get it out of the Impoundment Lot, and it still won't run. When you are flat broke, a car is no asset."

His car troubles were typical of the few others at the House of Charity who did own cars. Most here no longer had this symbol of their former lives. I was not completely sympathetic about this student's money troubles because others told me that when he did get money, the expenses of his addiction took priority over car parts. Since use of any chemicals— drugs or alcohol— was absolutely against the shelter rules, he was only at the House of Charity a short time. Of all the people I met at the House of Charity, he was the only one I knew of who was on hard drugs.

*

POST-OP AFTERCARE: "SQUARE SHOULDERS"

Next a man called "Square Shoulders" told his story. He had picked up the nickname because he always had time to listen to somebody's troubles. Here he was the unofficial counselor-in-residence. Square Shoulders was a slight, muscular man who had an aura of energy and purposefulness. We were eager to hear his story. He began, "I grew up here on the Southside. I got married at 18. Nancy, my bride, was 16. My buddies placed bets on how long the marriage would last. On our 20th wedding anniversary we called in all the bets. With compound interest, there was $1,000 in the till."

"In those years, everything was right. A few months after the wedding, I went into the Service and was trained as a nurse. I loved the work. I sent my pay home, and Nancy put it in the bank. When I came home from the war, we bought a house and a new car with the money we had saved. I was able to go to school on the GI Bill to study psychiatric nursing and got a Master's Degree in that and Social Work."

"We had it all. We had love, communication, common interests, fun and friends. She was pretty. She was small like me. I loved her beautiful long straight hair. She let it grow for me the whole time I was away."

"One night I had a nightmare that I was choking. I forced myself to wake up, but I continued to gasp for air. I couldn't breathe. Still half asleep, I was aware that I was being restrained, and I couldn't get air. I didn't know what was happening. It felt like a nightmare, but by then I knew I was awake. I flailed my arms and legs and the constriction in my throat got worse. I was losing consciousness, but Nancy woke up. She realized I was tangled in her hair. She had to roll me over and over to get my neck free so I could breathe again. After that I loved her beautiful short hair."

"When I graduated, I went to work in mental hospitals and worked especially with abused children. I worked up higher and higher in the child protection system and had progressively more responsibility and pressure. I was getting farther and farther away from patient care."

"I took up disco skating to work off tension and worked part-time at a skating rink. My competition skating got so good that I had a room of trophies and everything."

"Then Nancy got sick. I got irritable on the job. I wasn't sleeping good. I snapped at patients and clients. I was short with myself. There wasn't time for skating to let off tension, because I had to spend more and more time taking care of her. She was very ill. From the strain, I was turning into somebody else. I was turning into the worst possible me— a me I didn't even know existed, a me I didn't even want to be with."

"My wife died."

"When she died, my grief was too much. I got bleeding ulcers. I was sick, a physical wreck— I had lost 85 pounds. My grief was overwhelming. And I was burned out mentally. I had to take leave from my job to get my stomach fixed. But I was so sick and run down that I couldn't go back to work as fast as I had planned."

"There was a mix-up in the bureaucracy, and I lost my job. The worst part was that my severance and retirement pay got tied up in red tape, and I had to sue to get it. I have had no income whatsoever for six months. I'm not eligible for Unemployment or General Assistance as long as the court case is pending. With no money, no family living, I had no place to go after the surgery. The House of Charity took me in while I recuperate. The doctors have confined me to bed rest during the day, and I can't leave the building except for meals."

"So I was sick, burned out, without funds, grieving, recovering from surgery, and with no place to go. That's how I got here. As soon as the doctors say I can work and my checks come through, I can go back to my old job. In the meantime, I try to help out here whatever way I can."

✻

THE EX-CONVICT: MAX

Max looked about 65 years old, but he claimed to be 45. He was the short, scrawny, toothless ex-convict with thinning white hair. He told me a number of stories about what led to his incarceration, but the only theme that was the same in all of them was that he was a local preacher's son, an alcoholic, and had embezzled funds from some place. Max was a character and could easily have been a creation of Charles Dickens. He was slithery and ingratiating, constantly "borrowing" cigarettes, but never sharing or paying back. The other ex-cons treated him with contempt. Many said "Tooth-lessness is valued in prison prostitutes— probably the way Max kept himself in butts."

Max bummed cigarettes until every man at the House of Charity was ready to kill him on sight. Whatever he did that was annoying, he covered by saying, "I did it because I thought you wanted me to." No matter what a person said, he made it sound like he was martyring himself to please the other person— "I don't think I should do that, but I'll do it if you want me to."

Max was a trouble-instigator, a chaos-creating crazymaker.[8] He dropped little sly hints here and there that seemed to raise people's blood pressure. He was a short fuse setting other people off. But for all of his icky aspects, Max knew the ropes on the street and was very helpful to me: answering questions, introducing me to places

---

[8] Julia Cameron, *The Artist's Way: A Spiritual Path to Higher Creativity,* New York: G. P. Putnam & Sons, 1992, pp. 44-5, defines the term as follows:
Crazymakers are those personalities that create storm centers. They are often charismatic, frequently charming, highly inventive, and powerfully persuasive. And . . . enormously destructive. You know the type: charismatic but out of control, long on problems, but short on solutions. Crazymakers are the kind of people who can take over your whole life . . . . Crazymakers like drama.

open on Sunday such as the Hennepin County Medical Center (HCMC) canteen. He was also a willing listener to many of the young women who needed to talk.

*

DERANGED, DOWNWARDLY-MOBILE WOMAN MENTORS YOUNG GIRLS: "BENSON & HEDGES"

I had seen her about the Skyway throughout the day, a tangerine-colored crepe scarf and a lavender-colored silk scarf tied over her brassy dyed-orange hair. Her eyes were hidden behind mirror sunglasses, and thick eyebrow pencil covered the gray eyebrows. She wore a fitted rayon dress under a full length silver fox fur coat. The fur looked as if it supported a living ecosystem all its own.

Later I saw her in the crowded waiting room at the shelter where men and women were sitting on the window sills, the radiators, and the floor. She was sprawled lying on the floor beside her shopping bag of 'treasures,' with her knees bent and legs spread wide, rocking her legs from side to side bellowing a cloud of the peculiar sickly sweet odor of old urine, and of too many days in the same clothes. She was smoking cigarettes back to back, lighting one off the other so there was no interval unlit. Between puffs, she hacked, coughed, choked, and occasionally became blue in the face. When she paused between puffs and coughs, she would take a long drag, then sing-song muttering to herself as she exhaled.

Soon something pricked her memory and she rolled on her side. Without taking her head off the carpet, with the hand closest to the floor, she clawed through the red shopping bag, pulling out old underwear, apples, scraps of paper. The other hand held the bag open and the cigarette up. She pulled out lipstick and applied it with a sable brush. She rummaged again and found a series of four passport-style coin-op photos of herself, looking just as she did on the floor, a mirror image of mirrored glasses and crepe scarves tying back her matted gray hair. Rolling onto her pack, pushing her glasses up into her hair, she studied the photos at close range, singing a whiny lullaby to her image.

Later that night, as I headed for the bathroom, I heard her whiny singsong again, mixed with moans and groans. Afraid she was ill, I looked in her open door where she was laying on her bed with her hand fingering inside her blue bikini panties. She was wearing a black lace bra and was on the fur side of the tarnished silver fox. Her body seemed much younger than her old face. She did not care that the door was open.

The next morning as we waited in line for breakfast tickets, she was talking to the well-mannered African student, Togba, who had told me his troubles with his car. As she spoke, her hand, at first on his arm, slid up to his shoulder. He stepped back to the wall to disengage, but she ignored "social distance" and put her face directly in front of his and leaned against him as she whined an incoherent story in a too-loud singsong voice— a story in which certain words were emphasized for greater understanding.

"Would you believe a story of a mad man who tried to kill me because he loved me so much, but I, I mean, the woman in the story just loved to share literary interests with the man next door. And the angry man she was married to wanted to kill her, but, well, you're such a handsome young man, you really cannot know what it is like. I need you. Won't you please help me? Because the climax of the story— you know what a CLIMAX is— the climax to the story wasn't so important as understanding that there needed to be more stories so there could be other more accentuated climaxes. Because social intercourse is an important part of any good story, and you must save me from something awful that could happen at any time."

"Because after the angry husband and his wife found out about the climaxes to the stories during socially important engagements, his wife got jealous and came over to my house. And she climbed into my bed and really got close socially, if you know what I mean. And if you don't help me she might do that again, and that might be awful because I could like that kind of engagement better than bringing out a good plot and inserting the main dramatic point with someone who could make a good story with me as the star. Don't you agree? Isn't it important that we begin to share literary interests together?"

The student was pinned against the wall, and no man would do anything to assist him to extricate himself from this embarrassing predicament. They just turned aside grinning. She continued to lean on him during this rambling discourse, slowly working one hand down from his shoulder while the other massaged the back of his neck. The student was leaning away from her but that only resulted in arching his back, to her increasing delight. At last the line for breakfast tickets started moving, rescuing him from further literary discussions as we all passed through the line and out the door.

That evening, in the hall just outside my door, I heard her talking with Marla and Darleen. Marla was a street-smart woman about 18 years old who recently learned she was pregnant; her parents threw her out. Darleen, on the other hand, was shy and mentally much younger. She recently had been turned out of St. Peter's mental hospital.

With perfect diction, the woman said to them, "Young ladies, I know you don't know these things, so I must tell you. How else are you to learn how important some things are if not from a true lady? I see you both smoke, and that you smoke ordinary cigarettes. You must understand, girls, how this looks. You must be careful how you look to other people. Appearances are far more important than you realize. So while you are here, just follow my lead. For example, your cigarettes are a brand that is *declassé*. Always be aware that people are watching you. You must be an example of decorum, taste, and sophistication. If you are going to smoke, you should smoke only Benson and Hedges, as I do, so that people will recognize quality in you as they do in me. Now promise me you will do as I do. Remember, Benson and Hedges."

That lady checked out the next morning.

Several days later, the police asked us about that lady and showed her photograph. Marla and Darleen were now out somewhere. "Any of you ever see this person before?" the cop asked.

Cathy challenged the cop, "What do you wanna know for?" The cop said grimly, "That lady is a prime suspect in a multiple murder on Lowry Hill. We have reason to believe she murdered her neighbors and her husband and disposed of the bodies by carrying them off in pieces in plastic shopping bags. We found parts of them in dumpsters around town."

✳

UNWILLINGLY EMANCIPATED MINOR: CATHY

Cathy never really did tell me her story, but I heard her tell someone else. Cathy was a local, a St. Paul girl. Her mother decided to remarry; her step-father didn't like kids. Her mother told her "You and your brother have to go." So when Cathy's mom remarried, Cathy was out of a home and a family. Her brother hitch-hiked to Florida, and she lost track of him. She said she had been in and out of the shelter system for about a year and a half. After she was kicked out, she got into drugs. She said she had not been a user while living at home. Recently she had been in chemical dependency treatment. For her, the House of Charity was aftercare, because she could not afford a *bona fide* aftercare facility.

The kids in aftercare at the House of Charity got to eat fresh fruit, fresh vegetables, real meat, fresh bread, and whole milk. It was based on one theory that a malnourished body craves alcohol and drugs to make up for what is lacking, and a poorly fed spirit is more likely to give in to temptations. The kids in aftercare got no food discarded from a vending machine or moldy food like the rest of us got in the dinner bags. We all would have preferred to be on their aftercare diet.

*

AN UNASSIMILATED IMMIGRANT: "LUIGI'S SECRET"

One man I'll call Luigi was an Italian immigrant. According to the Street People, Luigi had come over on the boat in the 1920s as a young boy. They said he never learned English. No one knew if he had ever had a job or not. He never attempted conversation with anyone and was severely withdrawn. I began to notice Luigi, because it seemed no matter where I went, especially Legal Aid or the unemployment office, there was Luigi standing near the doorway in his baggy brown polyester suit and rundown wing tip shoes. Luigi had a unique quality about him that let you know when he was around. He munched garlic. His pockets bulged with garlic. His body reeked of garlic. Later, when I was doing research on the immune system, I realized that Luigi was probably onto something— garlic has antiviral and antifungal properties. Was garlic the secret to Luigi survival outdoors in windchill of 60 below, wearing only a cotton shirt and a threadbare polyester suit?

*

BATTERED WOMAN: BARBARA

In the living room at the House of Charity, it was evening. The staff had just posted Valentine Cupids and hearts on the glass and in the halls. Unfortunately it was a turn on for the men who began to leer at the outnumbered women. Jackson leered at Barbara, a young white woman, who had come here to escape battering and assault at home. Jackson edged closer to her.

Barbara turned away from him to talk to Max about her problem with shoes. Her shoes had come completely apart, and she needed to get some before she could go outside again. Max had found a pair of boots for himself at the Free Store earlier in the day, and had hidden them behind the couch to take to his own room later— but he saw that she needed shoes more than he did, so he gave them to her.

I thought about my situation. I had two pair of serviceable winter shoes with me. One pair was synthetic furry stuff inside and Eskimo style on the outside. They were warm enough but hard to walk in, day after day, because the arch support was inadequate. The other shoes were thick, crepe-soled, suede leather shoes from Kinney's. They were fleece-lined, came up to my ankles, and were warm and comfortable even to walk in them all day— a cross between Earth shoes and desert boots.

I looked around the room at what people were wearing on their feet. Dolly was wearing patent-leather Mary Jane's that looked like leftovers from a Shirley Temple movie. Some people wore plastic bags for socks. Many had thin sneakers with many holes in them.

As the days wore on, I felt more and more that it was inappropriate for me to have two pair of boots when I could only wear one at a time. Eventually I gave the second pair away to someone whose shoes looked like Swiss cheese. My reverie was abruptly interrupted when Jackson moved next to Barbara and she shouted at him, "Back off and stay away from me."

He said, "I ain't threatening you unless that's what turns you on. You want me to turn you on?" he said, putting his hand on her leg. She screamed and fled out of the room to find the staff, who had just escorted two drunks out the door. She filed a complaint against Jackson.

Max slithered over to me and whispered, "She's real edgy about men. Her father raped her when she was little, and she ain't been very cordial toward men since. When she got to be a teenager she was mugged, raped, and left for dead. She'd been angry at the world and at men ever since. She came to the shelter this week because her current old man beat her up. He's a real sleaze, he is."

I said, "It doesn't help that the staff put up Valentines posters all over and so tonight some men in the room are acting like its open season on women!"

Figure 3. Postcard view: Street People and shoppers sitting in the potted palms of the IDS Crystal Court.

Figure 4. Barbara, a battered housewife.

EXILES: "VIOLENCE IN THE HOUSE"

The particular Cuban Muriel Boat People who were at the House of Charity were a hostile and moody duo I called Romero and Domingo. They were in and out of the shelter from time to time when I was there. Romero was slippery. He used his exquisitely polished manners to antagonize everyone. Of the two, however, Domingo seemed like a more dangerous person.

One evening in the House of Charity livingroom, Romero said to Duluth, "*Senor,* you do not mind if I sit here next to you, *por favor.* I am small; I take but little room. *Gracias, gracias.*" He hastily plopped down in a grandiose manner onto Duluth's leather jacket, squishing the cigarettes in the pocket of the jacket.

"I do not mind your sitting next to me, but had you waited for my reply, I could have moved my coat out of your way," said Duluth.

"*Senor,* do not trouble yourself. Perhaps, if I smoked one of your cigarettes, you would have less to move."

"Cigarettes? You have cigarettes?" Max asked, sidling over to Duluth's chair and crouching down on haunches, looking up like a begging dog.

Romero sneered at Max, "I know you wouldn't lend one to him. I know that kind."

Max looked up at Duluth, "But seeing I'm such a special friend and all, would you mind giving me a smoke and a light?"

"Special friend and all? Who are you? I don't even know you. How can you say you are my friend?" said Duluth in astonishment.

Max kept pushing, "Well, it was worth a try. Sometimes it works. I just wanted a smoke," Duluth and Romero both ignored Max. Max habitually pestered every new arrival, trying to bum cigarettes.

Duluth attempted to return to reading a book he had taken off the shelf earlier. Romero wiggled and squirmed to gain advantage on the two-seater. Duluth could not read with this man bouncing around on the seat, purposely trying to annoy him into an altercation. Since Duluth was still recuperating from a drunk- driving accident in which he had broken his neck, he was reluctant to get into the fight Romero wanted. Duluth left the room. As soon as he had, Romero gloated and spread himself grandly on the yellow plastic two-seater. With this conquest achieved, he began again the process of using superficially good manners to annoy someone. This time he turned his attentions to Barbara, who was in the chair next to him; he seemed to regard her as ripe for conquest.

Two equally hostile drunks came in for emergency housing and took offense at the house rules— 'no alcohol, no drinking or smell of drink, no company in the rooms.' They huddled on the other side of the living room and loudly discussed the situation. "Look, man, we told those broads we had a place, man. How we gonna have an orgy tonight if we ain't got no housing pass?"

"Cool it, man. I got a plan." He then left the building with his buddy and returned a few minutes later with a different hat and scarf on. He signed the waiting list under a new name. The staff recognized them both and refused them a room, this time on the basis that they were drunk. Words were exchanged, while about seven staff members "helped" these two disappointed Don Juans out the door.

A few evenings later, they were back. That evening the two Cubans, Romero and Domingo, took Marla into their room. The small man on night duty suspected what was up, so he banged on the door and demanded a room check. Marla wasn't in the room (she was being hidden out on the fire escape). These Cubans did not speak much English, except when they wanted to antagonize, so they acted hostilely toward the staff man, intimidated him and claimed it was harassment, that it was all in his imagination. The night duty man gave up the search, and the hall quieted down.

Marla, wearing only a Teddy, climbed back into the room from the fire escape, and in a little while her "Alleluia chorus" from this *ménage à trois* echoed loudly through the first floor corridor. There was not a shadow of a doubt that the Cubans were having a woman in their room. The little night-duty man opened their door with a pass key and ordered all three to get dressed and leave the building. The Cuban burst into the hallway raving, shouting obscenities in Spanish and English, in hateful animal-like voices. Both Romero and Domingo brutally lunged for the night-duty clerk, slugging and punching him.

Marla, wrapped in a towel, raced down the hall and tried to stop the fight. Doddering old Father Blue opened his door, walked into their midst, and fearlessly began speaking Spanish to them, as if there were absolutely no danger. Romero pulled a switchblade. Square Shoulders crossed the hall from his room, gave a karate chop to Romero's arm. The knife clattered to the floor. Square Shoulders moved with lightning speed, attacking with hands and feet, *T'ai-kwon-do* style, to subdue these men.

Police sirens sounded. Three uniformed police ran up the hall, handcuffed the cursing Cubans. The men continued to shout obscenities as they were hauled off to jail. Fr. Blue stood there making the sign of the cross. The night-duty man turned to Square Shoulders: "You acted just in time. I'm really glad you are staying here," said the staff man.

"Think nothing of it. We had incidents like this all the time when I worked in the mental hospital. Besides, I learned what to do as a street fighter. But I almost forgot I was recovering from surgery," he said rubbing his side.

✻

High School Drop-Out: "Dennis' Job Interview"

Dennis, the young man about 20, came in complaining about a job interview he had been on in the morning. "They didn't ask me what jobs I've had or whether I work hard, whether I'm honest. They don't ask me nothin' but 'You finish high school?'

'No.'

'No? Well, we have so many applicants who have, we are not accepting drop-outs.'

'What if I got my GED, would you consider me then?'

'Not really. You see, we have to have some way to narrow the field.'

Dennis spent three hours at the unemployment office after the interview looking at the job screen. He said, "Although many of the jobs listed said 'No experience necessary, on-the-job training available' when I phoned them, they said a high school diploma was required and they would not accept a GED. How does that make sense? How will I ever get a chance? I talked to the employment office to see about paid schooling. They said school was a good idea, but they didn't know if I could get paid for it. How am I

supposed to pay for books and tuition if I can't get paid while I'm
in school, and I can't get a job either?"

He pulled his knit cap down over his eyes and stretched out in
the chair trying to feign a nap. "Only two more hours to wait until
I can get back into the room so I can really go to sleep. That's all
there is for me to do day after day. Stand in lines, get turned down
for jobs, or take naps all day until it is time to get back to the room
so I can sleep. Shit. Are these the best years of my life?"

*

DISGRACED OR UNDERCOVER COP? NICK

One evening a paunchy middle-aged man was in the living room
at the House of Charity chatting with Dennis, Cathy and others. He
said, "I had been a good career as a Minneapolis cop, but I seen too
much horror. I spent too many of my off-work hours hitting the
bottle, and eventually it interfered with my job. I like being out of
there. Now I can drink when I want, and no body can say boo. If
times get tough, I can always get picked up and thrown in the Work
House. I enjoy it 'cause I get to see my old buddies and shake 'em
up a bit that it could be them instead of me. Now I don't have to
hit the pavement, I hit the street." He would disappear for a week
at a time. When he returned, he'd say he had been arrested for
sleeping on a park bench and spent a week in the work house. His
story didn't jell because no Caucasian would sleep on a park bench
in those temperatures. [A few Native Americans were reputed to be
winter hardened enough to sleep outside.] Anyway, he'd hang out
with street people a while then disappear. Another reason his story
didn't hang too well was that he was loud and belligerent "a dry
drunk" but overly much— more so than the actual alcoholics there
who were in recovery.

One day, at the Crystal Court, he was sitting with the other street
people in the potted palms. The police on duty made it a habit to
come over to razz and ridicule him every hour or so, and to me
they seemed to be enjoying it too much. There were no prostitutes
in the potted palms that day or any other so far as I could tell, but
there were Caucasian business men, plastic shirtpocket protector
types, who would proposition any woman sitting in the palms.

When Nick was around, he would flash a signal, and the other cops would come over and bust the geek.

Based on that I didn't put a lot of faith in his story of being one of Minneapolis finest fallen off the wagon of grace.

*

DEVELOPMENTALLY DISABLED: THE-LADY-WHO-SEWS

One lady made her own clothes by piecing together used clothing. She didn't stay at the House of Charity while I was there. I had heard she stayed at a church shelter. I noticed her whenever I was near the Nicollet Mall, mostly in the library. She generally sat at a table on the top floor of the library in the far corner, somewhere between psychology, religion, and anthropology. She would put a book in front of herself and stare out the window. She never bothered anyone.

One day there was a new librarian on the third floor. She didn't want street people hanging out in her section. She didn't know I was one, I guess. Anyway the librarian marched over to The-Lady-Who-Sews. She stood with arms crossed and looked down her glasses and glared at The-Lady-Who-Sews. The-Lady-Who-Sews had been minding her own business and was within all rights to sit pondering in the library. Is the librarian against the equal right to ponder?

The librarian took a dramatic step closer to the lady and looked sternly at her, hoping the old glare technique would make her leave. But the lady held her ground. Then the prim librarian moved right up against the table and began to say, "You can't loiter here. You have to leave."

The-Lady-Who-Sews lifted her head high, pulled up her full stature, and let out a deep loud wolf-like growl, "Grrrrrh! Grrrrrhhh! Hisssss! Shrrrrooolll!" she hissed and snarled. She growled again with all her being, "Grrrrrhhhrrrroooull."

The Librarian screamed and fled. "Yeeeiiiii!— I didn't do a thing! She threatened me! Help."

The-Lady-Who-Sews settled back into her seat and arranged her parkas, and resumed pondering. A while later a second librarian, this time a male, returned with prim librarian. The-Lady-Who-Sews saw them coming. Stood up, packed up her stuff, held her head high and walked right past them and directly onto the elevator.

I was furious. The-Lady-Who-Sews had offended no patron by sitting there; she just wasn't in the periodical section where most of The Street People hang out. (I didn't blame her. That week the periodical section was full of lice.) And it was the librarian who had initiated the threatening postures.

*

ASPIRING GIGOLOS, WANNABE PIMPS, WANNABE HOUSE-HUSBANDS

After lunch, we drifted over to Burger King for coffee to rent a table so we could get out of the snow and wind. It was one of those blizzards where each flake of the snow is horizontal for miles before deciding where to settle down, transmute into glacial ice, and await for its eventual death with the arrival of spring sometime in the distant future. Conversation at lunch digressed to relationships. Washington said, "I been in eight major 'relationships' with fair-haired, blue-eyed white women. Three were long relationships. Five were feathers in my cap because I plucked their little feather away." I tried to tune out of the conversation but I was annoyed by his boasting and score-keeping.

"Yeah. The heights would be to find a rich, white, Scandinavian woman (mentally I translated, *you really mean a Barbie bimbo*) I could move in with and keep content."

"I have a lot to offer that way, a lot to give a relationship," one said.

Max offered, "I could even learn to read iffin it was necessary to bein' in such a fine relationship."

"You ain't gotta read to have a slow movin' hand."

Jackson said, "Get serious a minute. I have $200. Should I spend this bread on threads to look the part, or spend it on wine and dinner to win her, or as rent for a place to take her if I'm successful with this new mink?" (It didn't seem as if he had considered that there might be other options.)

His friend stressed, "Hey, man, get your own base, man. Get your own place, your own job, then you can screw a rich broad but you can be you, too, and you can tell her to go fuck herself when it's not going right. That way you don't have to upturn your whole existence."

Several guys stood up to leave, "Jeeze everybody like ta stay but we gotta go. We're goin' over to St. Paul for a few days. Gonna hunt around in the snow at Rice Park looking for that Winter Carnival Medallion. We find that, and we'll really be in the money. Anybody seen the clue for today in the Strib?"[9]

"Ain't been to the libarry yet today."

"Okay. Then we're takin' off."

"See ya 'round. Good luck— You're gonna need it."

"Don't freeze your nuts off."

Then the group resumed the previous conversation. Directing a comment toward me while lighting a cigarette, but talking to the air, said, "Not only can I keep a woman content, but I could also help a woman get a business going. She'd need a Black to get funding— after all I'm a Minority!"

I reminded him that "According to the government, as a white woman, I was already considered a Minority and I'm not interested in being in a relationship."

His friend said, "Ain't that the truth. Women is over half the population and still they're an official Minority. Bein' Black is bein' Black but bein' a woman is bein' too many all over the place and bein' dogged all the time. Fact some dogs get treated better 'en some women."

The other guy turned to Cathy: "Little lady, I could treat you right. Make you feel whole so you don't need to be alone wid yourself. I can make you feel real special. I would like that— I need someone to clean my house and fix me things. I could treat you real fine. I'd like that."

"Who you kidding, man? You is on the street like the rest of us. You forget you ain't got no house to clean!" Michael raved, and we all laughed, while Max sat there with a hang dog look trying to get the other guy to pass him a cigarette. With that, we all got up and started drifting out the door, disappearing behind the 6' mounds of snow piled on both sides of the street, and both sides of the sidewalk. The air was brisk and clean, a fresh wind was blowing my

---

[9] Minnesotan for the *Minneapolis Star-Tribune* daily newspaper.

hair but the snow was letting up as it briefly does in the midst of a blizzard or a hurricane. I pulled my knit hat down over my ears, and wrapped my scarf across my face. The walls of snow buffered the traffic noise so that it was strangely quiet.

Many of the men who were Street People staying at the House of Charity acted as if any woman at the House of Charity was an easy mark. They were mistaken, but they kept trying. Many expressed a desire for a home and family, but the particular Black men I spoke with that week said they want to be kept or be pimping. Many of the White men expressed a desire to be dependent on women too. Every man at the table was looking for some magic to provide them a home and an income. The Black men had said they were "more willing to earn it with their cocks." Some of the White men were older and had been in prison. Their perspective was that it was a selling point that although they wanted to be totally dependent on a woman, since their prison experiences, they were also willing to consider being dependent without putting out or being put upon now and then.

The next day I was glancing over the New Acquisitions shelf at the Library. There, on special display, was a new book— with Michael's picture on the cover, entitled *The 10 Most Eligible Bachelors in Minneapolis*. How could he be in that book and yet stay at the House of Charity and eat at the Food Service?

When I ran into him at lunch, I asked him about it. He said sheepishly, "I got to know somebody connected with publishing the book. Face it, what do I have to lose? They don't know where I live. I think it's pretty cool. Guess it all depends how you define "eligible." I can't think of anyone more eligible to make a change."

✳

THIEF: "LOUIE'S BURIED TREASURE"

Louie told this story. "I grew up in affluent Long Island. I had some college. My old man worked for The Family and was paid well. The next door neighbor man also worked for The Family. His kid was my friend. He hated his old man. Both of us were being raised to take over their role in The Family Business, and neither of us wanted that, even though it would be a guaranteed good income. We were determined to make it on our own, no matter what."

He went on to say, "I am having trouble getting a job since I came out here, and there is a temptation to rob. I robbed once, a few years ago. Got away with it. No sweat. The kid next door, I told you about, wanted me to steal from his old man 'cause he hated him. He told me when to go in their house to where the loot was hidden in his old man's sock in the top dresser drawer. I was such a dumb kid, I had to go back 2 more times because I kept looking in the back of the dresser and it was a sock in the front! $18,000. There was so much moola there it wouldn't stay in my jacket pockets, and I couldn't make myself take his socks. I left there and went to a bar because I couldn't go home 'til my folks went out later in the day."

"So there I was, sitting in the bar, trying to keep this stuff in my pockets hid. A squad car goes by with the sirens on. Some people come in and start drinking. 'Hey, did ya' hear? Tony's house got robbed. Ripped off $18,000 cash! Can you believe it?'"

"My hand was shakin' as I finished a beer. I felt I had to say something, so I said, 'Is that right, man? You're not shittin' me?'"

"'No shit. That's it. This morning. Knew just where it was hid, too.'"

"I looked up to see my old man come in with two guys and sit over in the corner."

"'Well, I gotta go. See ya around,' I said, and got outta the bar, keeping my hands holding against my jacket pockets."

"When my folks left, I took most of the money and put it under a floor board in the attic. With the few thousand I kept for myself, I led every kind of high life. I throwed parties at friend's places and lived good but always away from the house. I gave half of what I kept to the kid next door," Louis continued.

"Then I got bored with that and enlisted in the service for a five-year hitch. When I came back for my old man's funeral, my mom says, 'Louie, I'm gonna sell the house. I don't need all this room anymore.' I tell her 'Wait a year or so 'til you're over dad's dying. Take time to be sure.' I figured that was that."

"A few months later, I get a letter saying she's sold the house. I rush home. They were loading the moving van. The settlement was set for 4 o'clock that afternoon. So I go up into the attic. It's cleaned out. I remember the board was next to the trunk, but the trunk is gone, and the floor's been swept. I can't get my bearings. Mom calls up the stairs, 'Louie, none of your stuff up is up there; everything's packed, son.'"

"'Everything?,' I thought, 'Is that a code? Does mom know? I wondered. No, she can't know'." Louie took another sip of coffee and continued.

"I started pulling up floor boards with my bare hands. I didn't have any tools with me. I pulled and pulled. Guess what. It was all insulated with cellulose. Between every joist of the attic floor. I was frantic."

"'Son, come down here now. There's nothing up there. What's that ruckus you're makin'? Time to go, son.'"

"I pulled up all I could. I was covered with insulation, like confetti. I never did find the money. I guess Weatherization got it. Sometimes I think about going back there and robbing that house to get to the attic, but I don't think the money is there anymore. Still it haunts me like Captain Kidd's buried treasure. Even though I had the map, I couldn't find the buried treasure."

✳

SENIOR CITIZEN AND PARTNER ON DISABILITY: AENEAS AND DOLLY

Aeneas and Dolly were a striking couple. He was about 6'4", of indeterminate age but well over 65. He stood tall, distinguished, balding, with clear blue eyes and the polished manners of a gentleman. He and Dolly strolled down the street. Every time the Free Store opened, Aeneas and Dolly were first in line for new clothes. Dolly had fur coats, cloth coats, every color of spiked heels and fancy blouses. Aeneas had tailored shirts, top coats, and a Stetson hat. They dressed with great care. Dolly was a pretty woman also of undetermined age, maybe 48. She wore heavy make-up with lipstick applied all the way up to her nostrils. She had jet-black hair which she kept combed.

On Sundays when there was nothing to do, Aeneas and Dolly invited me to stroll. They would promenade, arm in arm, from the House of Charity to the Twin City Federal (TCF) lobby to the bus station to the luncheonette for a lemonade and donut, to Burger

King for the bathroom, to McDonald's to get warm, to the Hospital canteen. Then make the stroll again. They did this about three or four times a Sunday 'til it was time to get back into the House of Charity.

Aeneas told me that when he was a child, an elderly grandmother taught him how to crochet clothing without a pattern. As an adult, when he was broke he would go into a bar and begin to crochet. It always got attention. He would explain that he made his living making hand-crafted women's crocheted evening dresses, wide shell pattern. He would suggest to his audience that his company had so many orders, he was working overtime; that's why he had brought his work to the bar. He would hold the dress up to that man's date and suggest he buy it for his girl friend. He always got lots of orders. He charged about $150 a dress. He said he couldn't do that anymore because his hands were stiffening.

Now when he needed quick cash, he would drive a car cross-country for someone, and they would provide him with a fee and a bus ticket back. That way, he and Dolly could travel all around the country and sleep in the delivery cars or on the bus. But between runs, there were some times when it was too cold. They lived at the House of Charity.

They had lived this way for about 10 years except for when Dolly forgot to take her medicine and had a schizophrenic episode and had to check into St. Peter's or somewhere else to get her meds adjusted. She had a mental inventory of the mental institutions of the nation. She said, "My favorites are St. Peter's in St. Peter, Minnesota, and another in Arizona. I try to get committed to the Arizona one in the winter."

*

THE YOUNG FAMILY: "THE ELEVATION"

It was a Saturday near the end of the month, when (for many of the working poor) the food stamps are exhausted and there is no food, and the Food Service lunch was especially crowded. I estimated there were at least three seatings of 100 for lunch that day. I was seated beside a Native American family of two young parents and three kids— two boys and a girl. The food was the everyday fare— something like Creamettes (macaroni), peas, a box of salt, onions, and cream of mushroom soup. Okay food, filling, the usual of watered soup, donuts and sweet rolls of advanced age. The best part today was a good apple and a good orange.

The family waited. Then the beautiful young woman began. She held up the glass of water, "From the depths of the earth, this water is presented to us to refresh our spirits." Then she broke a piece of donut, held it up, "From the abundance of the earth this food is provided to us to become one with our body. Our Creator has provided for us to be together at this table to eat and drink from the abundance of the earth and to refresh our bodies and spirits." The feeding at the Food Service became a ceremony of spiritual rejuvenation.

*

FAILED BUSINESS VENTURE: MARK

During a blizzard, I was sitting with a group of men hanging out in McDonald's, waiting for the afternoon to pass. We stretched the afternoon by having each person get one item, but buying it about ½-hour after the other. With five of us, we were able to be there about 2½ hours. Mark said, "I came to Minneapolis to go into business with my cousin. It didn't work out. Now I'm in a bind until either we can get something going or I can get a steady job."

*

ON THE STREET BY CHOICE: "BURN-OUT"

William was a muscular, black man, about 40-years old, told his story. William said, "I'm not about to look for any job. I worked in a steel mill in Gary, Indiana. It's the only work I know how to do. I got the job right out of high school. I married my high school sweetheart. We had four kids. I loved my wife and family. I went to work every day, day after day, for them. They were my responsibility and I took that responsibility seriously," he continued.

"I made good money but the work was awful. I hated every day in the mill. I handled vats of molten ore. Even though I wore thick gloves and a welding mask, every day I got my hands burned.

Sometimes I got burned right through the gloves. One time it spilled all over me. Day after day, I went to that job. Each day I disliked it more."

William stretched, got up and bought his cup of coffee, then continued his story, "I put all 4 of my kids through college. They didn't have to pay a dime. I did it by doing that awful job that burned my hands. On the day my youngest child graduated, I told my wife, 'Now I've paid my dues. All four kids graduated from college. I ain't going back to that job again. I won't have to get my hands burned anymore.'"

"My wife said, 'You can't do that. You can't make that kind of wage anywhere else. We can't live here in this nice house if you don't go to work there. You have to work there.'"

William paused, then smiled and said, "So I said to her, 'Okay. The way it is, is that I ain't goin' back. So I guess I'm jus' goin'.' I walked out the door and never looked back. I haven't worked a day since and I don't intend to. To me the word "work" means "to get burned." I miss my kids sometimes but I raised them good, so I know, wherever they are, they are okay."

He paused, then added, "I don't know how long I've been on the street— five, maybe seven years. Compared to getting my hands burned every day, I love this life."

✳

CARE PROVIDER TO CHRONICALLY-ILL SPOUSE: "ALLEN'S WIFE GETS THE CHAIR"

"Allen, how are you today?" the shabby old man asked.

The young man across from him at breakfast replied, "Man, yesterday was the best day of my life." Allen's face was gaunt, malnourished. His remaining teeth were stubs, but his blue eyes were shining.

"Why, Allen? What made you feel so fine this morning?"

"Last night, they put my wife in the electric chair and it was the happiest moment of my life."

I choked on the reconstituted, powdered, scrambled eggs. The shabby old man tried to keep a blank look on his face as Allen continued, "My wife has MS. She's in the hospital now because using crutches damaged her backside. She won't be able to walk again. When she had to give up the crutches, that was a big downer for her. I never seen her so discouraged. It was hard, real hard on all of us when she was so down."

"Last night at the hospital they gave her an electric wheel chair. She was so beautiful. She was so happy that I've never felt so happy in my whole life." His smile was beautiful.

Several weeks later, Allen's wife was hospitalized for complications following influenza. Max and I were standing at the coffee machine when Allen came over.

"Hi, Allen. What ya' been doin'?"

"Yesterday, I was at the hospital all day. My wife really hangs on to my being there. But today, today was something else! I got a real good feelin' from today. I worked. I mean I worked a whole day at a job that paid me money. I washed ink off computer boards. It was fascinating."

"I recognized what they was 'cause once I took a pocket calculator apart. It looked that way inside."

"I hope they call me back. It felt so good to be working. That was the first full day I have been able to get in 3 years. It was so exciting washing those PC boards. They came in all different sizes. They let me work for 10 hours and I got paid for it all. I'd really like to get into that line of work. I know I could learn any of the jobs I saw there today. You know, like checking for flaws with a magnifying glass or inking boards. Or washing them. Stuff like that. What a super day!"

"Only trouble is my wife was real down that I wasn't there with her today. Real down. And I didn't have a quarter to call her from a pay phone. But it sure felt good to have a day of work."

Allen went on to tell me about why he was at the House of Charity. "We live far out in the country, and since I've been out of work there's no money for a motel or the YMCA when she has to be in the hospital here. I'm real lucky to be able to stay at the House of Charity."

"I used to have a job in a factory on the line. But my wife needed more of my time for her care. So I was late for work, or I missed too much time, or got called home from the job. There was never anybody else to take care of her. So I lost my job. After

Unemployment ran out, we had to go on Assistance. That don't go far. It would be real nice if there was someone to help take care of her days, when she is having a bad time, and I could have regular work."

Allen's story was typical of many families I encountered who were coping with major illness. The healthy one was willing to work, but there was no affordable back-up system to help with the care of the disabled spouse. The healthy one needed more help in order to stay afloat economically, emotionally, physically, and socially and to be able to continue to care for the disabled partner. Many men and women there had a totally disabled spouse— either mentally or physically disabled— and the spouse required constant care. The illness had contributed to the financial and emotional drain on both of them.

For the Working Poor as well as for people more financially established, the problem of home care assistance continues. There are still too few affordable back-up systems so that one partner can be at work and know that the home-bound partner is being well cared for. People don't realize how being a careprovider can put so much distress on jobs, budgets, employees and employers that in some cases providing needed loving care can also lead to homelessness.

✳

UNEMPLOYED WILLING WORKER: LEONARD'S INSIGHT

Yesterday at the Food Service lunch, I met Leonard. He was sitting across from me. It was a bitter cold January day, well below zero. We had plates full of meat-macaroni something that reminded me of asbestos fire retardant stucco. But it was hot and filling. He searched his pockets, pulling out little packets of mayonnaise, salt, catsup, mustard, salad dressing, crackers, a plastic fork and spoon.

"You have quite a kitchen in that pocket," I said.

"Yeah, everything but the pepper. That's what I'm lookin' for. Everything's here but the pepper. What you see here is what I am, what I'm on, and what I'm under. Everything's with me wherever I go and my pockets aren't even full. And there's farther down and worse and less to go. So eat your chow, girl, so you can make a turd."

"If you ain't et enough to make a turd a day, you ain't et enough to fuel your power 'n' keep you warm enough to make steam to do more work. If I ain't made a turd, I know I ain't gonna be able ta work a full day because I'm too empty a fuel."

"Can you say that, white girl?"

"You mean 'turd'?"

"Hey, you're real. For a minute, I thought you was too afraid of yourself to own your own turd. What's your name?"

"Pat."

"I'm Leonard. Where you livin'?"

"House of Charity."

"House of Charity. That's the Ritz. Wait 'til you really get down. You got it made. You got not only a bed, you got a door. That means you can be private. Once you live in a place that's just a line a' beds, you'll know just how high you is livin' now. 'Specially if dem beds is just mattresses on the floor with no space between and people walkin' all over you to get by."

"What knocked down your dominoes, Leonard?"

"I lost my job. Some middle-class Whitey took it."

"What were you doin'?"

He answered with annoyed impatience. "It was just a job. Just a job. But that Whitey had relations. I went to court on it twice but no mind, money talks. Empty pockets don't say nothin' to a court."

"So I lost my job, my apartment, my clothes, my car, even my stereo. In a month I went from being set to being out with no money, no car, no place to go, and no future."

"It's been a year now. A hard year. The best I've been able to do is to get day work here and there. Nothing steady."

"Only thing I got is what's here. My whole self. All together day and night."

"Sometimes a job is just a job. But when it ain't here no more, it's everything. 'Cause without it you find out how much more nothin' there is out here."

"So eat up, girl, and make a turd so you got enough inside you to keep you warm."

*

SILENT: "MAN-IN-THE-IRON-MASK"

Most of the mentally ill people staying at the House of Charity were anxious pacers, hand-wringing worriers, mutterers or compulsive talkers, but a few had become completely repressed, private, deeply within a shell. They were totally isolated by their own defenses and barriers. One of these was a man I named the Man-in-the-Iron-Mask. He was so remote he was almost eerie. He was there in the room, but in no way a part of it. He was so absent from himself, sitting next to him was like sitting next to an empty tomb. He seemed like he could have been a nice person, had he been present.

The first time I saw him, he was wearing an extra-long top coat and a carefully positioned knit ski cap pulled far down on his forehead. With a shopping bag at his side and a new quilt, tied bedroll fashion with twine, draped over his shoulder, he silently waited in line at the Food Service. Even when he ate, the expression on his face never changed, facial muscles always rigidly set. He never showed any aliveness at all, always deadpan. He didn't appear to listen in on other people's conversations either. He was exceptionally clean, orderly, and not stooped like most; he rarely sat down. He was at least 6'3" tall

I saw him almost daily over the course of several weeks— until one day, when he was sitting on the floor, possessions strewn around him. His anguished face was resting in his hands, and still he made no sound. Without his hat he no longer looked 100 years old, more like 45. This change in demeanor was such a radical departure from his iron face and rigid, statuesque stance that he seemed like he might be in crisis, a silent breakdown. Like the portrait of "The Scream," I could see his anguish but could not hear his cry.

For most other mentally ill at the House of Charity, its manifestation took the opposite tack. Instead of becoming locked in an Iron Mask, mute and rigid, infinitely sad and despairing, many went the other way. They turned inside out. Their conscious lives submerged and their unconscious selves became exposed. Their conscious state was one of such anxiety and pain that they buried these feelings deep inside. As a result, what would normally be inside now came to the surface, totally exposed. In writing this book, I thought of them as the "People-Who-Mutter."

Later a man who told us he was diagnosed as having schizophrenia, said what it was like: "I don't have an interior life. My inner process is my outer process and it's all apparent for everyone to see. Nothing's hidden. And I generally say what I am thinking. I don't seem to be able to control it. It isn't very nice, but at least people always know what I think about them."

✳

PARANOID VETERAN: "PERCY AND THE POLICE"

Several days later, Domingo was back with a Black Muslim friend, Percy. We knew he was a Black Muslim because, that day, he had a sign on his coat that said so. Percy was also a disgruntled Vietnam veteran. Percy was so eaten through with aggressive hostility, he made it a habit to take offense at everything, lest he miss something. He had spent most of the day in lines around town, just as I had, so I suppose he was tired and pissed off by the time he reached the House of Charity. Percy put his hat on the receptionist's desk while he signed the waiting list roster. He turned away without his hat. Silently the receptionist handed it to him.

"Look, lady, I'm a human bein' and if you has business witch me yous can communicate wid me. You understand? Communication, that's the thing. Don't forget it."

"I meant no offense," the old lady smiled weakly.

"Whether you meant it or not you gave offense. You're offensive. Next time COMMUNICATE your wishes with another human being."

Next Percy tried to provoke a hostile discussion of world politics with the African students. They were not interested in an argument, so Percy turned his attention to indirectly insulting the Whites in the room. "If the Blacks, and the Indians here were to become allied, the Whites would be the disadvantaged," he remarked. The Blacks, the Native Americans, and the Cubans were big-bodied and strong. And these particular Cubans seemed to have no limits to what they would do. The Whites, except for one who was a seasonally unemployed logger, were mostly decrepit, both in body and spirit.

I saw Percy around town a lot, although I went out of my way not to talk to him. Percy was lean and well-dressed but there was an aura of tension and tautness about him. When he talked, he bent slightly forward, clenching his fists, ready for action. His eyes traveled systematically across the waiting room, never looking at anyone directly but taking everyone in.

It was morning and the lobby was filling with the bedraggled who hoped a room would be vacant for them for the night. Percy was waiting, perched with one hip on the desk, reading the newspaper.

The headline riled him. He read it out loud and then exploded, "Mother-fucking establishment always out to do us in. Look here at this mother-fucking shit, even here in the paper is proof that the cock-sucking economic system keeps bearing its butt fucking Federal thumb down on us. Whoever called it the Great Federal Tit didn't know what kind of oppression government could dish out." He threw the newspaper aside and stomped out of the room.

He returned later wearing a Ranger beret and a camelhair coat with war medals on it. He made straight for the desk. "You mother-fucking social workers got a room for me for this shit-eating night?" he asked with as much politeness as he could muster. There was a vacancy, and he was assigned to the room next to mine.

That night, when the waiting room had changed to a TV room, he sat brooding in a chair on the side of the room. "Love Boat" was on. The staff had just put up more Cupid and Valentine hearts in the halls and on the window above the desk. Sullen men were leering at the women. There was an uneasy tension in the room. I was pissed that the staff would set women up for trouble this way in this place.

The commercials annoyed Percy, and he growled curses. Soon two young kids from the chemical abuse rehab program came in— horsing around, joshing, shoving, laughing— and plopped on the desk, unintentionally blocking the view of the TV of the old man using the desk chair. The old man was the kind who measured everything by how much energy it would extract if he did it. Silently, he moved to the chair beside Percy.

Percy had been scanning the room and had noticed that when the kids sat on the desk, the old man could no longer see the TV. It set Percy off. "Them punk fuckers. They shouldn't be here. They ain't paid no dues to society."

"Them mother-fucking bastard punk kids never mind to be considerate of other peoples. And you is old, and they thinks you is stupid, like asking you stupid-like, 'Can you see the TV?'— with their shit-asses in front of your face, there was no way you could see the fucking "Love Boat." The stupid assholes should be kicked out for their fucking, insolent, level of stupidity, ignorant s.o.b's."

The old man said, "Pay no mind, Percy. Kids 'as a right to be kids. They don't matter me. They asked nice iffin' I could see the tube okay. I can see it fine. I chose to moves over to here. Now quiet you'self and pay them kids no mind."

But Percy became incensed, erupting like a volcano, spewing curses with increasing volume, "Punk kids did that mother-fucking shit just to bother ME. They is here to get my mother-fucking goat." Percy continued to rave as he stomped down the hall to his room.

In the morning, when we all left for breakfast, the cleaning cart was in the hall outside his door. Percy stormed out of his room up to the front desk, "Give me my breakfast ticket, you s.o.b's. You shit-heads been discriminating against me. Last night you was against me. I could tell by that old sandwich you put in my dinner bag and what you did put in—putting in that little tiny apple. You just want to see if this mother-fucker knows what you pricks are doing to my fucking dinner bag. You lay off tampering with my food, you hear? You fuckers keep your shit outta my stuff."

"Percy, it's against house rules to talk to staff members that way. Everyone gets the same dinner," said Mike at the front desk. "It's all donated from vending machines. It's all old. We try to toss the worst before we bag it up. We do the best we can with what we get."

That evening when Percy came back to the House of Charity, all the rooms had fresh linen and towels, and a clean mopped floor. I could hear him banging drawers, moving clothes in the closet, and saying, "Where is it? I knowed them mother-fuckers were going to break into my room when I was out. Ain't no s.o.b.

supposed to be in my room when I ain't here." Percy seemed to find fault with something all the time. He was a cauldron of turmoil, hatred, and rage.

Percy went directly to the staff. "Some mother-fucking staff person been messing in my room. I got proof now you shit-heads been messing in my stuff. You're gonna pay for this. This is a warning. Keep out of my room."

"Nobody's been messing with your stuff. Nobody wants your stuff," Mike replied.

"How you know you don't want my stuff 'lessen you been goin' through it to see what's there. Now I know for sure that you been in my room. I know my rights. I'm gonna do something about this to put an end to this mother-fucking shit. I'm going out and there better not be any of my shit missing when I get back!"

"What's with him? Nobody's been messing with his stuff," Mike, the man on the night desk, said again.

"He's something else all right," replied the old man.

When Percy returned an hour later, he was still in an uproar. "Leave me alone. Don't disturb me. Tonight I have important business," he told the desk clerk. "I have papers here and when I'm through there is going to be an end to all this shit." He pulled a "Do not disturb" sign out of his coat pocket and hung it on his door, slamming the door shut.

Marla and Darleen were chatting as they walking up the hall heading for the ladies room. Percy opened his door and shouted at them, "I told you mother fuckers I am not to be disturbed. I have police paperwork to do. Important business. I'm gonna put a stop to this shit once and for all. So you shut up. I told you to be quiet before!" The two girls looked at each other and at him wondering who appointed him hall patrol. Why they weren't supposed to talk when they were walking up the hall. It was still early evening.

In his room, Percy continued talking loudly to himself for several hours about forms and reports. He searched through everything in his bedroom. At 11 p.m. he called to the night clerk and demanded, "I have the papers completed, Mike. Now, you mother fucker, please call the police to come here immediately."

Mike called the private duty-night guard who then went to Percy's room. "You wanted to see me?"

"No. You ain't no real cop. I asked that shit-head to call the Minneapolis police, and he sends me you. When I want the police I mean the shit-eating pigs. Can't that idiot on the desk do no fucking thing right? Do I have to do everything myself to get justice around this hole?"

By now Mike had come to the door too. "Hey, Percy, calm down. You're being too loud and it's waking people up."

"S'bout time somebody waked up to your mother-fucking crap. I asked this pig-faced cock-sucker to call the fucking police and you all stand around like pansies telling me to shut the fuck up. I ain't gonna shut up about nothin' 'til I gits this matter settled."

"Percy, what's eating you, man? If you keep insulting the staff like this, you're gonna get thrown out of here. You don't want that; it's cold out, man. Just settle down and get some sleep."

"You mother fuckers ransacked my room, stole my stuff, and now tell me to pipe down and get some sleep. I think you're trying to make a cover-up. There ain't going to be no fucking cover up, you hear? Now call the police!"

"I already have, but you'd better settle down and stop being so loud. You're not allowed to harass the staff. We don't have to take that. If you have a real problem, we will try to fix it, but don't go putting us down for doing our job."

A uniformed Minneapolis police officer joined the group. "What's the trouble here?"

"Come in here, Officer. We gotta talk more private." Percy and the Officer stepped into his room, leaving the private duty guard and Mike, the night desk clerk, in the hall. "The staff of this mother-fucking establishment," Percy says with careful diction, "has rummaged through my belongings, been frequenting my room, and stolen from me. I filled out this police report in complete detail."

"When did this theft occur?"

"Sometime between 8 a.m. and 4 p.m. today."

"Let me see the report. Is this your name? Percy?"

"Yes sir."

"Tell me again. What exactly is your specific complaint?"

"The mother-fucking staff entered my room after I had left the building, moved my belongings, searched my stuff and took stuff from my room."

The officer finally got to the bottom of the report. "Is this correct? You called me here to report the theft of a bath towel?"

"Yes sir."

"Why?"

"Why? You ask why? Don't you understand? They were in my room. They took my towel. If they would steal my bath towel and my wash cloth, they would steal other things. I demand justice from this mother-fucking system!"

"Where did you get the towel and wash cloth?"

"It came with the room."

"What room? Here? This room? "

"Yes sir."

"How did you get the police form?"

"I walked to the police station. The desk staff here refused to cooperate in this investigation and would not obtain any forms for me on my behalf. Obviously the assholes did not wish to report any fucking situation to which they were a party."

Changing tack, the officer asked, "What's your name?"

"You know my name. It's on the form."

"What's your name, anyway?"

"Percy Clark."

"What's your date of birth?"

"October 16, 1944."

"What's your social security number?"

"471-40-2160."

"What is today's date?"

"February 2, 1984."

By now, the desk clerk and guard, who had been listening to the exchange, entered Percy's room. "What's the trouble, Officer?"

"Percy, here, claims someone entered his room between 8 a.m. and 4 p.m. today and stole his bath towel."

"There they are, Officer! I wants to prove that staff honkies entered this here room between 8 a.m. and 4 p.m. today and stole my bath towel. Do ya here me? There they are, Officer! I want to press charges," Percy shouted. "Those s.o.b's stole my towel. Take them to jail. Lock 'em up."

"Percy, I can't lock them up for an alleged theft of a bath towel. It's not serious enough."

"You mean they got to steal more from me before you'll put an end to it?"

The desk clerk interrupted, "Percy, everybody, every guest, at the House of Charity gets clean towels and sheets issued every week. The cleaning man takes the dirty ones to the laundry once a week."

"See, Officer, that proves it. He admitted it. They entered my room and took my towel! I told you. Didn't I say they would take other things too! He admitted taking the sheets too. Lock him up!" He continued his tirade, keeping his cursing under unusual control.

Then Mike said, "Officer, we can't allow this belligerent uncooperative attitude and threats against the staff." Mike turned to Percy, "Percy, you have been warned several times. You are going to have to leave."

"What? They entered my room, took my towels, rifled my sheets, and I have to go? That's crazy!"

The officer pulled a pair of handcuffs from the back of his belt and held them in front of Percy's face. "You can proceed now, or I will escort you to the precinct police station."

"You honkey cop. No enforcement of the mother-fucking laws. The House of Charity staff paid you off, didn't they! There's no justice for a private citizen anywhere. I will have to make a report on you and file it with your Superior Officer. This will not end here, you can be sure of that."

"Come on, Percy. It's time to go."

"I ain't going no where without my stuff."

"You're going somewhere now, AND THAT'S OUT. You can get your stuff tomorrow."

The policeman cuffed him, and when he patted him down found a loaded Magnum.

Before the officer could comment on the gun, the night clerk said helpfully, "Yeah, we will pack up your stuff and you can pick it up from the front desk in the morning."

"First you rip off my towel, then sheets, and now you want another chance to go through my stuff. Officer, don't you see how they can't be trusted! They're out to do me in. And you are being duped into their cheating ways."

"Percy, you can go into the night or you can go into head-quarters. I can charge you with having a concealed weapon."

"Well, I refuse to leave. I ain't going to jail for their thieving. And you can't just throw me out on the street in the winter. It's cold out there. I have my rights."

"You have rights but that isn't one of them. You should have thought of this before you created such a disturbance. You were warned more than once," the officer said as he firmly escorted him out the front door and into the squad car.

Soon on-lookers drifted back to their rooms, and the halls were quiet. I was glad for the quiet so I could go to sleep. I hoped my next next-door neighbor would have a full deck.

Seven days later, Percy was standing at the front desk, draped in war medals, and a Veteran's ID card with an American Flag pinned to his lapel. He had newspaper clippings on discrimination displayed in Baggies and taped and safety pinned onto the back of his camelhair top coat. "Pardon me, ma'am," he said politely. "Do you mother-fucking social workers have a room in this establishment where I could stay?"

✳

MEN AND WOMEN WITH SCHIZOPHRENIA AND MULTIPLE PERSONALITY DISORDER: "WHO MUTTERS?"

Anne, more than most others with mental incapacities at the House of Charity, was dependent on the staff to remind her when to do things— like take a bath, change clothes, take her medication, etc. She was pleasant and cooperative but she took little initiative for her own self care. I had left Anne at the Food Service where she had been conversing with herself over breakfast. Three hours later, I was walking along the sidewalk. I heard her voice coming behind me.

"No one gives a shit if I live or I die," she said.

"You're damn right. I feel the same way," she answered.

"Can't even find anyone on a Sunday who cares enough to give you one damn cigarette," she replied.

On and on her selves went, talking to each other. It reminded me of Catanya, Duchess of Alba, who was baptized with 31 different names. Her lover-artist, Goya, made separate sketches to show a separate personality for each name. I wondered if all Anne's selves looked different.

In the frigid afternoon when I was heading back from the IDS Center, Anne was coming up the street toward me. She puffed steam like a locomotive. Her Navy pea-jacket was open, her hands on her hips. Her frayed red hair was braided down her back and tied with a shoelace with long wisps of hair sticking out above her ears. I could tell she was still talking to herself. Out of curiosity I wondered whether someone else could participate. I decided to try. I called to her, "Hey, Anne. What was for lunch?"

"Chicken," her first self said.

"Yeah, chicken. That's right," her second self confirmed.

"It's good too." (Was this the first self or a third self?)

"Thanks," I said. "That's where I'm heading. See you later."

I observed that when someone is muttering, the multiple selves are not necessarily oblivious to what is going on around them. Still, it continued to be disconcerting to hear a mutterer. I heard her continuing the conversation as we went our separate ways and her voices trailed away. I wondered how many also had the same problem.

Later, I went to the University campus. I heard a snatch of conversation coming up behind me like a puffing steam engine. I heard a breathy, panting conversation. "What shall we eat today?"

"The cafeteria has chicken. Does that sound good?" I heard the voices say.

"*Oh, no. Not here. Not more mutterers,*" I thought to myself. "*Not here, not at the University.*" I wondered if the campus had its share of mutterers too.

Then the two lady joggers passed me, wearing light yellow nylon racing suits with matching blue stripes on their matching yellow hats, suits, and shoes. They jogged in matched strides even up the steps of the Diehl building and off across the campus.

Was it two or one? Were they twins? Is Anne two or is she one? I heard another voice. A panting, deep singsong. It belonged to another jogger. He ran past, a man alone, his face immobile, determined, his blue hat and his beard covered with frost formed by his own exhaled breaths. With a Walkman on his belt and his head wired for sound, was he tuned in or was he tuned out? Had I not seen him coming toward me, singing with the radio, I might at first have mistaken him for a mutterer too. Did Anne and her other selves have a radio too? A radio inside her head that played the same theme over and over? Did she hear voices? Was she wired for sound?

Not all the seriously mentally ill at the House of Charity were mutterers or appeared to have multiple personality disorders. While many where schizophrenic with other types of manifestations, they were dependent on antipsychotic medication, and that usually controlled the symptoms from "public view." But no matter what the condition, the mentally ill always substantially outnumbered the rest of us. Some of the "crazy" people at House of Charity were "well-adjusted" in their way— in a loose sense of the term. They were functioning in the real world, a crazy environment that would tax even the sanest individual. They knew when they needed help or medication. They were sociable and pleasant. They might be lacking in certain social skills or work skills, but they were surviving and succeeding within the circumstances in which they had to deal. Others experienced episodic bouts alternating between functioning, near self-sufficiency, and the down side when it was not safe to be alone.

*

RELIGIOSITY DISORDER OR FLAMBOYANT STREET MINISTER?: "GREATCOAT"

It was surprising to me how much religion, the Bible, and belief in God were topics of conversation among the Street People, especially at the House of Charity coffee machine and by the escalators in the Crystal Court. These searching people had little hesitation in discussing their need for religion and spirituality. It was the last place I expected to find that kind of in-depth discussion. It was one of the few topics that had continuity in the conversation. Most other discussions were strictly brief exchanges of information, such as where to get food, clothing, bus tickets, and so forth.

While I have a strong belief system, I have never felt it necessary for people to have the same system I do. I believe God is very big and there is more than one way to find God. Some ways are easier than others.

I ran into a number of people who were preoccupied with organized religion or who felt that their religious expression was the only way, and if you didn't agree to believe/worship/express belief their way, there was something wrong with you and they therefore had a mission to "fix" you. I gave considerable thought to trying to come up with a way to separate those who were in fact doing God's will and those who were just religious fanatics who were "driven" to do this— an obsession, not necessarily prompted by God's will. At first, I thought it should be easy to separate those who were truly doing the will of God— even in the proverbial "strange and mysterious" ways— from those who were just kooks. But it was not so simple.

On the street corner at 8 a.m., a big man in a maroon greatcoat walked up to a well-to-do woman on her way to work. Urgently, he put his face close to hers. Greatcoat was a head and a half taller, so he kind of leaned over her and peered down. Loudly, intensely, he asked, "Have you accepted God as your personal Savior? If not, do it today before it is too late. God has plans for you. Get with it." Then he turned with a flourish of his ornate maroon wool greatcoat.

The woman was obviously uncomfortable and totally embarrassed. Simultaneously, humiliation and indignation flooded over her. She and I walked into the TCF building, heading toward the elevators to get to the Skyway. To ease her noticeable discomfort, I asked, "Did that make your day?"

"Well, I guess it's funny. But it's really an intrusion for those young people to be that way. He really was bold to say that to a stranger on the street corner like that. Why did he choose me?"

"I don't know," I replied, then kidded her, "Don't forget, get with it." We laughed as we stepped off the elevator into our separate lives.

To stay at the House of Charity longer than a week, a homeless person had to reapply once a week for an extension. Because of the line, it took up a whole afternoon once a week. When it was my first time to reapply, I still had not adjusted to being around Street People, and I was extremely uncomfortable knowing I did belong but feeling that I didn't. I was having an inner battle with myself about it. I had always felt it was not right to judge people by appearances, but I sat there doing it. I reminded myself that we were all in the same lifeboat, and broke, and it was too cold outside to be any place else (minus 30 degrees below zero).

The line was barely moving. I was already on the list, so I sat in front of the window by the receptionist's desk to read a magazine. It was the first day on the job for the receptionist, a dignified senior citizen, and she was obviously terrified.

I was getting sleepy from the smoky, stale air when he exploded into the room. With his maroon Greatcoat spread wide, he swooped down on the timid receptionist. I cringed when I remembered how this man had intimidated the lady on the street corner, earlier in the day. Greatcoat waved his worn red leather Bible in front of her face, hovering over her. "I am sent here by God," Greatcoat roared. "I am a man of God. I will deliver you from the wrath and perils of demons and lead you to righteousness." When he spoke, he bared his gums and great horse-teeth gnashed before her face. "It says right here in the Bible. . . ." He rattled off passage numbers and quotations to support his destiny, his mission to be right there at that moment. "Sister, repent! Call on the Lord to be your personal Savior. Can you accept Jesus Christ as your personal Lord and Savior?"

The receptionist's job required her to accept all the kinds of homeless who entered the world of this lobby. She concealed her fear and asked, "And what can I do for you, sir?"

Enunciating every syllable, Greatcoat said, "Oh! Accept the Lord, sister, I say unto you. Accept the Lord, now, as your personal Savior, before the days of wrath descend upon us. Surely sitting here you can see the wiles and effects of Satan all around you, EVEN IN THIS VERY PLACE. And the other thing I need is a room for the night. So let me put my name on this-here list." Unfortunately, in spite of God, the rooms were full, but the receptionist made arrangements for him to stay at Bethel Baptist Church shelter.

✳

COURT ORDER COMPLICATES FAMILY EMERGENCY: PAT

One evening a few weeks later when I was talking to Allen at the coffee machine, a young man named Ted came over to talk. Ted asked me, "Do you work here?"

"No. I don't work here. I'm one of the rest just like everybody else."

"You don't look like everybody else. Are you a social worker?"

"No, not now. I used to do work concerning housing problems. But now I'm unemployed."

"You look like you had money. How did you get on the street?" (This is the first time anybody had asked me the questions I had been asking everyone else.)

"I went through a messy divorce. My kids were taken by their father and brought from Pennsylvania to Minnesota and not returned after visitation. The daft old Pennsylvania judge and the sheriff didn't know how to enforce the newly enacted Uniform Child Custody Jurisdiction Act (UCCJA) to get my kids back, and it's a long story from there. Too long for now. Anyway when I applied for divorce to avoid going on welfare, I took a contract to work for a program in another city, in another state, where the cost of living was very high. With moving, divorce, court, legal fees, and other expenses connected with trips to court and the cost of moving, I got into financial difficulty."

"It was really hard to hold down a job and look for my kids and commute to court. I sold-off most all I had to raise funds. Then when my job contract ended, the unemployment checks didn't come through for three months. My debts rose even higher. Eventually I had no possessions left to sell for cash."

"I'm skipping over a lot of court actions because it takes too long to tell. Anyway I'm here in Minnesota because the Minnesota Court took jurisdiction. . . . My unemployment checks are being held up in Pennsylvania but I need to be here for the court, and my children and so forth. I live and work in Pennsylvania. I've applied for work here as a temp, and called on some ads, but nothing yet."

Again, as I spoke, I was aware that the more times I told my story, the more I spoke it in a monotone. I was beginning to sound like a tape-recording of my own story. That was scary. But it was just too painful to tell the story with the depth and mix of horror, misery, hope, and frustration I really felt.

"You'd better do some praying. I'll pray for you too. Things will work out for you. I have a feeling about it," Ted said.

"Thanks. I do pray. I'd like it if you would. That would be good. It's holding me up right now. That's one of the things I've learned from this time of trouble. I learned I need to pray," I said.

"I'll pray for you later tonight. Sometime, when I need it, I'll ask you to pray for me," Ted comforted.

✳

CHEMICALLY BRAIN-DAMAGED YOUTH: "TED MEETS GREATCOAT"

The day when he needed it came sooner than anticipated. The following morning was a Saturday. At breakfast Ted said, "I'm having a rough time inside myself this morning. Could you spend some time with me in a while? I'm afraid to be alone."

"Sure. I'll meet you at the Crystal Court about 10:30 a.m. if that's okay."

"I'll be there," he said.

At the IDS center, Ted was waiting. We walked over to the granite counter beside the escalators. It was slightly more private there than at the populated potted palms.

"I'm really having a bad time. I think you know I've been in mental health for a while. I'm not feeling right. I tried to get admitted at Hennepin County Medical Center last night, but they didn't have any bed space. Will you stay with me a few hours? I'll check back with the hospital later to see if they can admit me. If they can't, I have a room for the night at House of Charity, but I really need to be in the hospital. See, they changed my medicine, and I can tell it's not right."

"The reason I don't want to be alone," he said, "is because sometimes I get flashbacks. I get disoriented, sometimes blind. Sometimes instead of seeing what's around me, I see instead things like earthquakes and trees being exploded and knocked down like at Mt. St. Helen's. When that happens, I can't tell what's real. My brain plays tricks with my eyes." He had organic brain damage.

"Yeah, Ted, I'll stay with you today for as long as you say."

"Good."

"I've been in just about every kind of mental health facility they have in the Twin Cities: mental hospitals, day care programs, half-way houses. I've had a lot of psychiatric techniques tried, and I've weighed the pros and cons of each of them. I think I can say I've seen the mental health system from inside through every kind of therapy and every kind of facility. Medication helps some, and talking helps some, but I've reached a conclusion: that I did not respond to treatment until I found a doctor and a facility that both of them had a spiritual orientation, presenting religion as an important part of life. Until then I didn't get what I really needed to get, which was the coping skills to get better, and at least to manage this disease, even if I never get cured."

"Psychiatrists try hard; they really care about their patients, but their tools are limited. They mean well, but often they can't do much but listen. Until I got God in it, I didn't begin to get better. God helped me through a lot of this. I was looking for God all along I guess, but when I was younger I got into drugs and cults. I thought I'd find something myself. I didn't know I was searching for God. What I found was hell and the power of the devil. I got into every kind of drug, mostly speed, and it damaged my mind and changed my body chemistry. Eventually I had to go into the mental health system."

"Now, because I fooled with drugs, it looks like I will have to take prescription drugs for the rest of my life."

"Have you been able to hold a job?"

"I was in a fast food place. Doin' good. Moved up to Manager within six months, but then I had an attack right on the job, blinded with flashbacks. That ruined it. I haven't been able to get a job since, and I'm afraid it might happen again." We started walking toward the Dayton's Mall so we could be more private.

"I have told God I am sorry, over and over. I know and feel God's love. But no matter how hard I pray, He doesn't restore my mind and body to what it was before I did this to myself." He

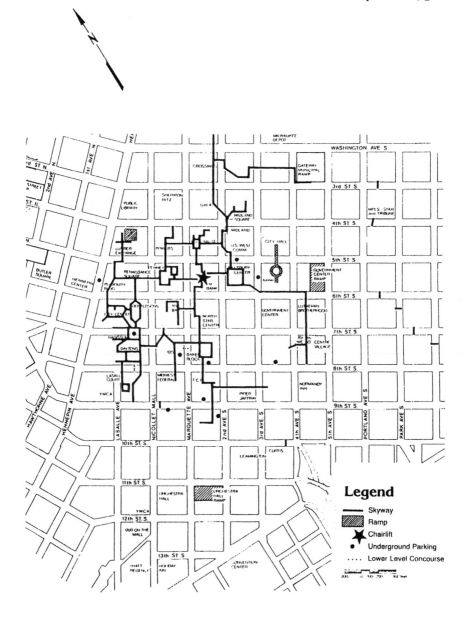

Figure 5. US*WEST* map of the Minneapolis Skyway System, circa 1990.

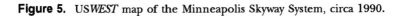

sighed. "It's real heavy that I did this to myself. I didn't start to get better until I started to pray. Now I have studied the New Testament. It contains a lot about healing. I think that psychiatry is short-changing itself from one of the most powerful tools— spiritual and emotional healing just like Jesus taught: 'Blessed are the poor in spirit'."[10]

"Psychiatrists, in their way, are there to cast out our personal demons, our personal faults, our personal obsessions, whatever is making our self sick. The terminology doesn't matter; they are trying to cast out demons so to speak, but a lot of 'em seem to get hung up on their own disbelief. And they also get themselves hung up on terminology. Too many psychiatrists think that a mental patient who turns to religion as a source of help is sick with 'religiosity'[11] or guilty of 'magical thinking.' I think many of them

---

[10] Paul Tournier in his book *The Meaning of Persons*, New York: Harper & Row, 1973, p. 107, wrote:

Thinking it over, one realizes that every psychotherapist sooner or later goes beyond the strictly psychological sphere—even the Freudians, in spite of their principles. The recounting of a life story, a mind thinking aloud, freed from the bonds of formalism, leads one inevitably to the consideration of problems which are no longer psychological but spiritual, problems such as the meaning of life and of the world, of disease and of death, of sin and of faith, or one's own scale of values. Dr. Igor Caruso has, I think, very clearly defined this inevitable passage of the psychotherapist from the technical and analytic to the synthetic and 'existential' . . .

[11] In some psychiatric circles, having eschewed all religion as unscientific and delusional, patients for whom religion was a significant focus or even preoccupation, rightly or wrongly were deemed to suffer from "Religiosity." At times, some medical practitioners abused power by labeling all belief in religion as delusional. Another common label was called "Magical Thinking" under which events which we might think of as Serendipity, Synchronicty or Coincidence could be classified as a manifestation of deranged thought.

By the time *DSM™-IV Diagnostic and Statistical Manual of Mental Disorders IV*, it had been soft pedaled to "Religion and Spiritual Problem" so that the fervent practice of a religion was no longer *ipso facto* a manifestation of mental illness.

(continued...)

label prayer of any kind as 'magical thinking.' I believe they are cutting themselves short of some of the powerful healing tools at their disposal. Think what a psychiatrist could do if he combined religious healing and casting out demons, with what he already knows of psychology and human needs. That would be a great physician."

"Instead most have tunnel vision when it comes to religion. Often they do not believe, so they think someone who does is nuts. And they assume a person is nuts if he mentions the possibility of demons, deliverance, or healing, or the power of belief and prayer. Yet they preach the power of positive thinking, and how a person must believe they can get well, to get well. They must believe, but should also realize that God is the healer."

"I'm not saying that everyone who prays will be healed of mental or physical illness or would no longer need drug therapy or support. But there can be some who would be helped. More than can be helped now. There is also healing of attitude— Attitude Adjustment. The really good doctors are the ones who do not think they have all the power. God has the power; they just administer, or minister it."

We went to a food stand and bought two Cokes, then headed back for Dayton's mini-mall. He lit another cigarette and said, "I read in the New Testament that we are to exchange our heavy burdens, our yoke, for His yoke, that His yoke is light. It has been bothering me a lot this week that I have made that commitment, but I still feel heavy about what I did to myself. It's been hard for me because I was hoping to be cured once I made a spiritual

---

[11] (...continued)

However, in 1984 when this was written, psychiatrists were 'zealously' labeling patients serious about religion as having a condition called "Religiosity," seemingly without actually determining whether the interest in religion was typical or did in fact demonstrated an imbalance. The conundrum here being that most psychiatrists were trained to discredit religion in favor of the Scientific Method.

Ted believed he had been caught in this paradox, that religion was helping him, but the psychiatrist was not open to the consideration that prayer and religious practice could have beneficial therapeutic effect. Studies in the 1990s demonstrated that prayer can have a positive effects such as accelerated healing, improved outlook on life, and in coping abilities.

commitment. But His time is not our time. Even so, I'm feeling very distraught about it. I understand in my mind, but my body feels tension and anxiety. It's real bad today."

"I know the problems I am having today are partly because my medication was changed, and it's not quite right. But I also feel that I need more spiritual help. I know I need prayer."

He was asking me to pray. I had seen healing services on Long Island and even knew a few of the words that the healers used, but I couldn't bring myself there on the bench at Dayton's to lay hands on him and pray out loud. I sat there with my hands limply in my lap, closed my eyes, and prayed, "God send me someone to help with Ted this afternoon."

I opened my eyes. Coming down the Dayton's Mall right toward us was Darleen's psychiatrist from the University Hospital. *"Wow,"* I thought. *"That was, yeah, wow, some speedy answer, God."*

I ran over to her and briefly explained, "This young man is having a difficult time. He was not able to be admitted to the hospital since there was no bed space available. He feels he is having a mental crisis. He needs some help. Would you help, please?"

She replied, "It's a lovely day. Saturday is my time to put sick people's problems out of my mind." She ordered a chocolate fudge cone at Baskin and Robbins. She passed a few pleasantries, and she went on her way. I felt completely deflated. Maybe Ted was right when he said, "Psychiatry can't help all that much, but God always answers."

Ted got up abruptly and was pacing again.

"I've decided to walk back over to HCMC. Thanks for sitting with me," Ted said. "I may see you later."

I felt relieved.

That night in the TV room at The House of Charity, Ted came in, still in distress. He paced the big room, wringing his hands. Ted sat for a minute or two, and then was back up pacing. He went out for a can of Classic Coke and cigarettes. When he returned, Greatcoat strode in dramatically waving the red leather Bible. I was in the hallway in line to get my feed bag. Greatcoat asked me, "Got 40¢ I can have?"

Remembering this man as he had been with the lady on the street corner and with the receptionist, I did not want to open myself to his raving, so I said, "No, I don't. I have just enough to get a can of pop to go with my sandwich."

In the living room, Ted and Greatcoat ended up beside each other because that's where the empty chairs were. Greatcoat, the self-proclaimed man of God, asked, "Can I pray with any of you brothers here? Anyone need prayers?"

Now we all knew we needed prayers, but like Brer Rabbit before the Fox, we lay low.

"Pipe down!" Percy shouted.

"Get lost!" Romero said.

"Pray on your own time but, not when the game is on TV," another said. Gently Ted turned to him, "I need prayer a whole lot. Especially today."

They walked together back into the hallway by the dinner bag line. Greatcoat placed his red Bible on one of Ted's shoulders and his big hand on the other shoulder and bowed his head over him. He prayed, "Oh God. This here brother is in distress. He is in mental anguish. He knows You said that Your yoke is easy, Lord. But this here boy is carrying a heavy load."

"He wants to do your will, Lord. But he can't take no more heavy. Ease his mind. Help him to rest in Your comfort. You can heal troubled minds, Lord, and broken bodies. This boy needs Your healing, Your leading, Your love, Your tenderness. This boy needs You. He needs You now."

"Don't mess around, Lord. Send Yourself to this boy here tonight. He needs You. He's calling You. He wants some answers. He don't need no more grief or anguish, and trouble or f'ustration. He needs to know he can trust You to take up his burden and he will take up Yours. And he will hold You to the promise that if he takes up Your yoke, You'll make it light. Lighten his load. Lead him. Help him. Comfort him. Love him. He loves You, Lord. Don't let him down."

"Let him know You are near and that You love him. Let him feel your caring, Lord. In the name of Jesus Christ deliver him from anguish. Deliver him from every evil. In the name of Jesus Christ, bind up and cast out from him any and every demon. Give him in place Your peace and healing love. Deliver him Lord. Help him, Lord. "

"In the name of the Father, the Son, and the Holy Spirit, take care of this child of yours, Lord God Almighty. Amen."

Greatcoat didn't know Ted, but his discerning prayer spoke to the concerns Ted had and his need. In those moments, a stillness fell over the people who had been carousing in the hall. Bystanders stood with heads bowed. Everyone was praying for Ted. It was moving in its penetrating simplicity. There we were: the sick, the lame, the maimed, the ex-convicts, the ex-addicts, the unemployed, the immigrants, the economically dislocated, the walking wounded, the mentally ill, the poor in spirit, the outcasts, the misfits, the unwanted, all praying together with love for another.

When the prayer was finished, Ted was noticeably calmed. "Thanks. I needed that," Ted said. He offered to buy Greatcoat a bottle of Classic Coke.

Accepting the Classic Coke, Greatcoat said, "Thanks brother. I needed this too," he said, upending the Coke bottle.

I felt humbled. One whom I had thought comical, when put to the test came through for Ted in the way that I had been unable to that very day. The flamboyant man I had judged a fanatic, a clown, had met Ted's spiritual needs in a special way. And in the process we all were blessed.[12]

*

EMOTIONALLY DISTURBED: A SINGLES ENCOUNTER

Bernie walked up to Darleen in the hallway. They were waiting in the line to use the pay phone. The conversational tone was casual, getting-acquainted talk. She said coyly, "Well, tell me about yourself."

He said, "I'm free of cancer. I don't have cancer. I'm healthy. The only thing I inherited was mental illness. My great-grand-

---

[12] At the library, I came across this quotation: "Do not think that because another man does not shine with the virtues which you perceive, he will not be precious in God's sight, for reasons you do not perceive." from E. Allison Peers, "Counsels of Light and Love," *The Complete Works of St. John of the Cross*, Paulist Press, New York, 1978, p. 51.

mother shot herself. My grandmother was mentally ill. So were my aunts and uncles on both sides."

"Oh. Someone in my family shot himself, too."

His face lit up; they had something in common. "Yeah? Every family has someone mentally ill somewhere."

"It's not that unusual," Darleen said.

"No, but suicide is," he added.

She became uneasy. She looked stunned. He said, "I'm sorry, but you asked about me. So now you know. Don't ask about what you can't handle," he turned away stomped down the hall.

✳

HOSPITAL PAROLEE: "BERNIE TELLS OF 1970'S HOT SUMMER"

In the summer of 1970, at the height of the Vietnam protests, Minneapolis, Madison, and Berkeley were hot spots of activity protesting the Vietnam War. I was then a bride in Minneapolis. Our first apartment was in the Stevens Square complex. The summer nights were sweltering. Our third floor apartment was often 120 degrees Fahrenheit in the living room. The only things that circulated were the bus fumes from the street below and the prostitutes down the hall.

Buildings were burning down every night. It was a terrifying time. There were nightly fires and frequent bombings. The Post Office was bombed. Our apartment building was evacuated several times with bomb scares, and searches. Government buildings were routinely evacuated and searched with each new bomb scare.

Just before a thunderstorm one night, a terrorist was walking toward Honeywell to set off a plastique bomb at the Honeywell plant, when the ionized air or static electricity caused it to blow up prematurely. When we walked the dog the next morning, the bomb carrier had become fly specs on 15 automobiles. My German Shepherd dog found the bomb carrier's cheek skin. It had a scar on it. Someone else found some of his teeth. From those items positive identification was made.

Every night we were awakened from sleep by something. Some nights it was Satanists doing ritual burnings on the front walk. Other nights it was a bomb search of our building. Some mornings it was dynamite blasts to dig new Interstate Highways 94 and 35W. But my clearest memory was of fires. As a young child, I had witnessed a playmate burn, after paint solvent exploded on him, and so I was especially concerned about nightly fires so close to our apartment. Every night there were fires. The dog would get antsy from the sirens, and my husband and I would get up and walk the dog and as often as not we would walk to see a fire. The result of all this was that we could not rest easy that summer.

Now 14 years later I was back in Minneapolis.

One morning at the Food Service, a well-groomed man about 35 sat beside me. He had a distracting recurrent muscle twitch that rippled through his eyebrow, moved in waves across his forehead, and faded into his receding hair line. I named him Bernie. Bernie was alarmingly open, overtly friendly, and too talkative. The other men squirmed with his too psychological jargon. To get into less revealing talk, conversation at the table was diverted to how it was that we were there. We each took a turn.

When it was Bernie's turn, he mentioned casually, "I had sort of an 'inflammatory career' leading up to incarceration in the psychiatric prison for the criminally insane." This got our undivided attention. He went on to describe his insanity as a teenager— as a compulsive arsonist. His goal had been to see how many fires he could set simultaneously without getting caught.

"I set one the first night, two the second night, and so on. I wanted to be Nero and watch Minneapolis burn. I even practiced the fiddle, so I would be ready," he said. "I got up to 18 an evening, all burning at the same time. That took a lot of planning and coordination. Setting 18 fires in different buildings took so much planning and coordination that I didn't get any time to fiddle or even watch. Later I figured out Nero must have had someone running around starting the fires for him so he only had to do the watchin' and the fiddlin'," Bernie said animatedly.

I began to feel queasy. I glanced at this seemingly ordinary, pleasant looking man and remembered my terror the summer of 1970 when our Stevens Park neighborhood was burning. I had to ask, "Say, Bernie, what year was that? What year did you set fires every night? The 18 fires at once— when was that?"

"Oh, let me think," he paused. "It was the summer of 1970. My favorite area was around Stevens Park— all the old apartments there."

I felt dumbfounded, flabbergasted, and horrified! I felt like throwing up. This Nero had stolen time and memories of my first year as a bride. And here we were, sitting at the same table. I sat mute, bereft of words while inside I was screaming. If I had a second chance, what would I tell him?

✳

COMPOSITION OF STREET POPULATION AT HOUSE OF CHARITY: WINTER DECEMBER 1983 TO MARCH 1984[13]

54% OF THE HOMELESS WERE SEVERELY MENTALLY ILL PEOPLE: forced out of mental hospitals. Many were elderly. A few were Vietnam veterans. Every type of mental illness was represented in this population.

30% WERE ECONOMICALLY DISLOCATED IN SOME WAY: dislocated farmers; displaced factory workers replaced by robots, reductions in force or company takeovers and mergers; seasonal workers; age discriminated workers; illiterates; high school drop outs; Vietnam veterans.

10% WERE EX-SOMETHING: ex-convicts recently paroled; ex-drug addicts; alcoholics in and out of recovery.

6% INCLUDED PHYSICALLY DISABLED OR DISPLACED FROM THEIR HOME OR HOMELAND: Caregivers of the chronically ill accompanied by that dependent person; long term post-op recovery patients with no family to assist; teenagers running away from physical or sexual abuse at home; pregnant teenagers; battered women with children; battered women unaccompanied by children; immigrants; mutes; persons required to be here by court; persons required to be here to seek specialized medical care.

---

[13] Author's original research and confirmed by Catholic Social Services census for HUD, March, 1984.

PART III: DELIVERY OF SOCIAL SERVICES

The System is the way to get basic needs met. In some ways, The System needs the poverty class in order to perpetuate itself. The System isn't even one agency, or one place, or one locus of power, or one abuser of power. The System is in fragments all over the place. But as fragmented as it is, this visible and invisible System has a control over access and distribution of many of the basic necessities to which Street People especially must somehow gain access, such as food, shelter, clothing, mail, check-cashing, medical and dental care, employment opportunities, and legal assistance.

In some ways, The System is us— "We, the People"— because we allow The System to be the ways it is. "We, the People" are ultimately responsible for public policy, administrative law, and federal, state, and local regulations and practices. Our economy is flawed. Our mental health system is flawed. Our criminal court system is flawed. Our delivery system for medical services is flawed. Our system for care of the elderly is flawed. Our civil and family court systems are flawed. Our governmental policy system is flawed. Even many family systems are flawed.

All these flaws affect people. Many of the flaws affect some individuals more than others. Some individuals are affected over and over. Our flawed and failed national policies, such as parts of the failed federal housing policy (evidenced by our need to implode federal housing project apartment buildings, by extensive corruption uncovered within HUD revealed several years ago, etc.), the weakened banking system (bank failures, indictment of prominent banking officials), the failure to address the povertization of women and children, the displacement of the mentally ill, the artificially low minimum wage rate, and the repercussions of "acceptable percentages" of unemployment, all especially impact one population, the Street People, in a multiplicity of ways.

Among the parts of the System which affected me directly in 1984 were the Bureau of Employment Security, the banking system (for check-cashing), the U.S. Post Office, medical and dental care, mass transit, temporary employment agencies, the shelter system, the legal and judicial systems, city and county governments, and churches. Other institutions which Street People encounter frequently include General Assistance, Social Security, detoxification centers for alcoholics, chemical dependency treatment, aftercare facilities, literacy services (GED), Food Stamps, the food shelves, the free stores (free clothing), single-room occupancy housing (SROs), The Plasma Center (to sell blood for cash), day-labor pools, group homes, the work house, and Goodwill, the Red Cross, certain church run programs, The United Way, and the Salvation Army. In addition to food, shelter, and clothing, other necessities that the System dispensed or withheld included proof of identity, door keys, access to telephones, access to bathrooms, access to places to sit, access to sources of heat, and access to drinking water.

*

RETURN TO THE UNEMPLOYMENT OFFICE

Dear Journal,

This day I had to report again to the Bureau of Employment Security (an oxymoron),which everyone knows is really the unemployment office. To keep a claim active, you must always report to the unemployment office on the same day of the week as the day you chose to walk into it the first time. This rule was the same in New York, Pennsylvania, and Minnesota. Perhaps it was an important obscure Federal administrative regulation. My "required by law" day was Thursday. While in Minnesota, I had to report in, each week, to meet the Pennsylvania claim requirements on Thursday, and to the same people on Friday every other week, to meet Minnesota's requirement. The unemployment office in Minneapolis resented having to do what was in their opinion "double work," to process an out-of-state claim known as a "Courtesy Claim." I resented having to stand in line three times to stay certified for each unemployment check (which was being held, currently inaccessible to me).

A lady unemployment-office worker was filling in the forms required for the Interstate Courtesy Claim. These had to be filed so that even though I was not receiving any checks, I would be able to receive them when I could return to Pennsylvania (which I continued to assume would be within two weeks). I was missing a completed "Low Earnings Report" for that week because you are not allowed to complete a Low Earnings Report until Friday and it must be completed EVERY WEEK. Although she had already filled in most of the forms, when she realized the Low Earnings Report form could not be completed and attached to the form she was working on, she irately put White-Out on all my forms, covering dates and signatures.

When I saw this I said, "Please, if it is not possible to complete all the paperwork today, just hold on to the forms until tomorrow morning. I can come back then and bring in the completed Low Earnings Report and you can complete the whole packet and mail it out. You would not have to put White-Out on anything, especially signatures.

She said, "No! I'll not have my signature or anyone else's on it on a Thursday! It's misleading."

I replied, "It won't be misleading as soon as I bring in the completed Low Earnings Report on a Friday. You just hang onto the forms until tomorrow. If you keep them here, you know I can't mail them or tamper with them."

Her face twisted up and she said, "No! I am not here to be your secretary!" She glared at me over the counter.

Her attitude really stunk, and by then mine did too. I barked back, "No, you aren't here to be my secretary; I wouldn't consider hiring you. But you're here, you're supposed to process my Courtesy Claim, and you're being a nit-picking bureaucrat!" This was the first time in my life I had ever snapped back over one of these bureaucratic nightmares. My finishing school finish was wearing thin.

On Friday, I found myself waiting in her line again. I wished I could change lines, but remembering what I went through the first time I applied because I had committed the Mortal Sin of changing lines, I stayed in her line waiting to show her my Low Income Report.

In the cubicle next to hers, a woman applicant nervously explained to the unemployment clerk: "I got sick, and I missed the interview, and . . . . Will I lose all my benefits?" the applicant asked. "If I do get cut off, I won't have nothin'."

The clerk replied, "Okay, lady, here's what you do. Do just what I tell you," he said, pulling out the forms. "First, take a deep breath. Second, don't worry. Third, the worst that will happen is you will lose one week's pay. Don't you feel better now?"

The applicant said, "Wow. I didn't think anyone in the Unemployment Office could be that nice." (I didn't believe anyone in the Employment Office could be that kind, either.)

He said, "Do you think I've never had a turn on your side of the counter? It will be okay for you. Don't panic and don't give up hope. Just fill in these forms. If you have a problem or any questions, I'll help you."

These incidents are reported verbatim, just as they happened. These two professional people were working side by side in the same office, doing the same tasks, and both were overloaded, as they saw several hundred people each day; but the difference in style was incredible. How differently they sent their clients out into the desolate world of being unemployed— where a job turndown for many seemed like a rejection of their whole being, a world where one feels unwanted, unneeded, unnecessary, a nothing— where, for many, sleeping eventually seemed to be the only answer to suppress the pain of piled-up bills and tumbled-down hopes, where a bureaucrat, dead to his/her own feelings, could tie up every feeling you had left— through delay, red tape, forms, denials, discouragement, and sub-humanness. Or he/she could let you know you are not alone: there are things that can be done to resolve the problem, and in so doing there need not be senseless delays. Knowing that someone cared about your case was enough to make a difference. Finding that he/she was willing to take steps to resolve the logjam could seem like a miracle.

How a person handles your case can affirm and validate an applicants worth (whether an employed person or a person who lacks paid employment). And it is not that all our affirmations or validations should come from others but, especially when dealing with persons who have fallen through the safety net, this worker on the front lines may be the only human contact the recipient has.

On many days, the social worker you have to report to on that day may be the only person who knows you exist, the only person you talked to. And if that person, like the example described above, is irritable, unfeeling, irascible, or obstreperous, it can be a pretty shitty experience— an experience that cuts away at a person's basic humanity.

As a street person or a social services recipient, every line on every day says you're under someone else's schedule and convenience. To survive, to get your needs met even minimally, you have to do it their way on their schedule. I know the maxim "Don't let another person take away your power," but on the street, you have no grasp of this concept. You have no idea that you have any power, because in almost every way throughout every day you are reminded that you are powerless and valueless.

✳

NEEDING TO CASH CHECKS

In the Twin Cities, checking accounts were expensive. At that time, the banks and savings & loan associations had a big hush-hush cash-flow problem. To compensate, banks usually would not cash a check that was unless it was deposited to an account in their financial institution AND had cleared the originating bank. Frequently this meant it took as much as ten days to get money drawn on a local check. On an out-of-state check, it could take as long as 30 days to get money. For a Street Person with no money, ten days could be an eternity. A checking account then required maintaining the minimum balance, which in Minneapolis usually ranged from $200 to $1,000; it was therefore a luxury we could not afford.

At the same time, if you were a Street Person, you were likely to be receiving some kind of government check such as Supplemental Security Income (SSI) or SSI-Disability, or straight Social Security. Even those who were lucky enough to get some work now and then were likely to be paid for the work with a check. Larger employers, such as the multinational corporations based in the Twin Cities, often did not use a local bank for payroll checks. The term "local" was often narrowly defined by banks to mean a very limited geographic area. For example, some of the checks from Manpower, Inc., came from Edina, an affluent Minneapolis suburb about eight miles from the Crystal Court banks. Yet these city banks often held up these checks before cashing them, as if they were from another country. Other Manpower checks were issued out of Milwaukee, Wisconsin. Then I really had problems cashing checks.

At that time, TCF (then a Savings and Loan) would not cash:

(1) any out-of-town check, or
(2) any check not deposited to an account, or
(3) any check that had not been held by them ten business days or longer and cleared.

When a person tried TCF or the now-defunct Midwest Federal, they were referred to the Skyway offices of Marquette Bank, which was slightly better about the time it took to clear a check. National City Bank and Norwest Bank were about the same as TCF and Midwest Federal, except then sometimes Norwest Bank held a check for 20 days.

National City Bank ("NCB") also required applicants for a checking account:

(1) to provide references from previous banks,
(2) to swear to having good credit, and
(3) to affirm that the applicant never had a checking account closed at the initiative of a bank.

At that time, I had my name on several NCB long-term trust certificates being held for my children (under the then Uniform Gift to Minors Act) which I had set up for my children and did not want to disturb. Even though I was a depositor this way, NCB would still not cash checks for me.

Some Street People told me that bars will cash paychecks if you're a regular.

I could find only one way to get a check cashed that was within the range I could get to. Through a Catholic Charities caseworker, I obtained a Letter of Introduction to First Bank System Minneapolis (FBS) pertaining to cashing one specific check for a specific

WAGES EARNED FOR HOURS WORKED IN MINNEAPOLIS
JANUARY 6 TO MARCH 31, 1984

I worked for wages during every opportunity when I was not required to be attending to my children's needs, or to court, to report somewhere for a basic necessity, and did not have pneumonia. There were three weeks when there was no work available for me through Manpower. My earnings record, based on pay stubs for that period, was:

WEEK ENDING	GROSS	HOURS
01/08/84	$ 70.00	14.00
01/15/85	58.75	11.45
01/22/84	172.00	42.00
01/29/84	204.49	44.00
02/05/84	60.00	12.00
02/29/84	0.00	0.00
02/26/84	60.00	12.00
03/04/84	30.00	6.00
	$655.24	141.45 HR

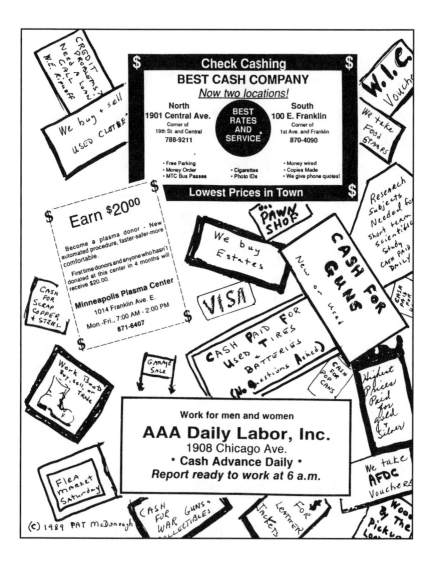

Figure 6. Non-traditional sources of cash.

amount. If you didn't have a caseworker to arrange such a letter, you were stuck.[14]

Since, being from out of state, I found no other way to cash a check, I started using the procedure. It took about half a day to wait in line to get to see the Catholic Charities caseworker. It took her five minutes or less to issue the letter. Then, because of the weather outdoors, to walk the longer way, indoors, through several segments of the Skyway maze: through the Government Center Skyway, through the Pillsbury Building Skyway, to FBS; take the escalator down to the street level. The lower lobby was about a half-block square. Over in the far southwest corner on this day was a yuppie Receptionist who screened people coming to see FBS Personal Bankers. She flinched whenever a Street Person walked up to her desk to ask to see Mrs. Pollock. Mrs. Pollock doesn't flinch. I am grateful to Mrs. Pollock, even now. In the arrogant maze of banking, she was gracious and decent, and she also signed for me to cash my checks.

This reception area had love seats to sit on and current magazines to read. The waiting in this sitting area took about half

---

[14] It was a widespread belief among Street People that by using this procedure to cash checks, one would jeopardize his/her shelter housing slot. I didn't verify this at the time, but it was so generally accepted that I presume it must have been the policy in some, if not all, of the shelters. Even assuming it to be true was enough to deter many Street People from making arrangements to cash checks this way, because it would reveal to Catholic Charities that he/she was about to get or had gotten a check. With no hope then of having enough for a security deposit, getting a check didn't mean that one could afford a rental unit, even for a short time. And because the act of asking whether it might be possible to get a check cashing voucher would imply that one might be expecting a check, most Street People feared it would be revealing too much, so many avoided this service. None of the Street People I asked knew whether it really would jeopardize their shelter placement.

Several years later, Catholic Charities and St. Olaf's Church purchased property to established the Exodus Hotel and a program to assist such homeless people to successfully transition into rental housing by assisting them with security deposit, and where possible, connecting them with rental subsidies and follow up support services.

an hour. The procedure was to meet with Mrs. Pollock and explain your circumstances in the privacy of her cubicle. She had a good memory. For example, you only had to tell her your whole life history once— the first time you came in. Then she personally escorted you to a teller, introduced you with grace and cordiality, and instructed the teller how to process the check. Thank God for that lady and that bank.

The bottom line was that after I had one 8-hour day of work, then it was necessary to spend at least half a day (4 hours) to get my check cashed. Those lucky enough to get a whole week of day work, who only had the weekend free, could forget it. Eat the check. On the weekend downtown (without rights to an ATM card), a check is worth nothing. On a weekday, it might have some value if it could be cashed. It also became important to know what days Mrs. Pollock worked and when she took vacations, attended funerals, and the like, because on those days I found no one else there who would or could cash Street People's checks.[15]

*

WELFARE: GENERAL ASSISTANCE

I can't say much good about Minnesota or Pennsylvania General Assistance, because as a Pennsylvania resident destitute in Minnesota under a Minnesota court order, the Minnesota General Assistance office only offered me scorn and derision. They accused me of coming to Minnesota for the sole purpose of aspiring to become a Minnesota welfare recipient. Months later Hennepin County Assistance was willing to provide me with a little more than scorn and derision— a one-way bus ticket out of the state. See Appendix II Handout: Summary of Hennepin County's "Bus Ticket Home" Policy.

*

---

[15] A year later, I learned that had I been able to walk far enough—outside, not in the Skyway system—at that time about four miles one way, there were money-changers who would cash a check for a 16% squeeze off the top.

PROOF OF IDENTITY

At that time on the main floor of The Government Center, there was a large U-shaped area where assorted licenses and identification cards were issued, such as drivers license, photo ID and such. If you were on the street, supporting a car was a liability, and driving anything was not affordable; therefore, street people mostly didn't own a current driver's license. To accommodate non-drivers, Minnesota offered Photo Identification Cards. This proof of identification should be just the answer for a Street Person— but it's not.

To obtain a card, it was necessary to fill out a form and show two proofs of who you are (or who you had been). These proofs must show where you currently reside. A Post Office Box was not acceptable. A Street Person, especially in the winter, doesn't know where he/she lives for more than seven days at a time. Unless such a person were lucky enough to have a friend whose circumstances were better, and who permitted the street person to pretend that such house was his or her residence so that it was then possible to fake two pieces of mail or other documents received at this place where he/she allegedly was living, a street person would not be eligible to get a Photo ID. On the other hand, the Street Person could opt to have his/her Photo ID say "House of Charity"— as if that would enhance your credibility when you had to show ID. The catch for this one was that most Street People were not allowed to stay at the shelter long enough to get the requisite two pieces of mail.

If you were able to fulfill all these requirements, proved that you existed and that you resided somewhere acceptable, and filled in the form, then for $6 Hennepin County would take your picture and put it on a card which could be mailed to you in about eight weeks. Of course, in eight weeks who knows where you would be. I don't understand why it takes eight weeks. In Pennsylvania, it was same-day service for the same type of photo ID that was offered in Minnesota at that time.[16]

---

[16] Since then, Minnesota has "improved" its procedure— now it takes three to fourteen months to receive a driver's license or identity card with iridescent loons, the Minnesota official bird, reflected on one's visage.

The obvious conclusion was that a Street Person could not obtain the needed ID. It appeared the system didn't want to identify those people who were living beneath the Safety Net. You don't count, if you are not landed gentry or at least have a leasehold interest. It seems to me that the constitution declared citizenship as apart from land-ownership more than two hundred years ago.

*

POLITICAL ECONOMY: THE SAFETY NET

In government parlance, "The Safety Net" is an economic concept used to group and describe the benefits and payments from federal, state, and local governments, and tax credits made to poor people as a last resort— to provide a minimum amount of funds for their maintenance at the poverty level. Since its inception, however, due to many factors, the federally defined poverty level rarely coincides with the actual poverty level, and the minimum payments have not been adjusted enough to keep up with the new actual poverty level. I suppose it is a reflection of a devalued worth of the dollar that each year it costs more to be poor. The minimum wage, of course, is trailing about 20 years behind.

The Hennepin County Government Center is a 24-story high office tower of mauve-colored granite and glass. Through the midsection of the building is open space, above which the towers are connected by with internal bridges on every other floor. The building has glass curtain-walls twenty-four stories high on two sides. There are interior windows on the insides of the H facing the Atrium and reflecting pond, and at the North and South ends of the building. These windows are washed on the outside during the summer and on the inside during the winter.

The boxy shape and bridges connecting the Administration Tower (A-Tower) with the Court Tower (B-Tower) resemble the shape of the letter H, and the particular shape of the "H" of the towers matches the "H" of the County logo. The letter and shape of "H" is symbolic in Minnesota: Vice President and former Minneapolis Mayor Hubert Horatio Humphrey, the Northern Pacific Railroad baron James J. Hill, the explorer Fr. Louis Hennepin, and multi-talented official Harley Hopkins, are among its favorite sons.

For a pedestrian entering the Government Center building from the street level walkway (rather than via the parking ramp), it was common to ride the escalator up to the main floor to reach the elevators to go social or court services, or General Assistance. I was riding up on the escalator from the street level to go up to the main level. Looking overhead, above me I saw a gigantic black safety net placed to catch any falling window washers. It was symbolic to me that I was entering this building *under* their safety net. It was symbolic to me that at that time most Street People coming to the county building to request General Assistance, Court Services, or Food Stamps entered this system from beneath this actual safety net.

✻

RECENT AMPUTEE

"We came here from California two weeks ago. My checks are held up in getting transferred to Minnesota. In California, I receive $541 per month in disability and here they tell me I will receive only $341 per month. How can the same Federal program for the same disability pay the same person different amounts in another state?"

"What's with your leg? MS?" I asked her.

"No. Car accident a year ago. Hurt my head and my leg. Left me crippled."

"Did you get any settlement from the one who hit you?"

"No one hit me. I was the driver. All I got was an invitation to the Special Olympics. That was really fun. I was good in the wheel-chair races."

✻

WITHOUT KEYS

I met Robert during lunch at the Food Service Center. He was commenting on what it is like for him, living under the Safety Net. Robert said, "We is on the street. We wasn't always on the streets though. Once some of us was somebody. But now, what we are is what you see. We is all together, just like a turtle is all together. We carry everything from here to there and back again."

"Each year there is less and less to carry— like keys. I don't carry keys no more. When you lives in a shelter, you gots a room, but only for the night. During the day you are locked out on the street— all day, every day. You may use the room at night but you may not use the key. The key is always part of somebody else's job."

"A key and a job are symbols of the other class. Most of all, a key implies that there is something else out there, 'cause there always has to be the other side for the key— like a house, a car, a post office box. Something. The key says you are not just what you see, because some of you is always locked up someplace else. Parts of you are here to see and parts of you are behind the other side of all the keys you carry. The more keys, the more fragments of yourself are all over the place. Each of those fragments is a fragment of power and control and structure that is yours, but apart from you."

"When you fall down through the cracks in this economy, your keys to the time when you was somebody do not fall through the cracks with you. Like Alice in Wonderland, YOU change size and slip through the gaps in the safety net, but the keys don't change. Keys don't pass through the net when you fall through it to the bottom of this society."

I never saw Robert again. I think of him every time I have a key in my hand.

✻

MEDICAL CARE: "THE MAKING OF A SURGEON"

A young man joined us in the breakfast line. He was the lumber-jack who had come into town because the camp shut down during this cold spell. Jack said, "Look at my hands. They are all swelled up this morning, and they hurt like hell."

Another man checked them gently and said, "They are frost-bitten. Go right away to the clinic. Mostly it's free. They have a salve for frostbite. If you don't use that salve, the skin will peel off. Your hands will ooze and gangrene is a real possibility. Don't mess around with the hospital. The hospital takes too long, and they won't have the right stuff. Go where I told you. You gotta watch where you go or you will just get beginners who don't really know how to doctor."

A few days later, I learned what he meant about beginning doctors. Something was growing on my back, rapidly, and changing shape and color. I knew it had to come off. My family has a history of skin problems— some such growths had gone to cancer. I walked to the Public Health Building downtown to see if they would check it. They wouldn't. They set up an appointment for me at Health Etc. Clinic on Lake Street and told me the clinic charge would be $5. Fine. I had $5.60 total so I could manage bus fare and the clinic fee. (My Jet Pass had expired.) It was brutally cold, and too far for me to walk. I had to take a bus down Nicollet Avenue and transfer at Lake Street, but when you have the Big C on your mind, you don't think about much else.

The Clinic was on a second floor over a store and offices. The Clinic did dentistry as well as traditional medicine. The waiting corner was overcrowded with obviously poor folks. I calmly sat down, glad for a chance to read magazines and warm up. But in the waiting area, men in their 30's and 40's had cheeks swollen out like hamster pouches. The men commiserated and analyzed the intensity of pain a tooth could cause and played "my toothache is bigger than yours." Another man returned to the room from the Dentistry area. He had a wad of bloody gauze showing from the corner of his mouth. He tried to join the conversation in a garbled way. Since this man had just had an extraction, that made him an authority ranking above the others.

As I remembered my past experiences, like having had the wrong tooth pulled, having abscesses and root canals, I began to feel uneasy with their "mine is worse than yours" stories. Not that I was unsympathetic; I was too sympathetic. The conversation about tooth pain, jaw pain, drill pain, pulling-the-tooth pain and its fateful-cracking noise of dental extraction triggered memories of my four root canals the previous year (a procedure I had just realized was available only to the wealthy), memories of dental bills, memories of the dislocated jaw when the dentist tried to climb into my mouth, and memories of allergic reactions to anesthetics. My heart began to beat faster, then pounded into my ears.

When I was little, new anesthetics were tested on me. That experimental dentistry left me permanently allergic to all the anesthetics that end in "-caine." (I know, "-caine" means a street substance now, but this was then.) The problem started because my permanent teeth were not lined up over my baby teeth. To realign the permanent teeth before eruption, while they were still under the gums, the orthodontist hammered balsa-wood spikes into my gum line— sixteen balsa-wood spikes a week, for a year. (By today's standards, that would have been child abuse!) It worked to realign the teeth. My permanent teeth came in all right. But I was sickly that whole year with many infections.

All this flooded over me as I listened to the men talk about their teeth, or lack of them. My pulse raced. Soon it was my turn to see the Doctor about the growth on my back. I knew it had to come off. I also knew I was allergic to local anesthesia.

A volunteer nurse took my blood pressure. It was the highest it had ever been. She took my temperature and cuffed my arm again. I got worried about the high reading and started deep breathing to try to calm myself. "I can't hear it well," she said. "I'll have to do the other arm."

"*Can't hear it?*", I thought, "*It sounds like 'Bolero,' to me.*" She took it three times on one arm and twice on the other. I continued controlled breathing, trying to tune out.

She looked confused, "Your blood pressure on your left arm is up. No surgery today. Your right arm, however, is within the range of normal." I guess the breathing worked on half of me. I couldn't resist asking her how she got separate readings from the same pump.[17]

The doctor looked at the growth and set the appointment for the next day. That confirmed to me that this might be serious. He said, "I have never done an excision before. I'm worried about trying it— especially since you don't want anesthesia."

I said, "It's okay, Doctor. I'm the one who will feel it. Just get a can of stuff to freeze it. I can take that."

He said, "But I've never cut anyone alive before." I had had another one removed last year, so I told him exactly how it was done. "Are you sure it's that easy?" he asked.

---

[17] I have asked several doctors about this, and their response has been that a slight difference in the reading from one arm to another is not unusual, but a more common error would be that the cuff itself was not the right size and therefore neither reading was reliable. Another possibility mentioned was that the cuff was malfunctioning.

"Yes," I said. "Just have the freezing stuff and a scalpel. I'm sure you won't have any trouble. You're the only doctor I've got here right now, and this has to come off."

He said, "Okay, I'll see you tomorrow."

Since they didn't do any procedure that day, they didn't ask for any money. From my $5.60 I took 25¢ to get to the clinic, 60¢ to get to visitation with my son, and 60¢ to get back to the House of Charity.

When I went to see my younger son, I started the conversation by asking, "What did you do today?"

"I got a blood test."

"What was it for?"

"To measure stress."

"Stress?"

"Yeah, stress. The doctor is really funny. The lawyers want to see if I have stress. Of course I have stress. Every kid has stress when he knows he has to have a blood test! And this test they had to do over and over again for a whole day. Lawyers, courts, divorce, doctors, clinics, blood tests— all this make stress!"

"Yes. I know exactly what you mean."

The next day I went back to the Health Etc. Clinic. I was preparing mentally for the surgery by using self-hypnosis and the controlled breathing (left over from the Lamaze I never got to use because I had C-Sections). It was working great. The nurse said, "No high blood pressure today."

But the Doctor was something else. "You know I've never done this before. You are my first operation. My first freezing. I've never heard of freezing tissue before. You're the first person I ever heard of, allergic to local anesthesia. I don't know if I can take it."

"Doctor, I have confidence in your training. I need you to do this. Just use a sharp scalpel, a steady hand, and flick it off. No trouble at all. You can do it, doctor."

"I'm really nervous. I don't know if I can keep my hand steady. It's not very steady right now."

The nurse also sensed his state, "Sure, doctor, you can do it. Don't be scared. There has to be a first time."

"Please, doctor, please cut it off. I can't do it by myself. I can't reach the center of my back."

"But it's right over the spinal column. What if it has roots?" he asked.

"The last one didn't have roots. Just cut crosswise and you will do fine. Don't go deep, just get it off," I coached him.

"I looked it up in the book last night. Bad ones have roots. If I don't get it all, it will grow back. If it grows back, or if the knife slips while it's on your spinal column, you might sue me for malpractice."

"Doctor, from what you have said, I already understand that this is practice for you. I have no money to pay anyone with a trained hand. I have to take you. You are going to bite the bullet and do this operation."

The nurse said, "When I spray this stuff on, Doctor, you start cutting. Just a steady crosswise sawing motion."

The nurse sprayed the freezing aerosol. "Okay, now cut," she prompted.

He began the excision as I did my pant-pant-blow routine. He said, "Don't hyperventilate, because if you pass out while I'm slicing, you'll be a paraplegic."

"Hope for the best, Doctor, and keep cutting," I snapped at him.

"Can my hypnosis continue in the face of his self-doubt?" I wondered.

He whined, "I can't. I can't go on. I can't see what I'm doing."

"What do you mean you can't go on?" I asked.

He replied, "I can't see. The frozen tissue turned white. Now the good skin matches the bad skin. I can't see what to cut. I'll have to defrost you to see what I have accomplished."

Then he cheered, "Hey, look! I can really see what I did. I'm half through with it. Isn't the blood a pretty red? I'll just circle the work area with this magic marker. Okay Nurse, spray it again." She sprayed the incision.

"Oh, my, my," he said. "The aerosol makes the magic marker run. I'll just have to cut that off. Does it hurt when I cut?"

"It's okay," I said.

"Does it hurt yet?" the doctor asked.

"Keep cutting," the nurse urged.

"Does this hurt?" the doctor questioned. "Doesn't that hurt? Why doesn't it hurt?"

"Okay, it hurts!" I snapped impatiently. "Is that what you wanted to hear?"

"Good, that's better," the doctor said. I didn't know if he meant it was better that it hurt, or he just liked his progress.

"How can I keep my mind off pain, if you keep asking me if it hurts?"

"Hey, this is easy. Just like cutting steak," he boasted.

"Am I well marbled? Grade A? Prime?" I prompted.

"No. I'd say it's 'economy grade'," he commented.

"Are you almost through?" I said irritably.

"Well, I could be, but I really want to do it right. I'm going to cut a little more here and there just to be sure," he said as he doubled the size of the excision.

"Are you done yet?"

"Nope. Not yet, I thought I'd just pretty it up a bit. I don't want to leave messy, ragged edges. Cuticle scissors, Nurse."

"Cuticle scissors?" the nurse raised her eyebrows.

"Yeah. Those itty-bitty ones that are really sharp," the doctor said. She handed them to him as he fancied up his creative work. "Okay, nurse. Styptic pencil."

"Styptic pencil?" the nurse said in amazement.

"Yeah. You know— to stop the blood from running all over."

"How about the traditional Red Cross method of applying dressings with direct pressure?"

"I thought this would be quicker. It always works when I cut myself shaving."

"Okay, this one is done. This is fun. I think I'll do this other one, too, while I'm at it." So I got two removed and a beaming, confident surgeon was born.

As I waited in the outer office for the bookkeeper, the doctor caught up with me and said, "Here are some dressings to take with you. Have someone change the dressing every four hours for the next week. Don't take a bath for a few days. Don't wear any clothing that would bind against it. And don't sleep on it. Keep an eye on it for the next 24 hours to be sure it doesn't start bleeding again and you'll be just fine. If you can't reach it, ask someone at home to help you."

I thought about what he said: "*Change the dressing every four hours. Keep it very clean. Go braless. Don't sleep on your back or your side. Keep an eye on the area of the incision. Ask someone at home to help you.*" I could see it now— going braless into the House of Charity living room every four hours and asking for volunteers to lift my blouse, clean the wound, and change my dressings. You bet.

"Well, Doctor, thanks for your help. I hope you do fine. Just study the vocabulary words a little harder."

"Don't forget to call me tomorrow, or the next day, so I can tell you if it's Cancer."

I sank into the chair in the lobby and looked around, trying to forget about the doctor. A young girl dressed her well-baby in a thin flannel and covered its head with a crocheted crib blanket. The baby didn't have a snow suit. The mother was wearing a short, loose coat. The wind could go right under it. How far does she have to walk? How would they stay warm? As they left, a man entered. The tips of his fingers are were crudely bandaged. Frost-bite.

The bookkeeper returned and called my name. She said, "That will be $12 for yesterday, $30 for two biopsies, and $12 for today. You must pay before you leave." I knew those prices were more than reasonable, but the city public health service had said it would only be $5.00 at Health, Etc. I said, "When I called for an appointment, they confirmed it would only be $5.00. I had $5.00 when I came here yesterday, but I had to come back today. I spent some of the $5.00 to get to see my son yesterday, and some to get here today."

I emptied my change purse on the counter and said, "Here is what I can pay today. Bill me for the rest. Take it or leave it . . . . Whoops, I forgot my bus fare." I quickly took back 60¢ from the dwindling pile of coins. I smiled weakly at her. She shot me a fierce glare and quickly scraped the money toward her like a croupier clearing a roulette table. I said, "I'll call you tomorrow about the biopsy."

The bookkeeper retorted, "I'll remember you when you call. Nobody comes here with money. Even when we tell them only $5 or $10. How are we supposed to collect enough to meet the payroll? We got to eat too. If we don't get some money coming in soon, this Clinic will have to close."

"I'll pay. I promise. I just can't pay today."

"Yeah. I've heard that before."

I did pay, eventually. Unfortunately, one of the growths grew back.

*

DENTAL CARE

I took two MTC buses back to the IDS building, and ate the last hoarded McGlynn's sweet roll that I had. The IDS building is a blue-glass building, taller than the Empire State Building. Tonight was my first night working for TCF as an ATM Monitor— watching the computer that watches eight teller machines. I worked two to four nights a week for the next several months. I had to obtain curfew extensions from the House of Charity to be able to stay out after 8:30 p.m.— otherwise I would have been locked out and my bed reassigned.

Today, I had not had breakfast, lunch, or dinner, partly because of the surgery, and I was now flat broke, so I couldn't buy anything to eat. Because I had to get to work, I missed the brown bag supper when it was distributed at House of Charity. So at the bank, when I was on break, the cleaning man said I should go into the lounge area. In the lounge at TCF a sign read "Help yourself to coffee and soft bread sticks," so I did. As I bit into the bread stick, I heard a ghastly crunch. I had broken my tooth— the one with the root canal I was still making payments on. The right incisor tooth was broken in half and dangling. I was 1,200 miles from my regular dentist. I felt sick at heart. What next?

The next morning, I walked to the University of Minnesota Dentistry Clinic on the East Bank of the Mississippi. After an hour's wait, I was assigned to a dentist. The short, round, young dentist argued vehemently with me: "You cannot possibly be allergic to anesthesia. That is a very rare allergy!"

"Well, I am a very rare person."

"If you are, in fact, allergic to anesthesia, which I seriously doubt, it would be to the Adrenalin, not to the 'caine product in it."

"Doctor, I know my body. I know the reaction is not to the Adrenalin but to the caine part of the anesthesia. I know it is the sulfa chain which makes up the caine family drugs. I have had tests to confirm it. And I am not going into anaphylactic shock just to prove you wrong." With this exchange cementing our trust relationship, he proceeded to examine my broken tooth.

"I haven't seen one like this before. I can't tell exactly how to fix it. Just lean your head back while I pull it out, and that will solve the problem quick and easy."

"You can't pull it out; it's not paid for yet. I can't afford to lose another tooth. I have collapsing-bite problem already, and my orthodontist is adamant that if I lose another tooth, all the other teeth will topple over and my bite will cave in. I need this one fixed, not pulled. Can't you glue the halves together or put a plastic cap on it?"

He ordered X-rays to be taken, but failed to order the proper angle or the right-sized film, so the photo failed to locate the break or to show how far up into the gum line it was broken. "It will be necessary to cut up into the gum line to explore the root of the tooth to locate where the break is. I'm just going to give you this injection of Novocaine so you won't be bothered by my probing."

"No Novocaine. No Lidocaine. I'll be fine. No caine, period."

"But I inject all my patients."

"That does it! Excuse me, but I really must leave. The tooth will wait until I get back to my REAL dentist, who has experience, believes what I say, and knows which X-rays are necessary for the job."

"You're mighty fussy for a charity case."

Yesterday's novice doctor was at least pleasant and cooperative, but today I was in such discomfort from yesterday's minor surgery and the distress of the broken tooth, I had no patience left to coach another beginner— especially one whose arrogance and anesthesia could put me into anaphylactic shock.

I decided to cope with the broken tooth until I could be with a trusted dentist— but what about the people here, who have no one else?[18]

After the episode with the University Dental Clinic, I crossed over the frozen Mississippi River on the double decker bridge, made the wide arc around the Hubert H. Humphrey Metrodome, where men were on the fabric roof shoveling snow to prevent its collapse. Then over to the old Kasota-stone, gold-colored Grain Exchange building, through the elegant doors, up the curving marble staircase to the modest offices of Legal Aid. I could no longer afford my fee-for-service attorney. His predecessor had been so impressed with the spousal duress and the tax code aspects of my story that he resigned from the firm to research and write a book on the subject. The junior attorney assigned to represent me didn't want to do "domestic work," so he tripled the hourly rate, making it impossible for pay. Hence, Legal Aid to the rescue.

From there, I crossed 4th Street and 4th Avenue at each corner, because despite the Walk and Don't-Walk signals, Minneapolis considers diagonal crossing at such intersections as jaywalking. Many other cities set the Walk light to afford pedestrians the opportunity to cross in any of six directions. The old clock tower showed it was 1:30 p.m. I went into the brownstone fortress of City Hall, touched Mr. Mississippi's toe for luck (in Italy the similar statue without the ears of corn is Neptune), passed the pop machines standing sentry in the corner. The long white marble pedestrian hallway wound past Sheriff Don Omodt's office and became a tunnel passing under the Street, the plaza, and winterized fountain that marks the entrance of the Hennepin County Government Center. Briefly admiring the Native American art on display in the glass cases, I glanced at the civil servants, judges, and attorneys dining in the employee cafeteria, reassuringly I reached into my parka pocket to see if I still had a McGlynn's sweet roll. Nope.

---

[18]   As it turned out, it was May of 1986 before I paid off the root canal and could afford to get this one reconstructed for $500 so that the others didn't fall over. It was extremely inconvenient to have a broken tooth dangling all that time, but I'm glad I waited.

At the in-the-wall U.S. Postal Center, I deposited some letters home, then proceeded up to tiers of escalators, nodded to some Street People trying to be invisible under the trees by the indoor reflecting pool, then over to the A-tower bank of elevators— most of which were shut down for repair or didn't stop at the floor you needed. I checked in with the office of my son's caseworker to set up an appointment for a progress report.

Although the temperature was about 20 degrees below zero, winter temperature means nothing here. Every day is business-as-usual. At both places, I was put down for coming by without calling first. Having paid all my money to the Clinic for yesterday's surgery, I did not have the quarters to call. All I had was my feet.

*

Dear Journal,

Why do so many male medical professionals create a power struggle when a female patient tries to convey germane medical information? Many doctors need training in listening skills so that they do not bring ego-baggage into the dyad.

I can't believe how I spoke to the doctor and dentist. Profound changes are occurring inside me. I am changing from a polite, patient, soft-spoken person to impatient, assertive, and self-protective. The age-old dictum that 'nice girls don't get angry' is crumbling. Maybe nice girls don't get the message. Time will tell whether this skill will be a virtue or an impediment. I am experiencing a lot of feelings— anger, resentment, self-protectiveness, rage, festering frustration, dejection, disillusionment, dismay, and being disrespected. I feel such resentment in response to the looks that professionals, who don't have a clue concerning what it is like, give. I feel so much consternation with the red tape, the lines, the hassle just to do simple straight-forward things.

I have been so resilient throughout my life; I didn't think this experience would make much difference. But I am changing on a deep level, beneath the level of attitude, even beneath the place where ideas become words. Is it that we are changed by what we experience, whether we intend it or not? Even when, perhaps, certain such changes are not welcome.

*

MEDICAL CARE: "TO THE ER FOR AN RX"

Aeneas had to walk up 8th Street to the HCMC for his cancer surgery. He asked me to look after Dolly but when I agreed, I really made a mistake. I did spend time with her Thursday and Friday mornings. By Friday afternoon I came down sick, and by Saturday I could hardly hold my head up. I came down with bronchial pneumonia so bad I was having severe difficulty breathing, and pain.

I called the Health Etc. Clinic, whose answering service advised me, "Hennepin County Medical Center is covering for the Clinic. The Clinic is closed on weekends. Go to the HCMC." Getting change for phone calls, getting to a phone, getting a turn to use the phone, and getting the run-around took up the morning, and I am still angry about it. At least I don't have to take a bus to get to HCMC; it's just up the street across from the Food Service.

I was past taking a decongestant, which could clear my head but probably make my cough worse, or cough medicine, which would loosen up my chest and fill up my head. Because decongestants are drying and cough medicines are moisturizing, taking them both at the same time usually doesn't work for me. From the fever and the varieties of green mucus, I judged that I was past the viral stage and well into a secondary bacterial infection. My ears were so congested that my balance was affected. I knew I needed an antibiotic. On a Saturday, there are even fewer places to go for medical help. My only option was the HCMC, which was within walking distance.

The Emergency Room (ER) Intake Desk at the HCMC is not called a reception area, or an intake office, or even Station One— it's called the Triage Desk! (Triage refer to quickly deciding who gets life sustaining care and who doesn't.)[19] What made me most uncomfortable in this hospital admitting room is that it felt like the

---

[19] In 1966, at WETA-TV (Washington, D.C.), I served on an Emmy Awards Committee. We reviewed an Army Training film at Walter Reed Army Medical Center on the French system of medicine used on the battlefields in Vietnam— *triage medicine.* Amid all the gore, the film stressed that under the triage medicine system, one decides as quickly as possible who is likely to die and lets them, so that more time is available to spend on those who have a good chance of surviving with standard First Aid procedures such as applying clean dressings and pressure to bleeding wounds.

triage was ranking who could pay rather than what was the urgency of the condition.

Figure 7. In case of emergency.

I waited in the chair next to the elevated platform for the Triage Desk for a while, until it was my turn to tell my symptoms in the direction of the platform. I couldn't see the face of the person asking me the questions. Eventually another person in blue pajamas (scrubs) asked me more questions and filled out a history and physical form, then took my temperature and blood pressure. As soon as it was decided that I could still walk, I had to go directly to the Accounting Office. I suspect other ones— people who might not be able to walk, can bypass the blood pressure-temperature-history-and-physical interview and be wheeled right to the Accounting Department.

Next I had to "settle my account" before I even had an account. If I didn't, I wouldn't be allowed to have an account or, for that matter, to see a doctor either. The Accounting person looked over her horn-rimmed glasses and said, "That will be $60." I hadn't even seen the doctor yet.

Once again I had to tell my life story. I showed her all the court documents, and explained all the Catch 22's why I didn't have any income— even though I was working two jobs— and how I had become a charity case. This was not, however, the first time I had been here, and this was the second time I had told this person my situation. I had been to the clinic in this hospital one night when I discovered gangrene in my surgical incision from the surgery by the doctor who was afraid to operate. That particular night I had been issued a Purple Card. I could not have the standard General Assistance Medical Assistance Card that 'most everyone else uses, because I was from out-of-state. Minnesota doesn't like people from the place called out-of-state.

I showed the lady my Purple Card that I had gotten last time. That was a mistake. She took it away because I had already used it last month, and it was a one-time-only card. I didn't know that. About an eternity later, she settled the matter by deciding that I should see the doctor today but report to the hospital's caseworker on Monday.

The caseworker was great and knew her stuff. I wish I could say as much for the doctor I got in the Emergency Room. I felt embarrassed to be using the ER for a respiratory infection, but my options were limited, and I was very sick. When I got to go to the

ER itself, I waited for an hour or so. That was okay with me, because the person ahead of me was seeking treatment for bleeding knife wounds. After he was released, there weren't any other emergencies waiting— just a number of us from The House of Charity with the same flu and pneumonia.

Keg, a stocky, blue-eyed man with honey-colored hair under a seaman's cap, was there, sitting beside me. He recognized me; we nodded but couldn't hold a conversation. The only English words I ever heard him say were on my first day at the House of Charity: "De ol' man, he reely cut one." When Keg did speak, he spoke Spanish. Since there were no bilingual staff members in the ER, he gave his history and physical in pantomime. Three persons in lab coats crowded round him to figure out what he was saying. Finally Keg got graphic. He coughed. He pretended to heave. He blew his nose and offered them the contents. They got the point. We sat and sat while the staff had their coffee break and munched Danish, just three feet in front of us. We were so sick of stale Danish and so sick, period, that the munching away (on our waiting time) was disgusting enough to make us even sicker.

Then we were ushered behind the little pink, striped curtains that make privacy in the ER. Only this cubicle had two beds in the area I was assigned to, and I wasn't too pleased about doing a strip in front of Keg to put on that skimpy little tiny hospital gown— one with Velcro I couldn't reach. (It didn't even have the little tiny strings I couldn't reach.) Somebody could make a fast million designing a new hospital gown. After some commotion, at last, a nurse re-partitioned the room, moving the little pink striped curtains between the beds. Then I sat on the bed shivering in that little postage-stamp-sized gown to wait some more for the Doctor.

The "Doctor" was a nice-looking young man. He had written his questions on a card so he would get it all right, so I decided to let him figure out what was wrong. Doctors don't like you to give them the answer before they've had a turn. So I let him go through his list and try his new toys. I have to give him credit for being thoughtful: he did warm the stethoscope first.

"Let me hear your heart. Now take deep breaths and let me hear you wheeze. Let me look into your eyes with my flashlight. Let me play with this tuning fork by hitting you on the side of the head. Did that make you hear music? Let me put this fireplace tong down your throat to get a culture for a strep screen."

I knew I had been exposed to tuberculosis, which was then becoming endemic among Street People, and to strep, and flu viruses A and B— the people at the House of Charity aren't the healthiest. They smoked and hacked constantly. I had also been exposed to strep when I went to visit my son, who had caught a strep throat cold from the kids who were getting strep screens the day he had to get blood tests for stress. While I hacked and wheezed, the doctor got all his reports filled out neatly so he could get good grades. Then he said, "I'm sure you'll feel better in a few days. I would rather let the illness take its course. If you're not better by next week, come back and see me."

That did it. I said, "Doctor, I have a secondary bacterial infection with obstructed air passages, and a fluid accumulation in my right side of my lungs and a bleeding ear infection." It was hard to get all that out and breathe too. "I need an antibiotic. What works best for me is erythromycin 250 mg. four times a day for ten to 14 days, and I need to begin it today," I wheezed at him. "If I can't have that, then I need tetracycline or eurythrocin on the same dosage and schedule. (Penicillin products are likely to give me an allergic reaction.)"

"You do have a fever of 102.5 degrees. All you need is a week of bed-rest and you'll be fine. You're run down. Just go home and relax. Let your family do the cooking, cleaning, and housework for a few days and you'll be fine."

"*Fat chance,*" I thought to myself. I felt my temperature rising at the phrase "bed rest." *How do you get "a week of bed rest" when you are locked out on the street in sub-freezing weather!* But I didn't say any of the things I was thinking. "Doctor, I am 1,200 miles from home and I am temporarily at the House of Charity."

"Good. Then you won't have to worry about housework this week."

"Doctor, I need an antibiotic. I cannot get bed rest: I have to keep going. Do you want me to bring you the wastebasket of green Kleenex to show you proof of a acute bacterial buildup?"

"Well. Since you insist, I'll give you a prescription for Actifed and Robitussin."

"Doctor, those are over-the-counter medicines which do not require a prescription, and I have already taken Actifed when this infection was only in my sinus. Would I pay $60 here for something I can get at the corner pharmacy for $5? I can get Robitussin and Actifed on my own without a whopping ER bill. I'm here for necessary medicine."

"It's not the policy here to dispense antibiotics because you run the risk of becoming resistant to them. And there is the chance of allergies developing. If you got an allergic reaction, you might sue me for malpractice."

"Believe me, I can't afford to sue anybody."

"But still. You could possibly develop an allergy."

"I know all about that. I need an antibiotic, preferably erythromycin."

"How would you know what you need? You said you're from the House of Charity."

"Believe me, I know what I need. I know enough about respiratory infections to tell a virus from a bacteria and know that bacteria usually responds to antibiotic. And I can teach you a lot more about allergies too. I have raised two children through rhinitis, allergies, obstructed air passages, pharyngitis, mycoplasma, pneumonia, otitis media, and I could go on and on. I doctored to a family allergic to sunlight (due to an ingredient in Lifebuoy soap), allergic to sulfa drugs, to local anesthesia, chocolate, onions, polyester fiberfill, lanolin, perfume, lactose, mercury vapor lights, dust, and vapors of cleaning solutions. And I'm sure I have had more experience with doctor's offices than you have."

"Well, I could put codeine in the cough medicine prescription. That's what you really want, isn't it? Everyone who comes here for a prescription wants the hard drugs."

"I'm not here for codeine. I am here for an antibiotic and I'm not leaving until I get it."

"Oh. Not leaving until you get it? I'll go write the prescription."

He handed me a prescription, "Here is a prescription for you. I prescribed penicillin 250 mg. 4 times a day x ten days, Robitussin with codeine three times a day, and Actifed four times a day."

"An antibiotic is just what I needed (I recalled telling him before that I was allergic to penicillin— but I was too exhausted to press the point.) Thank you, Doctor. But Doctor, just because a person is poor, don't make the assumption that they're stupid or addicted."

"Good-bye. Hope you get over the pneumonia and feel better, so you don't have to come back," he said. As I was getting my layers of winter clothing on, I heard his superior reprimanding him for dispensing an antibiotic— but saying nothing about the narcotic-containing cough medicine.

At the House of Charity, if you are on any medication, you must turn it in to the desk, and one must remember to report to the staff who are to dispense the medication to you on the prescribed schedule; but that's hard, since you're technically locked out during the day. Anyway, I hadn't been back inside The House yet, so technically I wasn't breaking any rules by having my own sinus prescriptions on my person.

I left the ER and got my prescription filled in the basement of the hospital, where they handed me my medicines in a plain brown wrapper. I took the medicine, went across the street to the Food Service, and then went to the public library. I got the biggest book I could find and took it to a desk in a remote corner, put my head down on the book and went to sleep. That's why I didn't "take care of Dolly" Saturday.

In the afternoon I stopped by the Harvest House for some coffee to take the next pill. I wondered if I might run into Dolly there. She likes to pour the coffee. They had a bottomless cup policy. She flits from table to table pretending to work there, filling coffee cups and flirting with the old men. But she avoids any of the Street People who are shabby— she has her standards. Dolly's the kind who flirts more when her husband is with her.

In any case, I selected a booth in the far dining room around the corner so I would have less chance of being seen taking a pill. I struggled with the childproof cap, and it came off with a loud pop. I took the medicine and downed the horse capsules with coffee. I heard Dolly's booming voice, "Look, Max. That's Pat over there, and she's popping pills. I always thought she was a nice girl. I didn't think she'd be on drugs. She must have a habit to be popping pills where everybody can see."

"Jackson, did you see her? Think she is on drugs?" she continued loudly. What she said was bad enough, but did she have to have such a loud voice? I purposely started coughing and hacking to try to show my side of the story, but it probably wouldn't make any difference.

Then I went back to the House of Charity lobby, which was now open, but it was too early for the rooms to be unlocked. I found a space in front of the broom closet and lay down on the dirty floor. I spread my parka over me to conceal as much as possible—only my feet were sticking out. I made myself as small as possible. I wanted to be invisible. With this pneumonia, I was as sick as a dog. Just as the first day I arrived, I had seen others sleeping on the floor like dogs, now I, too, was like a sick homeless dog sleeping on the floor. I said a silent prayer, "*Just leave me alone and let me sleep. Let me heal, or let me die. Let me out of here before I lose all human qualities.*" And I drifted off in a fevered sleep.

By morning, the fever was gone but I was still feeling sick and tired. I was weak but feeling slightly better, and I was itchy from a penicillin reaction. But Sunday was Sunday, and everyone had to be out on the street. It didn't matter that I was sick, because it was Sunday. Being locked out of a shelter on a Sunday is the pits. Most downtown buildings are closed. That means most bathrooms and most heated places are closed. There is little to do but hang out 'til you're thrown out, and keep walking so you don't freeze. I was still feeling like shit with the bronchial pneumonia. I didn't feel like doing much at all, but the library was closed, and it was the only place, besides the Skyway movie, where a person could sometimes sleep a little without getting noticed; unless you have a fake bus ticket, then you can sleep in a chair at the bus station if the bus ticket is showing in your hand.

I recalled that I had promised Aeneas, who was still in the hospital, that I would keep an eye on Dolly on Sunday. He said worrying about her was slowing down his healing, so I had promised him I would spend the entire day with her so he would not have to worry at all. I should have kept my mouth shut. Anyway, keeping track of Dolly would give some purpose to the day and help me keep my mind off of how rotten I felt.

In the morning, I headed for the bus station, because Aeneas and Dolly usually spend a few hours there together every Sunday morning, watching the people. I had been hanging out with them on Sundays for about three weeks, so it seemed to be best to keep the routine. I went to the bus station and looked for Dolly in her lavender coat. "Yes. I know who you mean. She left here about a half hour ago."

From the bus station, I walked around the corner to the donut shop, where the lemonade, but not the donuts, is a bargain. You get an extra-large cup for the price everyone else charges for a small one. Dolly's anti-psychotic medicine is dehydrating, so she requires a high fluid intake every day or the side-effects of the medicine will take over. "Yes. She's been here. But she didn't buy anything this time."

I walked a couple of blocks to Burger King, where we usually use the bathrooms after the extra-large lemonade. No, she wasn't there. I was exhausted.

Then I walked over to The City Center. That's a wonderful place to people-watch because there are tiers of balconies, skyways, and all kinds of exotic eateries— a waterfall of light, and fascinating escalators. From the Street Person's perspective the eateries are nice, but the whole thing seems opulent, almost decadent. Most days, I enjoyed browsing at the Brookstone's Store. Today it was locked. So I walked along Hennepin Avenue. I checked the windows of the Jesus People's Bookstore. I talked with the staff for a while about the LaSalle Book Store in South Bend, Indiana.

It was snowing pretty hard now. I had a few dollars on me, so I bought a $2.00 Skyway movie theater matinee ticket for some movie with Michael Caine, "Blame it on Rio," went into the theater, sank into the seat, and fell asleep until the usher told me the movie was over. I noticed some of the men there coughing and snoring in the theater, and they were the ones who had been in the ER yesterday. There were also several policemen asleep in the backrow. When I went downstairs to leave, a fight had broken out at the front doorway. No policemen in sight there.

I walked every place else I could think of where Dolly might be. I went to Woolworth's Harvest House Cafeteria about five times because she might go there to pour the coffee. No one had seen Dolly, in the Harvest House or down in the potted palms in the Crystal Court. I knew she would never consider sitting in the palms of the Crystal Court, but she had gone there sometimes to bum cigarettes and visit. No Dolly. On weekdays she frequently walked to the Post Office or the free stores. She likes to dress well, and is a careful shopper even for the free items.

I really was getting concerned, because Aeneas had told me a little of her medical history. Sometimes she gets a fugue (amnesia) and hops a plane or a bus to wherever the ticket reads. Then he has to guess where she went, and find a way to get there, and get enough money for the round trip. She likes Tucson, Seattle, San Francisco, and most urban centers. It's a nasty version of hide and seek. One time she took a trip, he had an intuitive feeling that she had gone south, so he headed for Houston. While he was there, a movie studio put out a casting call for extras for a Western film. Although Aeneas is 70 years old, he is tall, muscular, and has a western look about him. He was flat broke from the bus ticket to get there, so if he were going to search for her, he needed money. So he went to the movie location and asked the Director for a part as an extra.

The Director said, "You're hired. Just sit over there in the shade, and we will call you when we are ready. It will take a while." So Aeneas sat and waited. He waited there for 4 days. On the fourth day, the Director said, "We have changed the scene. We won't be needing any extras, but here's a few bucks for your trouble."

Then Aeneas had his travel money, and he still had vibes that Dolly was in the South and that it was somehow connected with a movie. He intuitively felt she must be sleeping in the airport, so each day he checked a major airport in a Texas city. No one had seen Dolly. And he was eager to tell her he had almost been in a Western.

Finally he had covered Texas and felt she must be in some other southern state, so he headed for Alabama on a hunch. He found her in Birmingham. She was loaded with money and content. She had been working as an extra on the film "Airport II," and they had had to shoot the scene many times. Each time she got an airplane ride, beverages, and an in-flight meal. "Aren't you surprised? I'm a movie star!"

"Well, I knowed you're pretty— the prettiest of all your sisters— and I knowed you used to be a model. I guess it fits that now you're a movie star. It doesn't surprise me." He didn't tell her how close he had come to being in pictures, too.

So with this fugueing wanderlust apt to strike Dolly when she is under stress, and Aeneas having cancer surgery, she might have flipped right out of town. The responsibility was weighing heavily on my mind. By 5 p.m. I decided it was useless to search further. It was after 4 p.m. Unless she had fugued the coop, she would know she could get into her room at the House now. Aeneas had arranged for her room assignment to be moved to the one across the hall from mine so it would be more convenient for me to keep an eye on her.

About 9 p.m. she came in the House, talking loud, and draped in Hawaiian leis and orchids. "Dolly, where have you been! I've looked all over town for you."

"Isn't that nice. You must really care about me."

"Dolly, answer the question."

"You really want to know."

"Yes, I do. I know you were at the bus station. I know you were at the donut place."

"But you won't know where else I was. You won't even be able to guess."

"I told Aeneas I'd spend the whole day with you, and I let him down. I couldn't find you anywhere."

"Well, I didn't have any money, ya know. I needed cigarettes. I have to smoke, ya know. Jeez, I didn't know what to do. Really, I didn't want to get Aeneas mad about whatever I did. So I tried to figure where I could go where I wouldn't get in any trouble with him. Yah, and I finally did. I went to the 'GAY 90's' gay bar over on Hennepin Avenue. I had a great time. I think I was the only woman there who wasn't wearing falsies of some kind. So I sold my wedding ring to some guys who wanted to get married and that gave me money for cigarettes. They were so happy, they bought me dinner and all the drinks I wanted. With my medicine, my regular doctor told me to drink a lot every day. So I drank a lot of beer. We had a really great time."

"Dolly, don't tell me any more right now. Just be quiet or you will be in trouble." Her voice was always too loud.

"Trouble? You betcha I'd get in trouble if I told Bill on the desk that I was drinking beer at the Gay 90's bar?" her voice boomed down the hall.

"Shhhh, Dolly, don't say another word," I cautioned.

"Bill, would I get in trouble here if I told you I was at the Gay 90s bar? We didn't DO anything. All we did was eat pineapples, poi, and other funny foods, and drink beer. Of course, I did drink two bottles of cough medicine first— mine and Aeneas'. It has codeine in it. But you know what? After I drank both bottles, my cough didn't bother me at all. That's wonderful stuff. I didn't even want the cough medicine for my chest cold. I wanted an antibiotic, but cough medicine is all you can get at the ER."

"Yeah. I know. But didn't he ask you what other medicines you have to take? Codeine doesn't go with them. Didn't he ask?"

"No. He didn't ask."

"Well. I think I'll go to my room now. See you tomorrow."

"You betcha."

When I saw her in the morning, she was being kicked out for having coming in drunk the night before. At least they had let her stay the night. I let Aeneas know what had happened and that she was gone. She gets by, living life in a Mr. Magoo-type bubble of protection. She puts all the responsibility for her living on Aeneas and takes no responsibility for herself at all. "After all, I'm a certified crazy, ya know!" When she wants something, she whines 'til she gets it, but she doesn't ask for much— some cigarettes, a new blouse at the free store, a walk to the bus station, and attention, constant attention— even if she has to be outrageous to get it.

Aeneas seems like a good egg. But sometimes she is so naughty. He has a full time job keeping up with her. When they walk down the street together, he walks so straight and tall, and she is so petite walking along beside him with her hand in the bend of his arm— the old-fashioned way men and women used to stroll together. You can almost see an aura of love about them. Somehow when they are together, parading arm-in-arm along the Nicollet Mall, they seem so good for each other. I really do feel affection for them. I hope he pulls through the surgery okay.

Since no one in the shelter is permitted to possess or take pills of any kind, even aspirin, one of the functions of the front desk staff volunteers is to store and dispense prescribed medicines. Persons needing to take their own prescription medication have to remember to get in line for it in the morning and evening. But how many prescriptions has anyone had that require taking only one tablet twice a day? Almost everything I ever had for sinus is three or four times a day. Too bad.

I wonder at the legality of having shelter staff dispense meds. In a hospital, to do the same thing, I believe it requires a nursing degree or a licensed medical technologist degree and a doctor's supervision. It is not right that our "least restrictive setting" rule is making shelter personnel function as trained, licensed medical personnel because the institutions where trained, licensed medical personnel are are the very places the mentally ill have been turned out of.

✻

MEDICAL STUDENT'S VIEW

Dear Journal,

Medical care for Street People is frequently done by green medical students, some of whom view Street People as the supply line for their practice of laboratory autopsies.[20]

✻

THE SCHEDULE

Dear Journal,

To keep track of their required appointments and optional opportunities, almost every Street Person I met has a method of keeping their schedule— a notebook, a little black book, a professional schedule book, a calendar, or notes scribbled on a paper napkin. I find keeping up the schedule as arduous as a college curriculum or scheduling a construction project. The coordination is as complex as many CEO's responsibilities. Even if willing to work, the schedule is so complex that there are no large blocks of time when one could go to work without losing some part of the mini-

---

[20] In many teaching hospitals, cadavers for anatomy and autopsy training are supplied by "the indigent."

mum necessities (e.g. shower, shelter, shoes, nourishment) that make it possible to work.

*

Dear Journal,

I figured it out: The bottom line is that I average more than 90 hours in every week struggling to meet basic requirements to maintain my situation and to keep from falling into even more dire straits. Most of that 90 hours is standing, waiting time.

While my situation is not identical, it is comparable to the Street Person's. They also have unique situations and complex schedules. Even with a Street Person who might be employable, there is little uncommitted time in which to do paid work without jeopardizing some *required* recertification appointments. Those who do work usually take day labor, e.g. shoveling snow from 4 a.m., until they have to leave to get into line for some other required essential recertification. Unfortunately, even with the heavy annual Minnesota snowfall, there is no guarantee of a reasonable work-schedule shoveling snow. So they are dependent on both for existence, but can't serve either work or recertification fully.

*

Dear Journal,

The System required you to follow "The Schedule." You had to fulfill The Schedule. The Schedule is set by the people in authority. You have to make phone calls to set up and maintain The Schedule. You have to wait in line 5 or 6 days a week. You get dumped on for not calling and dumped on for appearing in person to make the arrangements that would have been taken care of over the phone if you had the money for a call and access to a telephone to make the call. The Schedule helps you get the necessities, but it works against your being able to obtain and maintain employment. The Schedule itself, in effect, is an element that perpetuates a person being on the street.

*

USPS : POST OFFICE BOX

Most people I met on the street received some kind of check in the mail, but receiving the mail can be a real problem for those who do not have a home. In order to rent a post office box, one had to have a *bona fide* permanent residence. Although I was on the street in Minneapolis, because I still had my residence in Pennsylvania, the Loop Station postmaster made an exception, allowing me to apply to rent a box (when I had enough money). To apply to rent a box, the post office had a form to fill in, which was mailed to the post office where the permanent residence was located. The post office there was required to verify that such an address existed, and that the person was known to be to living there— or at least was currently listed to receive mail there. This form was completed by the original post office and mailed back to the post office to which the person had made a request for a post office box.

It took eighteen days for that card to make the trip from Minneapolis to central Pennsylvania and back. Obviously, United Parcel, Federal Express, even Pony Express, could have processed this more efficiently. In 1983, the post office hadn't yet enlisted the eagle to fly Express Mail.

When this verification was complete, my name was added to a waiting list for a post office box to become available. In a few days, a box became available, but it still wasn't officially mine because its lock had to be changed and a new key made. So, twenty-five days after I applied for a post office box, I finally got one. I still haven't figured out why a person must be receiving mail at a permanent residence some place else to get a post office box.

Now I was eligible to have my mail from Pennsylvania forwarded to the post office box at Loop Station, Minneapolis 55402. I completed the form requesting my mail to be forwarded, and I mailed the form to the local Postmaster in Pennsylvania. The post office in Pennsylvania bundled up all of my accumulated mail, put it in an envelope, and forwarded it to my Minneapolis Loop Station post office Box. Because, however, the mail was bundled by the post office in Pennsylvania, each individual piece of mail did not have the exact number of my new post office box written on it: the big outer envelope had something like Pat McDonough c/o Postmaster, Loop Station, Minneapolis, MN 55402, rather than saying

Post Office Box 2608, Loop Station, Minneapolis, MN 55402. Instead of looking up the box number on the list of box-renters at Loop Station, the Minneapolis Loop Station postal employee took all the letters addressed to me out of the large envelope and mailed every individual piece of mail back to the Pennsylvania post office and asked them to fill out the box number on each piece and then send each back to the Loop Station Minneapolis post office. That required each letter to make two round trips and took thirty-six days. In total, it took fifty-nine days from the time I applied for the post office box for me to receive my first piece of mail. I received my first bundle of mail— Christmas cards, checks, and all— on March 31, the day I took the bus home to Pennsylvania.

In the middle of the three month long process of trying to get a Post Office Box and my mail an interesting thing happened. I left the Loop Station Post Office Branch in the Peavy Building and went upstairs into the Skyway. In the place of Mrs. Field's Cookies, a new company had opened up shop. It was decorated in purple and orange and the sales rep was eager for me to share free coffee and cookies. He asked me if I would do him the favor of signing up with their company as he had a quota to meet of sales calls and since it was 4 p.m. and they were just getting opened for the day on their first day, it was unlikely anyone but me would be able to help him out. So then and there, I opened a Fedex account, giving my Pennsylvania address. [That Fedex account has served me well over the years.] Unfortunately, there was no way to get my U.S. mail intercepted and transferred to Fedex for overnight delivery. I just had to wait it out.

*

LEGALISM: GOVERNMENT CHECKS AND USPS GENERAL DELIVERY

I was not only the only one with post office problems. Since Aeneas and Dolly have had no fixed address for the last five years, they could not get a post office box at all. They had to walk the extra mile (literally) to the Minneapolis main post office building, where they were permitted to receive mail designated "General Delivery."

Something was wrong in Aeneas' throat; it was always sore and hoarse. He feared cancer. His doctor instructed him to go immediately to Rochester, MN, to the Mayo Clinic for tests. He and Dolly took the bus. They were away for two weeks.

Somewhere there was a rule that Government checks not claimed within a month must be returned to the Government. The rule is written somewhere on the check or envelope. For (in)convenience, the post office interprets the rule to mean that checks not claimed on or before the last day of the month. There is also another rule that Government checks may not be forwarded by the post office.

According to Post Office record, the check arrived at the post office on the 28th of the month and was placed in the General Delivery pigeon hole at the main post office the same day. Three days later, it being the 30th of the month, the postal clerk returned Dolly's check to Social Security. (The Street People called the Social Security Administration 'the federal repository of red tape.')

When Dolly and Aeneas returned from Rochester, they were exhausted. The tests had confirmed malignancy. They got off the bus at the station and started to walk: first, to the Main post office, no check; then, to the Social Security Office on Chicago Avenue, a distance of several miles. It took three trips to Social Security before it was straightened out. The first trip was unproductive because the check itself was still trying to drive the three miles from the Minneapolis Main post office to the Minneapolis Social Security Office. I suppose it had to go by way of Washington, D.C.

Then a tracer had to be put on the check to find out where it landed within the Social Security (SS) system. Eventually the check was reissued, but Dolly was not allowed to come pick it up. The Office of SS (OSS perhaps?) required it to be mailed to her again at General Delivery. By this time, it was February 28 and if the check should arrive at the post office via General Delivery it was in immediate danger of being sent back again! During that month, when the check was held up, they had absolutely no cash money. None. Aeneas was a senior citizen with cancer and she was on mental disability. Neither one had the option of working. Without the check, she had no money to survive on while he would be in the hospital.

I mentioned earlier that her room assignment had changed. The management's logic of it was that since he had to go in for surgery, he would not be present at Bed-check at the House of Charity. Since they occupied one of the few rooms set up for a couple, she had to move out of the double room into a single while he was in the hospital.

*

Concerning receiving mail, there was another alternative for the Street People in Minneapolis who were in and out of the shelter system. For those who were clients of Catholic Social Services, that service could receive mail and hold it. With this system, the recipients had to come to the House of Charity between 11 a.m. and 12:30 p.m. or 1:30 p.m. and 4 p.m. and wait in line to see their social workers. Those were the times set for both social workers to come over from the Catholic Social Services Offices up the street. Unfortunately, the office at the House of Charity was not open on exactly that schedule because the workers only showed up if there were room vacancies to reassign. So, recipients might walk back to the House of Charity from clear across town to see if they had any mail, only to find out that they could not find out. If the social workers were in, it frequently required several hours of waiting for a turn to see if one might have any mail. Then there was the additional problem that if the mail did arrive, and if it was apparent that it contained a check, the recipient might become ineligible to continue to stay in a shelter because the person now had money, and the shelter supervisors would know it.[21] It was an awful system, but is sometimes better than trusting a check to General Delivery.

*

Major parts of The System are broken and in a state of decrepitude. The System is unfair. The System is oppressive. The System is unpopular. The System is all we got 'til we finish reinventing government. But The System, as bumpy as it is, did deliver

---

[21]   See discussion and footnote in earlier subsection entitled "Needing to Cash Checks."

social services so that I could function, however marginally, until I was free to leave Minnesota to return home.

*

SUNDAY AND LIBRARY SERVICES

Dear Journal,

It's Sunday, and I'm out on the street. The library is closed— a public disservice to Street People, who read a lot and use the library regularly. We have time to read, we need the food it gives our minds; and most of all we need the escape it provides. It doesn't do damage, like alcohol or drugs. Unfortunately, with no fixed address, I could not get a library card to take books out of the library; but I could read a lot when I was there. I spent as much of my free time as possible at the public library. I also read as much humor, sociology, spirituality, anthropology, and biography as I possibly could as well as several books by Thomas Merton, Henri J. M. Nouwen, Dorothy Day, and writings of the Desert Fathers. Stories of strong men and women sustained me. At the House of Charity I read almost everything on the shelf.

*

WIDOWED MOTHER CAUGHT IN THE SYSTEM: SYLVIA

This day, I was required by the court to give information to AFDC to establish to the satisfaction of the court that I was not eligible for welfare. Since I knew that as soon as the safety of my children was guaranteed, I would be able to focus on earning a living, I did not want welfare. In the court's logic, I had to be on welfare before it would consider a change of custody for my children. Anyway, the court required me to go fill out the paperwork. I made my way to the yellow welfare building at the corner of Franklin and Nicollet Avenues. (As predicted, I was turned down because I did not already have my children living with me.)

While sitting in the narrow crowded waiting area, I joined in conversation with several mothers who were surrounded by their children in this stuffy corner of the AFDC offices complex. The last to tell her story was Sylvia. She was an alert Black woman with rounded features and a maternal loveliness about her. Her story was one that was hard to get out of my mind.

Sylvia said, "My Randolph was a manager of a large agri-business equipment company. The company sent him for a routine annual physical in anticipation of a substantial promotion and transfer. At the time, we were living in a large house in the suburbs. Our oldest was in private school. I was pregnant with our fourth child. I really didn't feel like he needed this promotion, getting up rooted and all, but the company said it was important for his career advancement. The physical was of the type that the patient stays in the hospital overnight. The physical determined that he was a healthy man. However he had had four bouts of strep throat over the winter, so the doctor felt he would benefit from a tonsillectomy. When the doctor called the surgeon to schedule it, he learned that the surgeon had an opening the next morning due to a cancellation, so the operation was scheduled for the next day. He stayed in the hospital."

"During the operation, there was a malfunction of the equipment under the control of the anesthesiologist. This malfunction caused an inappropriate amount of anesthesia to be administered. Randolph did not regain consciousness. When the doctor came out to tell me what happened, the anesthesiologist told me about the malfunction— he said, 'That piece of equipment is scheduled to be scrapped as soon as the replacement equipment arrives, but we have been told to continue to use it 'til it gets here.' The anesthesiologist was extremely upset and wasn't able to continue. At that point the surgeon cut in to say, 'The result is that your husband is in a vegetative state and the prognosis for recovery is not good.' From there, I was ushered right into the hospital services offices to prepare a care plan—not to a counselor or to the chapel, but to the office to make long-term care decisions. Needless to say, I was in shock, but I do remember them saying 'The hospital is going to try to stand by you since it came about by an *administrative oversight.*' With that remark I was about to lose my composure— oversight, my foot! Well, it was all set up. The hospital said it would provide extended bed space, but that if Randy remained comatose for more than a month, I would have to provide and pay for around-the-clock nursing care even though he was in the hospital. Me, provide round the clock nursing care— with 3 children at home and one on the way! Somehow I found the resources to pay for it for the next 10 months. But I'm getting ahead of myself."

Figure 8. Sylvia, recently widowed, with two of her four children.

"The next day, the lawyers and the insurance agents of the company swooped down on me without warning, to claim that the insurance company had no responsibility because infected tonsils were a pre-existing condition. I fought that one, and so the insurance continued for several more months. Eventually, the number of days provided by the insurance came to an end and the hospital wanted to transfer my husband to a hospice, only there weren't any beds available anywhere, yet the insurance company wanted to end payment for in-hospital care. I went to court to fight that one. Me and my lawyer in court against all those corporate suits— 10 of them— My God, how I prayed for the judge to have wisdom! And God answered. We won an extension. The insurance company rep at court was livid at the extension ruling and made death threats against me on the way out of court. Can you imagine the gall of that man? On top of trying to care for my husband and children, I now had to be looking over my shoulder all the time."

"I went home exhausted to try to give the kids dinner and regain my composure. Then I went to the hospital to sit with my husband a while. Although he was said to be vegetative, I knew he heard me when I talked to him because his eyes would flicker, and sometimes he had a little smile. One time he squeezed my hand just a little. It's those little moments that you live for, that give you hope. Well, I chatted with the nurse a while to bring her up to date on the court extension. Then I went down to the cafeteria for a cup of coffee, and when I went back up to the room to see him, the nurse I had arranged for was gone. A strange nurse in a different kind of uniform and cap was there messing with the IV trying to put an injection into it. I intercepted her, demanding to know who she was and why she was there. She showed me her license— it wasn't even a license from this state. I called security and she fled the room. Although they alerted the guards at all the doors, she escaped. The investigation later determined that her license in that state had been suspended because she was what they called 'an angel of death' and in this case she had been hired by the insurance company."

"Believe you me, after that I didn't want to leave Randolph's side. My sister helped me with the kids as much as she could. Eventually the agri-business said they couldn't pay Randy's salary any longer, and gave him severance pay. They did the best they could and I have no contention with them— but the insurance company was another matter. When Randy's income stopped, I was really in a tough place. I had been a homemaker. My job skills were minimal, and my energy had to be with my children and Randy's care. Needless to say I was exhausted."

"This little baby was born. I took the baby down the hall to see Randy. I know he recognized him, his eyes flickered and he got that little smile. How I wished he could have held his little baby and watched him grow up. But it was not to be. Two months later Randy died of a hospital infection— something that started around the Hickman feeding tube. He had lasted 11 months since the surgery."

"I thought then, I could grieve and get on with it, but the next shoe dropped. I learned that when Randy was paid the severance pay, the insurance provider cancelled his company life insurance policy. It got cancelled and I didn't know it. Since we had that policy through the company, we didn't buy mortgage insurance when we bought the house. With no money coming in, I was totally strapped and couldn't continue to keep up the mortgage payments. HUD took back the house from the bank under the FHA mortgage, and if I can't get it caught up, we have to move out.

We're going to be homeless in two months unless I can get a miracle. So here I am to see if welfare can help me— welfare, a government program— to help me stay in my home, so the same government doesn't take it out from under us."

*

LIBRARY SERVICES

While I was spending quality time in libraries, as if I were a professor on a sabbatical, I also became more cognizant of the distress on the entire library system of the United States because there are so few other options for many of the most hard-pressed Homeless people during the day. While spending quality time at the library is an excellent use of time, whether homeless or housed, it is clear that Libraries are not set up to be Day Care Centers for incapacitated mentally ill, chronic inebriates, and other such populations. In addition, they have other populations who, while not Homeless, nevertheless present a problem. For example, one sunny cold day, near the Sports, Religion, and Sociology shelves the following situation occurred:

Upstairs in the library a young man sat at a small table by the window. He smelled like a skunk. His clothes were soiled but not ragged. His hair was straggly and matted. I was searching the shelf numbers for a certain book in the religion/sociology/sports section— How did they decide on this grouping? He seemed restless, squirming in his seat. My back was to him. The odor of him was horrendous. I wished I could find the book and move away. I turned around to look at the shelves that had been behind me and unfortunately that way I was also facing him through the open shelving. It was then I saw that he was masturbating. *"Fuck the book,"* I thought, *"I'll look for it another day.* I tried to pretend I didn't notice what he was doing, but a post and a patron blocked ability to my exit without walking past him. With each hasty stroke, more putrid odor wafted through the library. He was aware that I had seen him, he grimaced, then his cum squished into his hand. He quickly zipped up his fly and trying to appear nonchalant, he looked out the window as he patted his juices into his matted hair."

There was nothing to indicate to me that this man was a Street Person. There was some evidence to indicate he was or had been a student— U of MN maroon and gold bookcovers, notebook, and the like— I concluded a student whose elevator didn't reach the top floor.

Men I discussed this with concluded he had been enjoying the *Sports Illustrated* "Swim Suit Edition." Women were universally disgusted. Moreover, his behavior reinforced the perception that homeless library patrons are a problem, without any evidence that he was, in fact, actually a homeless person.

✳

LEGALISM: VAGRANCY AND SITTING

Dear Journal,

The topic is sitting down, but excludes dozing off while sitting down, which is a separate issue. Except for the palm trees at the Crystal Court, the Minneapolis Public Library, and the lobby of the Government Center, there were no other places to sit unless a person had money to rent a place to sit, such as a restaurant, a movie theater, or the bus station. It was possible to rent a place to sit at the Harvest House Cafeteria above Woolworth's, at McDonald's, at Burger King, or in City Center, by buying a cup of coffee. A place to sit could be rented by buying a movie ticket for the Skyway theater, or a place to sit down for a half-an-hour at the bus station by paying for the coin-operated TV attached to the chair. If challenged at the bus station, however, one also had to be able to show a *bona fide* bus ticket. Some Street People would obtain a "bus ticket out" from Hennepin County, just to have it to hold on to, so as to be able to have a place to sit down when there was no other place to sit— especially on Sunday.

On Sundays, the City Center, the Government Center, the library, and the cafeteria were closed. On Sundays, about the only place to go was the canteen at the HCMC, but one couldn't stay there more than an hour. During the week it was possible to sit in the back of St. Olaf's Church, but on Sunday, to sit there through all the Sunday services was questionable. So most of the time a Street Person just keeps walking, even if it is just walking around and around the block, very slowly.

*

MANDATED INVISIBILITY

Dear Journal,

Today Nick showed up at the House of Charity. He said, "There are dignitaries from the White House coming to Minneapolis." He never said whether the dignitary would be the Cheese Pres himself or not. Anyway, he said, "The word it out. The Mayor doesn't want any street people visible when this hot shot is in town. If the police see anyone loitering or looking like a street person, they'll be arrested and jailed for the time this entourage is in town."

*

Dear Journal,

While it ruffled our feathers to be told to stay invisible while the very policy makers who could make a difference were in town, in the short term it worked in our favor, because the House of Charity remained open for TV viewing Saturday and Sunday, although the sleeping rooms are still locked.

*

SUPERFICIAL COMMUNICATION AND ALONE-NESS

Dear Journal,

I find the "guests" at the House of Charity a happy and supportive community, most of the time. They are really resourceful when
someone can state a specific tangible need: for example, "Where do
I go to get a Jet pass?" (That's the transit bus discount voucher.)
But most talk in lines is exchange of survival information. They
don't generally open up to tell their stories unless we are all seated
somewhere for a long time, such waiting out a blizzard in the
House of Charity living room, killing a cold afternoon drinking
coffee in the far corner of fast food establishment. If we are
someplace more public, conversation is more reserved. I have
enjoyed my conversations with the Street People, especially listening
to their stories

But on a deeper level, more than I would have thought, I seem
to have a need for me to have someone to talk to; Not just chit
chat— I need some companionship with people "like me." Except
that we are in the same situation, I do not feel that I am "like" the
Street People. But I am becoming so isolated that I am beginning
to feel my differences from *all* people more than my similarities.
I am beginning to feel that there is no one "like me," for example,
no one going through the same experiences (hurt, pain, suffering,
disillusionment with the courts, and the like.) This sense of isolation is deepening the longer I am in this situation. Is this the
beginning of alienation? or just loneliness? or culture shock?

I'm not feeling sorry for myself or having a self-pity party. I'm
not playing "Poor little ole me." I know I am not the only person
that bad things have happened to, but at the same time living with
the Street People has its fascination. All that isn't it. It is deeper.
It is a deep-seated grief and isolation. I have even wonder that
perhaps, left in this situation too long, like the others, I too might
start muttering to myself. I think this has to do with some primal
knowledge of belonging. I don't *belong* here as in "not my family,
my group, my tribe" or some such thing. It is a feeling of being cut
off from invisible interior "supply lines" or communications-
pathways to my "real" life.

Since most of each day is concerned with taking care of business
and arrangements, I don't spend a lot of time with anybody or

anybody in particular. On really dead days, like Sundays, I hang out with Street People and listen to their stories. But most of the time I am alone or feel that I am very alone. On most weekdays my only verbalizations are "having to tell my story" to someone else I don't know who has discretionary control over something that I need.

*

SUNDAYS

Dear Journal,
   Homelessness strikes deepest on a Sunday. On Sundays a Street Person is locked out of the shelter and also locked out of almost all places a Street Person could go on a weekday. Most places are locked up on Sunday. It was really miserable today. Sunday is the deepest lonely of the street.
   Loneliness and alienation are pervasive. The spirit of loneliness and alienation sinks deeper and deeper, almost taking over your own spirit. Loneliness and alienation are dark, thick, bleak, and heavy. They make it harder to move, to feel, to hear, to interact, to respond appropriately, to be real. For some Street People, this loneliness seems to have extinguished their spirits and has robbed them of viable life force, except for the robotic motions of survival.
   Sundays on the street can feel like the penetrating deep cold of walking into a boarded, vacant, unheated house when it's 14 degrees below zero. There is no light to guide your footsteps, only penetrating chill. It's like death of a soul who, getting lost along the way, didn't enter heaven, wanders— but this place is too cold to be hell, like those in Milton's *Paradise Lost* where the deepest regions are frozen, not fire. It is the great empty place where there is no beyond.
   Is this what life is supposed to be?

*

PART IV: NECESSITIES AND SURVIVAL

When restricted to what a person can carry comfortably, priorities take on a new clarity.

SPIRITUAL SUSTENANCE

Dear Journal,

My priorities are emerging, are quite revealing. I think first is spirituality. It has become my steady anchor.

I want reassurance that justice will be accomplished, that there will be justice, relief, and repose from this ordeal of endless court and the homelessness it has imposed upon me. I want and need it so deeply in my core self that it is not possible for any human person to resolve it. There are no helping professionals or social workers who can take away my suffering (about my children and their care, an endless court mess, bureaucratic red tape, withheld checks and financial insecurity); the bottom line is: there is only one power that is big enough now to bring me any consolation: God.

I find that keeping in touch with my feelings and keeping my inner self in balance requires nurturing my inner harmony, feeding my spirituality as well as my face. Attending Mass has become more important than attending a meal— so many of the charity food services are more like "feedings" than "dining" anyway. The Bread of Life is more nourishing to me than the food service's salt-and-water soup, mushroom-colored goulash, or sulfur-fart-producing reconstituted eggs.

The Mass, daily Mass that is, and Communion have become my real food— not by Danish alone does a person live. It is the Mass, the Eucharist, that is feeding my spirit— and my love for my kids that keeps me going. I hunger for the Word at daily Mass, trying each day to find some passage of scripture from the day's liturgy to hang on to. By attending Mass each day, I am discovering that the scripture readings have continuity and the stories continue from one day to the next. It is now in context and becoming meaningful.

✳

JOURNAL

Dear Journal,

I want to talk to you about how expensive you are. Supplies to enable me to journal and to write letters are a big expense— spiral notebooks, stamps, envelopes, pens, writing paper, and typing papers. Thank goodness there is time and opportunity to do extensive writing. Without that, I know I would not have fared as well. Writing is giving me a chance to sort through the insanities of the day, and of the system, to keep my sense of humor and my sense of the ridiculous, and gives me a safe place to vent my frustration over the absurdly difficult situation I am in. I guess you are worth it, Journal.

✳

CORRECTIVE EYEWEAR

Dear Journal,

What would I do if I broke my prescription eyeglasses?

✳

TOILETING

Dear Journal,

I am angry that there are almost no toilets open to the general public. Toileting, after all, is a basic human necessity. It is not an optional activity. Access to unlocked, clean, proper disposal sites should be a basic human right. Maybe we should amend "Life, liberty, and the pursuit of happiness" to include some provision for this necessity. Perhaps, "Life, liberty, and a private, accessible place to dump."

Finding accessible toilets is difficult. Finding bathrooms that do not require executive passkeys is nearly impossible. The alternatives— to go outdoors by the sidewalk, in the basement of an office tower, or along the Skyway— are not only socially taboo and illegal, but would also be nearly impossible to do without getting arrested, perhaps frostbitten, or both.

Because I suffer from irritable bowel— if this life style isn't irritating, I don't know what is— I need frequent access to a toilet; It's very important on my priority list. Being sure the bathroom has toilet paper or that I can bring something to use for toilet paper is becoming nearly an obsession. Public bathrooms rarely have enough to fill the normal demand. (Who decided the miserly size of toilet paper rolls? Who decides how many rolls per week per stall is appropriate for a public facility?) Who decides who shall be entitled to bathroom keys and who shall not be entitled to relief.

Even at the House of Charity, it is hard to get a turn to use the bathroom. Today it lacked toilet paper. The building is so large, it was a block's walk from the bathroom to the front desk to stand in line to ask for the use of a roll of toilet paper. By the time I got back to the bathroom, it was occupied.

*

FACIAL TISSUES

Dear Journal,

In Minneapolis in the winter, it is not unusual to go from 26 degrees below zero outside to +65 degrees inside— a difference of 91 degrees. Such rapid changes in temperature and relative humidity makes noses run a lot. I never see (free) Kleenex around where I can get some.

*

SANITARY PRODUCTS

Dear Journal,

For women of child-bearing age, sufficient appropriate feminine sanitary products are a recurring need. The House of Charity was able to provided one sample box (containing three pads) per woman per month. The Public Health Service recommends such items be changed every four hours, or more frequently as needed. It doesn't take much math to realize that three would not be sufficient.

For infants, disposable diapers are equally necessary on a daily basis.

A significant number of older people would smell a lot better if they could abolish polyester fiber in slacks (urine odors don't wash out as well as with other fabrics) and provide products for adult incontinence such as Depends or Attends.

I know these items would be received gratefully if donated to Food Shelf and Canned Goods collections.

✻

CLOTHING

Dear Journal,

On the street, a coat can mean the difference between coping, or pneumonia and an appointment with the grim reaper.

The Twin Cities is trendy and style-conscious, but for people here in the deepest winter, most set style aside in favor of survival value. Gender-specific clothing isn't a big consideration— boots are boots. In Minnesota, the prime consideration for winter clothing is warmth. The best measure of warmth is usually thickness and breathe-ability— practical, utilitarian, and affordable clothing to keep out the cold. To be warm enough, clothing is generally thick, bulky, heavy, and often not machine washable. The silhouette of a Minnesotan in winter is generally puffy and rounded with enormous feet— sort of an Alfred Hitchcock profile.

The first day Dolly arrived, she was wearing a yellow dress, nylons, and white pump-style shoes. The temperature was 25 degrees below zero, and in her '60s-style cloth coat was fashionable and she was freezing. The next day, however, she was wearing several layers of men's trousers, several hats, and a thick ladies' coat with fur collar, all from the Free Store. The Free Store is for the homeless who cannot afford even the low prices of the Salvation Army or church thrift stores. After the temperature rose above zero, Dolly went back into frilly fashionable and feminine clothing.

✻

OUTDOOR CLOTHING AND WARM BOOTS: "MY DADDY'S BOOTIES"

In clothing, I think the epitome of practicality was The-Lady-Who-Sews. Her clothing was always hand-stitched and color-coordinated. Even her canvas bag matched the color of the day.

When she walked, it was like a slow-moving tank. You could almost hear the gears grinding and creaking with each shuffling step. When I looked more closely, I could see the reason for the shuffling walk. She had made part of her shoes. She was wearing socks under rubber buckle-boots, the buckles long gone. To hold them on and cover the torn places, she had made cloth booties that were tied on with bits of string and paper clips. To keep the whole apparatus from falling off as she walked, she slid her feet with deliberation, her double-parka-padded, great encumberment swayed from side to side.

Great bulk? Maybe not. Maybe she was so covered with fur and greatcoats that the small person inside no longer showed. Her coats were a mastery of ingenuity. She wore a cape made from a short jacket. This covered a standard, heavy-duty parka. To cut the edge of the wind on her legs, she had sewed a second parka upside down around the bottom edge of the first coat. She had removed the second set of sleeves for bootie parts. To decorate the double-parka and conceal the seams, she had appliqued a stripe of fake fur and another of ostrich boa, so that even this horribly practical arrangement had the artistic touch of this craftswoman.

I know I could not sew one parka to another by hand-stitching in such a way that the sewing would hold the weight. I believe she had shown creativity, ingenuity, and great skill in doing what she did. With proper supplies and training, her life might have been very different.

Of the women Street People, this lady received the most ridicule from Women in the Middle. I compared her resourceful sewing, which was ridiculed, to one of my mother's resourceful sewing projects, which was held in high esteem.

I remember growing up in Chevy Chase, MD, during a bitter-cold windy winter, when my father was Superintendent Electrician on the construction of the Nuclear Reactor on the Atomic Energy Commission site at Gaithersburg, Maryland. The reactor was to be located on a piedmont meadow, isolated, except for the new Interstate 70S and Sam Eig's motel complex. My father had to stand long hours in an unheated shed doing take-offs on the blueprints. His clothing was not adequate, as his most recent previous jobs had been indoors. Then there were no "outdoor clothing" specialty stores in the Washington, DC area.

My mother had once worked in sewing and alterations at Garfinkel's Department store. She was very frugal: throwing anything away was a cardinal sin. She accepted everyone's cast-offs and squirreled them away in the attic until the livingroom ceiling began to sag. She kept things in the hopes of someday finding someone who needed just that item. If she waited long enough, amazingly someone would show up at our house asking for just that thing.

Much of what she saved was junk. Similarly my friend Helen Drotning Miller's mom had boxes of string labeled by size with the last box labeled: "string pieces too short to use." My mom was especially adept at scrounging Persian rugs and old fur coats. Her bridge club friends would discard any full-length fur coat which was balding at the derriere. Mother would shorten the coat to a jacket by cutting away the worn area. With the fur remnants from the bottom of the coat, she created hats, headbands, and muffs for my cousins and me.

When Daddy was enduring the cold at work, but coming home nearly frozen from the ordeal, Mother decided to fix him a proper survival wardrobe. She lined a pair of chino workpants with a U.S. Army Surplus khaki wool blanket. She removed the alpaca lining from a worn out Army Polar Expedition Parka that had accompanied Admiral Byrd on at least one mission. The alpaca lining had survived, even though the outer shell of the parka had not. She inserted this alpaca lining into another Army-issue windbreaker. For additional insulation, she tucked a mohair inner lining between the alpaca and the khaki shell.

She made boot liners for his leather, steel-toed construction boots by creating mink socks with the mink fur turned to the inside. It gave us all a good joke to think he was the only rugged contractor in the metropolitan area wearing mink booties in his clodhoppers. But then, how many contractors had Persian carpets on the floor of their on-site workshed.

*

APPROPRIATE CLOTHING THAT FITS

Dear Journal,

On my way to Church this morning I saw Eric standing behind a snow drift. He had a face and beard like Santa Claus. He was a huge man, but today looked unusually short. I peered over the piled snow to say hello, and noticed he was standing over the sidewalk grate.

"Is it warmer there, Eric?"

"Yep. When there is no place to go, like Sundays, my feets get hu-hurtin' cold, standing on concrete."

It was zero and windy. I was wearing a hat, regular underwear, long underwear, shirt, heavy sweater, regular slacks, boot socks, fleece-lined thick-soled boots, mittens, and a parka with the hood up. I was still very cold. Eric was wearing a Stetson, a plaid raincoat that too small and was pinned with a large brass commercial-laundry safety pin that left a three-inch gap over his Tee-shirt, which was too short to cover his tummy. I knew he would be outside for hours, until the Food Service served lunch. How could he keep warm, so thinly dressed? The only insulation on him was his beard and his tummy. The Free Store doesn't usually get the top or bottom ends of the size ranges. He probably needed XX-Large and X-Tall.

✽

Monday, Max was reading the newspaper in the Public Library and saw a notice in the obituary section that his father had passed away. He has spent this evening trying to borrow clothing that is clean, presentable, fits reasonably well, and is appropriate to wear to the wake and funeral. It has turned out to be quite a challenge to put together a borrowed wardrobe for the occasion but the men are really going all out to help him.

✽

CLOTHING REPAIRS

Dear Journal,

A young man walking up the street toward me was wearing a coat that was in shreds. I thought of the rope-caulk we put along the windows in Pennsylvania to keep out the cold air. His coat needed caulking, to seal air leaks. Later I saw a similar coat repaired with bits of duct tape. Street People generally get pre-owned clothing, so more than most folks they need mending supplies just to be able to wear their "new" clothes.

The man with the coat full of holes had shoes in about the same condition. The soles were coming off his shoes. He had no socks. Socks hardly ever make it to the used clothing stores, and never reach the free store. Mending supplies are also something people could donate.

*

CLOTHING: LAUNDRY, DRY CLEANING, AND APPEARANCE

Dear Journal,

My Sierra Designs lifetime-warranty, navy-blue parka has become very, very soiled. I cannot do without it to have it dry-cleaned, and I don't have that much money anyway. My parka had never been dirty before. Though it has been in the wind several hours a day, it holds a terrible staleness, deep in the fibers, from all the exposure to smokers. My other clothing I wash in the sink at night, or in the basement in the laundromat. But my once-proud coat has become heavier and shabbier as the winter wears on. It now appears more brown than navy blue. I mended the pockets, but the holes and tears seem to have reappeared. I am glad my identity and self-esteem are not dependent on my clothing.

Coats vs. lack-of-coats is a visual difference between the Street People in the Skyway and almost everyone else in the Skyway. The others do not have to wear or carry their coats in the Skyway. The Street People wear their coats like another hide. The coat seems to become an integral part of the Street Person.

*

COATS, HATS AND SCARVES AS SYMBOLS

Dear Journal,

Back on Christmas Eve, each "guest" of the House of Charity received a gift of some kind of wearing apparel. When I returned to my room, a staff Santa had left on my bed a new, soft, black scarf with white letters that spelled "EEZY-FLOW," which I think is a type of cellulose insulation, and a crocheted white hat and mittens. (Unfortunately, the hat was too small, but the thought was there.)

The red, white, and blue hats and scarfs many had received had "Minnesota Winter Fest" woven on them. Some hats said "Burton True Blue," "Toro," or "Snap-on Tools," making the wearers walking billboards for these companies— for products the Street People were not likely to buy. They must be an advertising write-off for the donor companies. Whatever the hats and scarves said, they also became the hallmark of a fraternity. They provided admittance without question to many social services and free-meal places around town.

After a while I grew to love my scarf. It was warm and soft. Many times it protected my face from the ravages of freezing winds. It protected me from frozen flesh and frostbite. At the same time, my scarf was a problem. I needed it and even loved it, but I felt compelled to hide it on the days when I worked in the bank or had to meet with government and court officials.

I learned that, when I wore my scarf, Street People acquaintances recognized and greeted me, but the People of the Middle, that I knew, did not. When I hid the scarf, stood straight, left any plastic tote bags at the House of Charity, but carried a notebook or file-folder (even empty), the People in the Middle with whom I was working would see and greet me. In the Skyway, if I wore a suit but no coat I was generally recognized by them. If I wore my regular parka but walked fast, I was occasionally recognized. On the other days, when I was more obviously like a Street Person and walked slowly, those same people did not recognize me, avoided eye-contact as much as possible, and made a wide arc to avoid passing near me. I am told by handicapped people that they also experience the same averted-eyes treatment.

I knew that, every day, I was the same person. So what changed? Could it be that those people changed?

Are they were as divided as the People-Who-Mutter? The people who mutter keep their inside self on the outside. But in the Skyway the people who look past us seem as if BOTH their inside self and outside self are encased on the inside. Their faces showed only scorn, disdain, and smugness, even though (were I to know them today, perhaps as their colleague or consultant) they would most likely not reveal that self-righteous, judgmental look toward me. Yet I am basically the same.

Could it be that the space between us changed?

If I work all day at the bank, I wear my tailored navy-blue suit, pantyhose, black pumps, and a paisley blouse. Sometimes I wear tailored navy-blue slacks and a matching blazer. I was criticized today by my supervisor for wearing this blue suit, and told next time to dress appropriately for work. Many of the places where I was assigned to work as a Temporary had dress codes for their employees which was posted in the ladies room and dictated that "All bank employees shall wear gray suits. Female employees may buy women's suits that are in compliance, at a discount through the bank." The least expensive women's suit available this way was $200, the average $450, the most expensive on the list $600.

Everyone, except me, wore the "Dress for Success" uniform, and the women all had on look-alike soft, silken, droopy bow-ties. I did my best to be clean, deodorized, shaved, mended, and polished so that I would present the best possible appearance under these most difficult circumstances. But I was aware that the supervisors gave me disapproving looks. They did not, of course, know my situation or where I was staying— only that I was "a Temporary."

And what if they had seen my coat?

✻

PRESENTATION

I have been asked how I dressed "to be a bag lady." Did I wear a wig, or some elaborate disguise? No, most days I dressed the same way that I would have anyway. Sometimes, my slacks were less tailored, and I mentioned the EEZY-FLOW scarf earlier.

Posture made a big difference. I walked bent at the shoulders and walked slowly, as a Street Person. That was not an act. I felt bent-over those days. My pockets were loaded and heavy. My shoulders ached under the weight of the parka, and sometimes the weight of the court documents I carried in plastic bags or in a rucksack. In addition, I think I stuffed a lot of my frustration and anger between my shoulder blades and in my lower back. My back and shoulders ached relentlessly.

✳

KEEPING CLEAN

Dear Journal,

Washing myself adequately is a problem. The food and the stale cigarette smoke in the air make my body and clothing smell funny. If it hadn't been for the House of Charity, I might not have been able to keep clean at all. At the House of Charity, the facilities are not adequate for the number of people. There are two or three small bathrooms for men, but only one that I know of for women— one bathroom, one toilet, one tub without stopper or shower components.

✳

PERSONAL HYGIENE: "THE CANTANKEROUS DOOR"

Trying to find time to take a bath is a scheduling problem of major proportions. We were allowed back in the building at 4 p.m., so there was a rush for the facilities from 4 to 6 p.m. Each resident also had to wait for and return the door key for the room, and wait for a brown-bag dinner between 4 and 6 p.m. Often I worked ATM-monitoring in the evening, returning at 11:30 p.m., but the night-owls usually had the bathroom for hair-washing then. I tried in the morning, but from 5:30 to 8 a.m. was rush hour, and I was lucky to get even a few seconds in, then, since we had to wait in line to return the door key to the room, wait in line for a breakfast ticket, and also be out of the building by 8 a.m. to head for the Food Service or wherever.

One morning, I set my pocket alarm for 4 a.m. and tiptoed up the hall to have my turn. I got into the ladies bathroom and realized I had forgotten my towel, so I knew I had to go back. When I tried to open the bathroom door, the bolt mechanism of the lock broke off in my hand. I was locked in. The House of Charity was a long narrow building. This bathroom was on the first floor by the chapel, and the night desk was at the front of the building, nearly a block away. The night guard would not check this end of the hall for 2½ more hours.

If I sat quietly on the toilet seat, I might be able to doze off, but it was cold and uncomfortable. The door hinges were tamper-proof style, and, on the inside where I was, there was nothing available to use to pry them off. There wasn't a thing in the bathroom at that time except the tub, the toilet, and the basin. No tub-stopper, no toilet paper, no nothing that wasn't bolted to the floor or the wall.

I banged on the door, "Help! Help!" and kept up the racket for a good eternity before one of the night guards meandered up the hall. "Help! I'm locked in," I yelled.

"You gotta be kidding! Just unlock the door," a voice said.

"Help! Would I kid about this? I'm locked in! The bolt broke!"

"Unlock the other lock," he suggested.

"I tried that!"

"Take the hinges off," he advised.

"With what? They're tamper-proof. Are you gonna get help or just give advice? Get me out of here!"

"Okay, I'll see what I can do. Why don't you take a shower and cool off? This may take a while," he suggested. "Maybe you could make yourself a water bed."

"Hey, guys, guess what? Pat's locked in the john," another voice called. I started counting the white tiles on the wall, studying the water spots on the ceiling, analyzing the pattern of white and colored tiles on the floor. Someone also named Pat, and Bill, the night-duty clerk, came back to the bathroom door. They tried forcing the bolt, prying the door, and Case-knifing it with a pen-knife. "Stand back, we have to break the door down."

I stood back, while the three rammed the door. The two-inch-thick solid wood door didn't give. They tried several times more. I was getting a little uncomfortable. How much air supply would a person need in a bathroom with no ventilator and no window, during an indefinite confinement? (Code requires a window or mechanical exhaust. This had neither.)

"Get the fire department. Call a locksmith. Call the police."

"I am the police."

"Oh," I said, crestfallen.

Finally, they got a crowbar and the other Pat leveraged the bottom corner of the door enough to pass me a steak knife and a screwdriver with a broken handle. "Here. Try these." I thought the steak knife was ludicrous, since I hadn't seen a recognizable piece of meat in weeks, and nothing that was served at the Food Service had enough resistance to require cutting. Besides, most people here didn't have teeth anyway. Teeth are for rich people. They take a lot of upkeep.

Anyway, I took the knife and the screwdriver and worked at dismembering the lock and door from the inside, while he took off the parts on the other side. Between us, we got the bolt exposed and, using the steak knife and force, we managed to spring the lock. I was thankful to be free. And I bagged the idea of a bath. From then on, I was content to take PTA (pits, twat, and ass) baths in the sink in my room. I did keep clean, but I went the rest of the three months without what I consider to be a satisfactory shower or bath. Don't ever fail to appreciate the luxury of a shower or a long soak in a clean tub of clean hot bath-water.

The next morning, I examined the door. It was now bowed at the bottom, and would no longer close at the striker-plate. It had admirably withstood the onslaughts of three husky men. Later that day we heard a loud crash. By itself, the cantankerous door broke completely off the hinge and crashed onto the floor. For the rest of the week, there was no door on the ladies room that could be closed.

※

CELL HYDRATION: THIRST

Dear Journal,

I find I am thirsty a lot of the time. Access to drinking water is especially significant, because dehydration is possible in severe cold just as it is in the heat of summer. [The Society for Prevention of Cruelty to Animals here will have arrested anyone allowing an *animal* to get dehydrated in the cold.]

Factors accelerating dehydration included:

(1) walking in wind and sub-zero temperatures,

(2) breathing-in very dry air, exhaling (moist air),

(3) wearing many layers of clothes and a heavy parka outdoors,

(4) wearing many layers of clothing and a heavy parka in the heated Skyway,

(5) the continual runny nose, and

(6) normal bladder function.

Coffee is more readily available for those who have the money to buy a cup, but drinking quantities of coffee can be dehydrating, too. Fast-food booths in the City Center are closed on Sundays. The Government Center and The Crystal Court are fenced off on Sundays. For me on Sundays, the only accessible drinking fountains are at St. Olaf's church and at HCMC.

✳

FOOD QUALITY

Dear Journal,

Since food is a necessity and there is dependency on The System to get food most of the time, it is a huge frustration to be given food that isn't safe to eat.

When I got my evening dinner in a brown bag at the House of Charity, I noticed that the fish sandwich had a "freshness date" which had expired over a month previous. There was no way I was going to eat it. I had experienced exceptionally violent bowel-troubles all week. From then on, I paid a lot of attention to the type of sandwich and the freshness date. We received old chicken-pattie sandwiches, old pork-pattie sandwiches, and old fish sandwiches. The bag also contained an apple or an orange and a sweet roll with heavy icing.

I went down by the coffee machine and threw my sandwich in the trash. Max and the African student scrambled into the trash can to get it. "Why are you throwing food away?" Max demanded.

"I can't eat food that is that old. It goes through me in less than an hour, makes me feel real sick. Are you guys able to eat the stuff?" I asked.

Max replied, "Even if I don't eat it, I can usually trade it for a cigarette.[22]"

Togba, the student, said, "I always eat it. Why don't you do what we do in my country? You know in my country in Africa, meat never has a little purple (USDA) stamp on it, so there is no way to know if the meat ever has been wholesome. In this country, you know that at one time that meat in that sandwich was inspected and was wholesome, so it's got to be better to eat than meat which has never been wholesome."

"What good is it if I can't digest it?"

"You must do as I do. In our country, half-an-hour before each meal, we take those little pink tablets called Pepto-Bismol. Then, as the food moves through your system, it has more time to extract the nutrients before it is expelled. We use Pepto-Bismol in my country whenever we have meat at a meal. It's a wonderful product!"

"*That takes guts,*" I thought.

---

[22] In Viktor E. Frankl's book *Man's Search for Meaning: an Introduction to Logotherapy*, New York: Simon & Schuster Pocket Books, 1972, from the chapter entitled, "Experiences in a Concentration Camp," pp. 10-11, he speaks about the uses and meanings of cigarettes.

As this story is about my experiences as an ordinary prisoner, . . . most of the time I was digging and laying tracks for railway lines. At one time, my job was to dig a tunnel, without help, for a water main under a road. This feat did not go unrewarded. . . I was presented with a gift of so called "premium coupons" . . . . The coupons cost the [construction] firm fifty pfennings each and could be exchanged for six cigarettes, often weeks later . . . . I became the proud owner of a token worth twelve cigarettes. But more important, the cigarettes could be exchanged for twelve soups, and twelve soups were often a very real respite from starvation.

The privilege of actually smoking cigarettes was reserved for the Capo, who had his assured quota of weekly coupons; or possibly for a prisoner who worked as a foreman in a warehouse or workshop and received a few cigarettes in exchange for doing dangerous jobs. The only exceptions to this were those who had lost the will to live and wanted to "enjoy" their last days. Thus, when we saw a comrade smoking his own cigarettes, we knew he had given up faith in his strength to carry on, and, once lost, the will to live seldom returned.

DISTRIBUTION OF FOOD

Dear Journal,

In the vestibule at St. Olaf's church I had to pass the food baskets to get to the magazine rack for a free copy of *Catholic Bulletin* newspaper. Under a large poster ("Feed the Hungry," with an arrow pointing down) there were wicker laundry baskets for donated food. One basket was full of groceries in brown-paper bags. I wondered if there were any fresh fruit or vegetables in the food basket. I hadn't had much in the way of vegetables lately. The Food Service, when I can get there, sometimes has potatoes, and little snippets of tomato or one or two peas on a plate, but not a farm-fresh pile of honest-to-goodness vegetables or a really fresh salad or raw carrots, or even meals based on the Basic Four Food Groups I taught in 4-H. The fact that I was tempted even to look to see what was in the basket surprised me. I didn't follow through. I avoided the basket.

An elderly couple came in and walked directly toward the food basket. They were presentably dressed and clean but not wealthy-looking, but definitely not Street People— probably on fixed income, social insecurity. The man leaned toward the lady: "Look, Ma! For us! Let's. Quick!" Without further words or discussion, they deftly put most of the bags full of groceries under their coats, tucked up under their armpits, and carried only one bag each in front of them. So they had all the food, but it looked as if they had each taken only one bag. They left the church and the food baskets empty. I could not tell if they came back for the church service. I suppose they gave thanks at home.

I am sensitive about remarks I have heard from people, that those who get food from church or social service distribution programs "do not really need the food." If people based the distribution of food on appearances, they would say I do not belong in food-lines and soup-kitchens (I look well fed), but for a while it was a necessity. Sometimes it is hard to tell from the outside who is really hungry, but if you could see the faces of persons eating at the Food Service, you would be ashamed to suggest that they were there just because it was a FREE meal.

∗

ETHICS AND HUNGER

Dear Journal,

Seeing elderly people steal from the food baskets presented me with the ethical dilemma of equitable distribution, of fairness— the Animal Farm approach to equality (some are more equal than others). The System wasn't fair, but stealing the food before it got into the distribution system wasn't fair either. It was almost as if they were stealing from me. A professor who read this manuscript commented, "It's to the government's advantage to have the poor turn against the poor. It keeps the pressure off the government to change or make improvements."

I am against pitting the poor and the middle class against each other. After all, right now, the middle class is getting poorer every day.

∗

LEGALISM: APPROPRIATE USES OF RESTAURANT AND VENDING MACHINE REMAINS

Dear Journal,

I remembered yesterday's trip with my son to the Como Park Zoo in St. Paul. We went on the transit bus, which required a lot of transferring to get there from Minneapolis. The bus was painted dark green, with a professionally painted graffiti of a monkey leaping through space having just let go of a monkey vine. I enjoyed the walk through the zoological park and seeing the animals, but the thing that really made an impression on me was that the wolves and the lions had day-old burgers from McDonald's and Burger King spread on the snow in their den. The wolves' dinner was fresher than mine (even fresh frozen), and they got more meat and vegetables (even that famous Reagan vegetable "tomato sauce.")

The wolves got a selection of two all-beef patties, lettuce, cheese, special sauce, tomato, pickle, onion, mustard, catsup, on a sesame-seed bun. I got salt-water soup with two beans to the bowl.

I learned the reason it was safe to give day-old anything to the lions and wolves is because they might not sue for food poisoning. Many Twin Cities corporations used to donate discarded food but someone complained about it being a dangerous practice, so now many restaurants will not even allow a patron to take home a "doggie bag."

Why is it not okay to use food an hour-old or a day-old from a restaurant but okay to serve it when month-old, cast off from a vending machine. Why don't these rules pertain to the discarded vending machine sandwiches that appear nightly in the brown-bag dinners?

✻

Dear Journal,

As I mentioned earlier, the Food Service donuts were often moldy and stale. The package on the table today had a freshness date of a year ago! The other day, we got one that was moldy, but the freshness date would not expire until this month next year! If you relate these two tidbits to each other, some of these donuts may be two years old.

I met entire families who survived on Rocky Rococo pizza and raw dough discards alone. In Minneapolis, the easiest foodstuff for nonprofit food services to obtain is old white bread products, rarely whole grain. It's not the kind that would sustain life.

Some food establishments will have any Lazarus arrested for pilfering through the trash outside, for a morsel. There are rumors that some companies sprinkle Drano and lawn chemicals in the trash to discourage pilfering of "day-old" foods.

✻

MALNUTRITION

Dear Journal,

I am losing my ability to experience joy and delight. According to A. H. Maslow, delight is a key indicator of a fully developed personality.[23] Everything is getting damped down from stress. I am loosing capacity for delight. Is this, perhaps, a form of depersonalization?

I am getting a lot of physical symptoms: diminished stamina, increased intensity and frequency of allergic reactions, back pain, toothaches, intestinal distress, fatigue. My response time is slowed. Even my joints ache. I've developed incredible fatigue. My teeth are breaking and loose. I think I am in a type of shock that I am even on the street.

Many days I have to put my full concentration into the process of walking. By the end of the second month, I could no longer count on being able to walk briskly. This experience of the street is draining me. An old injury has flared: my left leg is beginning to drag. To get where I must go, I move with sheer determination of will and an interior monologue telling myself: *"Lift the right foot, swing the leg forward; put it down; now move the left foot forward. Good. Do it again. You are a step closer now. Do it again."* I say this continually, now, to keep my legs moving, to get from appointment to appointment.

Much of the food is harmful to me, because often the products are moldy and because the meat sandwiches are often too old to be safe to eat, and because of my food allergies, and because it is lacking in vegetables. The carbohydrates help keep me warm, but the diet is making me progressively weaker.[24]

＊

---

[23] Maslow, Abraham H., *Toward a Psychology of Being*, 2nd edn, New York: Van Nostrand Reinhold, 1968, p. 31.

   The observation . . . is based [on] that self-actualizing people enjoy life in general, and in practically all its aspects, while most other people enjoy only stray moments of triumph, of achievement or of climax or peak experience.

[24] Not long after this, I got pneumonia. The penicillin I was prescribed—I had requested Eurythromycin—both helped and harmed me by allowing this poor diet, consisting 90% of Danish sweet rolls with globs of icing, to stimulate a yeast condition. It flourished in my mouth and other areas and by then was systemically debilitating me.

HUNGER

Dear Journal,

When I was growing up, there was never even one time when I was hungry. In my adult life, that certainly has changed. Hunger is an interesting thing. The fear of hunger is more devastating than the hunger itself. After three days without food, I didn't really hunger— unless I ate something. Then the hunger pains started all over again with a vengeance. *After I let go of the fear of hunger, the suffering from being hungry seems to have left me.*

*

Dear Journal,

I have always accepted the maxim "If life gives you lemons, make lemonade." But the Street People take it literally. One taught me, "Try to order tea with lemon, and get a glass of water on the side. Drink the tea. Make lemonade in the water glass. Then eat the pulp of the lemon wedge to ward off scurvy."

*

NUTRITION AND WELL-BEING

Dear Journal,

Some thoughts on "craving veggies." A diet consisting mainly of sweet rolls and coffee does not provide essential nutrients. I believe that many Street People are made sicker and crazier by the diets and handouts which provide almost unlimited sugary sweet rolls but not vegetables. Vegetables, especially fresh vegetables, can be expensive. I crave broccoli, pumpkin pie, alfalfa sprouts, cucumbers, and garden ripe tomatoes. I think my body wants Vitamins A and C. I also want salad, and even bacon.

When possible, I drink tomato juice with breakfast, and that fills some need. Once or twice I had enough money to buy a sandwich at the Cayol's health food store— and afterward I felt better for days. I would buy a sandwich on homemade brown bread (without preservatives), with alfalfa sprouts, cucumber, and generally something else like turkey salad, tuna salad, Provolone cheese, or roast beef on it. And I would drink a vegetable juice concoction that they made up in the store and gave as a little free sample. Another favorite at Cayol's juice bar in the LaSalle Building Food Court was carrot-parsley-celery juice. I felt so much better after eating there.

I learned clearly that without fresh vegetables and fresh fruit, I feel yucky— I feel bad about myself, I feel anxious, I have lower energy, and I tire more easily. Important lessons. Years of malnutrition must take their toll on Street People.

*

Dear Journal,

I am excited about a possibility. Because of my persistent food allergies, I have for a long time been thinking about going on an "Elimination Diet."[25] My diet is so restricted during this time that such a complicated process is suddenly simple.

*

Dear Journal,

The elimination diet experiment is going well. I started it several weeks ago, and now I can quickly observe what foods trigger a negative reaction and what foods promote a sense of well-being. Maybe I can learn enough that I won't be at the mercy of sudden unexpected allergic reactions anymore.

*

MASTICATION

Dear Journal,

Some thoughts on special diets. Is the reason that these diets we receive are so heavily into the carbohydrates, and light on meats and veggies, that most Street People have no teeth? Saving teeth is a domain of the wealthy. With no teeth, or loose teeth, masti-

---

[25] An Elimination Diet is a diet where all foods are eliminated from availability and use, and then only one food is reintroduced each week, to observe how the body responds to reintroduction of that food.

Figure 9. One tooth left.

cation is not good. Only one Street Person that I know of has dentures. I don't think dentures are available to Street People.[26]

*

NUTRITION AND MENTAL HEALTH

Dear Journal,
I had some free time so I spent time in University Medical Library perusing journals.[27,28,29] What I learned was very interesting. My diet on the street lacked vegetables. Most days I got an apple, an orange, and two sweet rolls as my food intake for 24 hours. Had I been able to digest the sandwiches in the dinner bag (which were over a month old), I would also have had some protein intake. While breakfast was available, most days I didn't get any because of my scheduling requirements to meet the lawyer or social worker before they were taken up with other court duties, or my need to report for work by 8 a.m. I had the same problem getting to the Food Service for lunch. If I were working or had to report to unemployment or go to any other lines, I couldn't get there.
This was not atypical. Street People who signed up to work at Day Labor had to begin snow-shoveling around 4 a.m.; to get construction work they had to be there about 5 a.m., so they also missed breakfast and lunch at the Food Service.
As far as I can tell, most weeks my diet completely lacks folic acid, which is found in green leafy plants.

---

[26] Sometime later certain rules were changed to allow welfare recipients to get teeth.

[27] D. Flynn & W. Bazzell, Matthew J. Wagner, (eds.): Psychiatric Aspects of Abnormal Movement Disorders. *Brain Research Bulletin* 2(2):238 1983.

[28] [Author unknown]: Differences in Intermediary Metabolism in Mental Illness. *Psychological Reports* 17(M2-V17):563-582, 1965.

[29] George Watson: Psychochemical Test. *Nutrition and Your Mind*, New York: Harper & Row, Inc., 1972, pp. 76-78.

Folic acid appears to be crucial for mental and emotional health, but little is yet known as to the exact mechanism .... When carbohydrate foods constitute too large a portion of the diet, folate deficiency may develop because these foods contain only traces of iron and folate.[30]

Another chemical that is essential for mental stability is serotonin. Our body manufactures that, if we feed it vegetables separately— not in the presence of carbohydrates. Direct sunlight is also believed to be a factor in its production by the body.

Serotonin is essential for mental stability and for almost all mental activity. It is stored in the synapses of the brain, and is activated each time an electrical impulse needs to cross from one synapse to another. It is essential to the hypothalamus, which uses it to maintain body temperature, and it prevents the body from dreaming at inappropriate times. Many Street People and others who are mentally ill hallucinate (a type of dreaming at inappropriate times).

The book went on to say:

Folate and other pleridine derivatives also function as coenzymes in the biosynthesis of norepinephrine and serotonin, substances which are believed to be brain neurotransmitters (between nerve-cell communicators) .... Considerable evidence indicates that alterations in norepinephrine levels in the brain, possibly in conjunction with serotonin and dopamine, may play a part in the etiology of manic-depressive disorders. . . .[31]

*

---

[30] Carl C. Pheiffer and the Publications Committee of the Brain-Bio Center: "Mental and Elemental Nutrients." *A Physician's Guide to Nutrition and Health Care*, New Canaan, CT: Keats Publishing, Inc., 1975, pp. 163-164.

[31] *Ibid.*, p. 163.

FOOD INTERACTION WITH CERTAIN PRESCRIPTION MEDICATION

Dear Journal,

Many Street People have mental illness, and must take necessary prescribed anti-psychotic drugs to manage the illness. Many anti-psychotic medications require a special diet called an MAO-inhibitor diet, which is rigid and difficult to follow. Basically, the diet requires that all foods be fresh, because tyramine is produced as a natural by-product of aging. This fermentation by-product causes a toxic reaction to occur in the liver, if one is on these certain medications. This also affects persons who suffer from certain types of migraine headaches triggered by the tyramine. A buildup of tyramine from the breakdown of food can also trigger high blood pressure, which can trigger strokes and/or heart attacks. In other words, much of the food offered to Street People who are on certain medications is hazardous to their health and may even be life-threatening.

How can a Street Person manage to stay on a MAO-inhibitor diet when they have no control over what food they get and what is in it and how old it is? Many on the street are time-bombs of rage, hostility, and resentment. How many angry people have untreated high blood pressure? How much of their health problem is aggravated by the interplay of untreated high blood pressure and a daily ration of soup that is primarily heavily salted water?

Many on the streets are alive, but long ago their spirits fled (disassociated) in terror, pain, despair, depression, or other overwhelming suffering. Yet the body walks on. How many would be different if they had the proper trace-minerals? I've never seen multi-vitamins dispensed at the Food Service, or in the Food Baskets, or at the Food Shelves. If Street People are stuck with such marginal diets, wouldn't multi-vitamins make a big difference?

✳

Dear Journal,

Some animal studies indicate that standard antidepressants such as chlorimepramine and amitriptyline significantly inhibit H-serotonin activity.[32]

With regard to depletion of zinc in the hippocampus, McLardy, in 1973,

> found a decrease in the cells of the hippocampus in both schizophrenics and alcoholics. Any deficiency in mossy fiber cells, or of zinc or histamine in the cells, might result in schizophrenic behavior.[33] . . . if treated with birth control pills (to . . . regulate the cycle) the patient will have a rise . . . in serum copper which may precipitate depression . . . and intensify disperceptions . . . . In the zinc deficient patient, there may be joint pain, cold extremities with poor peripheral circulation . . . .[34] Care should be taken to recognize zinc deficiency in a patient before elective operations as there may be slow healing of wounds . . . .[35]

. . . stress of any kind depletes the body of zinc and in some people stress causes excretion in the urine of kryptopyriole, which takes with it both zinc and vitamin B-6.[36]

(Zinc will not work without other nutrients including B-6.) In our clinical experience, patients with loss of taste should be given B-6 for the first two days. Otherwise zinc alone can increase hallucination experiences and/or depression. Patients

---

[32]   Smriti Izengar and Jamshid Rabil, "Role of serotonin in estrogen-progesterone induced lutenizing hormone release in ovariectomized rats," *Brain Research Bulletin* 10:342, 1983.

[33]   Pheiffer, p. 224.

[34]   *Ibid.*, p. 225.

[35]   *Ibid.*, p. 235.

[36]   *Ibid.*, p. 226.

with loss of taste are usually severely depressed, and for good reason: The food they eat tastes like so much sawdust.[37]

Zinc-containing foods are peas, carrots, pork liver, beef liver, lamb, beef, chicken, wheat bran, oysters, clams, rye, whole wheat, eggs, cow's milk, whole nuts, peanut butter, oatmeal, wheat germ, whole corn and whole rice.[38]

Eating too much starch blocks the absorption of these vital nutrients and of amino acids. Since donuts, breads, and sweet rolls are the foods most readily available to the Street Person, I don't think their diet is conducive to mental health. Many Street People are mental patients who have been dumped out of the mental health care facilities, and many have also been cut from their government disability income. A diet based primarily on pastries works against them by exacerbating their already-fragile mental state.

The treatment of choice today, for the mentally ill, is adjustment of their body chemistry through drug therapy. This treatment works well for a great majority of the mentally ill persons. It is this treatment that is so effective that many mentally ill persons can cope with independent, if sheltered, living as long as the medication and resultant body chemistry is consistent and continued. Doesn't it make sense also to provide nutrients to maintain body balance?

Especially during the time I was on the street, many eligible mentally ill persons had recently been arbitrarily removed from the list of recipients for social security disability payments. At the time, it was a stated government public policy to remove as many people as possible. Quotas were set for regional offices. (Later, years later, the government apologized, and a few were reinstated.) But since many of these people had experienced having had their income cruelly revoked by the government, they were forced to accept whatever food they could get for free. That meant that stale donuts, toast, and sweet rolls, by necessity, became a large part of their diets.

---

[37] *Ibid.*, p. 228.

[38] *USDA Agricultural Handbook #8 and Garden Bulletin #72* Washington, DC: USDA, 1963.

SUMMARY OF MENTAL CONDITIONS OBSERVED AT HOUSE OF CHARITY, WINTER DECEMBER, 1983, TO MARCH, 1984[39]

More than half of the guests in the shelter were mentally ill and unable to function in independent living situations. Of those who were mentally ill, the women were predominantly elderly, and the men were middle-aged or younger. Among the mental conditions I observed were:

- Serious mental illnesses, including schizophrenia in many forms, echolalia, multiple personality disorder, disassociative disorders

- Delusional (paranoid) disorders, dementia,

- Adjustment disorders following service in Vietnam,

- Organic brain disorders such as bi-polar disorder (a/k/a manic-depression), severe depression,

- Dementia (and brain damage) following abuse of drugs or alcohol,

- Behavior disorders, paranoid personality disorder, antisocial disorder, hostility

As a person on the street myself, I was the first to appreciate the ready availability of the donuts, breads, and sweet rolls. They do fill the stomach and give calories necessary to keeping warm. But other foods work better in the temperature-regulators of the brain. I wonder if this "diet of the street" promotes mental illness in these walking-wounded, who are already overburdened. So many people in the street carry on conversations with themselves. Maybe, in the end, if everyone is hungry, if population and food supply go

---

[39] Some terminology and descriptive phrases from the *American Psychiatric Association, Diagnostic and Statistical Manual of Mental Disorders: DSM-III-R (Third Edition-Revised)*, Washington, D.C.: American Psychiatric Association, 1987.

completely off the Malthusian graph, we will all be surviving on donuts and muttering.

*

A. H. Maslow, in defining "basic need" interestingly enough linked neurosis with deficiency using a nutritional analogy:

> My original question was . . . . "What makes people neurotic?" My answer . . . was, in brief, that neurosis seemed at its core, and in its beginning, to be a deficiency disease; that it was born out of being deprived of certain satisfactions which I called needs in the same sense that water and amino acids and calcium are needs, namely that their absence produces illness. Most neuroses involved, along with other complex determinants, ungratified wishes for safety, for belongingness and identification, for close love relationships and for respect and prestige.[40]

*

SPROUTING AND NUTRITION

Dear Journal,

In the library, I was reading about The Desert Fathers, an early monastic group, and it seems that many of them lived on Essene bread. Essene Bread, bread made with sprouted seeds, has a long historical basis. The Essenes were a spiritual community of early desert hermits who depended on the hearty bread they made from sprouted grain (Essene bread). Bread prepared this way can still be

---

[40] Maslow, A. H., Toward a Psychology . . ., p. 21.

purchased today at specialty bakeries such as Brownberry's and many health food stores. It is also easy to make.[41]

*

OBESITY AND POVERTY

Dear Journal,

Many persons assume that being fat is the result of overeating and being skinny is from not eating. Numerous Street People I met, however, were fat. Some were obese, but not so much from consuming food as from the alternating cycles of starvation, pig-out,

---

[41] The year after my street experience, I continued to look into ways to provide high nutrition at low cost for persons with few or no usable teeth. This led to dinner-table discussions among friends Roger and Ellen Sue Spivack (co-owners of Deep Roots Trading Co., Williamsport, PA), C. B. T. Burgess III, and me. What grew out of these discussions was "The Johnny Alfalfa Sprout Project" to provide technical assistance and introductory supplies of seed and grains for sprouting to world missions and U.S. soup kitchens. Sprouting seeds and grains increases the nutrition of the seed or grain with only the addition of water. No soil is necessary, so it is possible to "farm" even in urban centers.

I also experimented using sprouted soybeans and sprouted alfalfa, run through a blender, then added to bread dough. It made the bread rise higher, faster, and produced a more moist loaf. The flavor was delicious. Food services could add a cereal and sprouting supplement in the preparation of the dough of sweet rolls; this would make a tremendous nutritional impact on the population in general and on street people in particular.

I once read a synopsis of a study (issued through the University of Washington at Seattle) of two studies in India which found that:

(1)   sprouting edible seeds and/or edible grains increased the sprouts nutritional content and benefit to humans between 200 and 450% (depending on which nutrient was being measured). The amount of nutrition available increased in every vitamin and trace mineral. The sprouts absorbed nutrients from the water in which they are sprouted and manufactured chlorophyll.

(2)   Sprouts provided the nutrition of a complete protein when combined one-part sprouted seeds with two-parts cereal grains (such as rice or wheat).

(3)   Persons in hospitals who were fed this mixture (for example in soup, or cereal, or bread) recovered faster, especially from certain diseases affecting the bowels, such as cholera.

and from the change in body chemistry from all those starches ingested. Continued over a long period, these cycles had taught their physical plants to be more food-efficient when they did get food— burning off calories at a lower rate and storing every possible amount of food-energy as fat. In other words, their weight set-point was adjusted for long-term survival by creating fat, but not necessarily related to maintain optimal body weight for health in the short term. The abuse of such involuntary dieting had changed it.

Cathy was talking about it today, too. She said, "Everybody knows that calories aren't necessarily nutritious. The rich can get seafood, fruits, and veggies; the poor like us eat grease, starch, and sugar because we need something to keep going. Take me, for instance. I ended up fat, but not well nourished. I gained all this weight since I been on the street. "For some, obesity can be an indicator of poverty.

Some Street People are fat and for some that is the result of periodically starving when food was not available, teaching the body to be conscientious as possible in putting as many calories into storage as fat. In our society, however, fat is more than just something which pads the body. It is misinterpreted by some as a symbol of an unexamined life.[42] There is little or no account taken of metabolism, hypothyroidism, genetics, limitations on motion (arthritis), and the phenomenon of "protective fat" persons who have been in violated sexually, and the opposite viewpoint that fat is a declaration of a liberated body.

*

---

[42] John Hanson Mitchell: *Ceremonial Time: Fifteen Thousand Years on One Square Mile* New York: Warner Books, 1984, p. 247.

Fat seemed to be something of a metaphor . . ., as if to have even an extra ounce or two was the sign of a lost human being, an individual who had never come to terms with himself and was living the unexamined life.

RECONSTITUTED EGGS

Dear Journal,

Breakfast at the Food Service was cold toast, powdered eggs, fermented applesauce, fragmented donuts, coffee, and grapefruit juice. The juice was delicious. Even though I'm critical of the food, I am very thankful for the generous portions, for without it, just now there would be no food for me.

Nevertheless, I am developing an aversion to powdered eggs sliced with a plastic fork and to never having a knife on the table, even a plastic knife, and to eating elbow-to-elbow, sandwiched at the table. It could be worse. At the Drake Hotel Shelter, the tables and chairs are so close together you cannot move the fork up to your mouth, so you just keep your mouth close to the fork. But the Drake provides large serving portions of vegetables with the meals.

I am getting an even greater aversion to powdered eggs, because they produce gas and leave everyone's clothes smelling of sulfur like an Artesian well in Florida.

*

INCONGRUENT VALUES

Dear Journal,

General health maintenance and maintenance of dental care are somewhat dependent on clean and healthy food, adequate rest, reasonable levels of stress, wholesome living, and good heredity. I know a lot of people who are health-conscious, and who exercise and eat right, but who smoke cigarettes constantly— so what a person values and what they do about it can get kind of crazy.

*

FOOD ECONOMICS

Dear Journal,

There still aren't enough paying jobs to go around. There still isn't enough money to go around. One of the staff said, "There is enough money to go around. It is in the Pentagon, in boardrooms, in buildings, in debts, and in pockets that lose it!"

I see old men searching trash cans for cement-like pieces of old toast. I see people hunched and silent over beanless bean soup, thankful for the heat of it, in a room with others just as desperate. Old people who go hungry because checks don't come on time when there is a four-day weekend or federal holiday. It is young families hungry at the end of the month because the food stamps didn't stretch that far, even with careful budgeting. Yet a well-fed President Reagan and his comfortable advisors said, "There is no hunger." It sounded to me like saying, "Let them eat cake" (or is it donuts?)

✳

CASH

Dear Journal,

Money is only on the list of priorities when there isn't any, but I do need it for telephone calls to set up appointments, for bus fare, and to buy sanitary products, journaling supplies, envelopes, and coffee (so as to rent a chair or get access to a bathroom). A typical budget for me is to send the $185 rent home per month, and to send a fuel-oil payment of approximately $200/month.[43] I am always short of cash, and my bills are piling up in Pennsylvania. I generally have $11 per week for phone calls, transportation, and coffee, and about $15 per month for toilet necessities, spiral-notebook paper, and pens. I really need $30 more per month for all those things.

✳

TELEPHONES

Dear Journal,

The frustrating challenge of telephone calls— making calls and receiving calls— is a daily challenge. I need to make and receive calls during in the daytime as follows: to my older son, for medical appointments concerning my children and myself, for legal and court appointments, for job interviews, and in other necessary

---

[43] Today when I was out in the cold, my empty apartment at home in Pennsylvania was cozy and warm.

coordination of daily life. Public phones should be accessible to the public.

*

COMMUNICATIONS: TELEPHONES AND POWER

Dear Journal,

I keep thinking about access (telephones and appointments) and power. A telephone is a status symbol of the affluent, and a control, for those in a position to abuse power. People with phones at work and at home are absolutely arrogant about presuming one's ability to afford and make phone calls. They are also absolutely arbitrary to Street People about appointment times. When you are not a Street Person, it is normal and customary to negotiate a convenient appointment time. But when speaking to a Street Person, the person on the power side of the desk is also an enforcer of the adage that beggars can't be choosers. Standing in line, itself, is now a full-time job. ("They also serve who only stand and wait."[44])

When I have the money and make the required phone calls, it consistently takes four phone calls to finally connect with someone. There is no way anyone can phone me, and that makes people angry (with me). If they were to leave a message for me at the House of Charity, I would not be likely to receive it until after the close of their business day, because Street People were locked out all day and when readmitted it would be after the shift-change at the House of Charity, and also due at times just to the logistics of getting back to the House of Charity from some other appointment— so the chance of successfully getting a daytime phone message is not good. I did try it a few times, but it just didn't work out.

Many days it takes $4.00 or more to connect with four people. My total disposable income for the week is about $15.00, and I expended $4.00 for every four people who needed to call— a 25% decrease in my total cash position. It is apparent that I cannot afford to phone them, and I can't afford to take a bus to see them—

---

[44] John Milton, Sonnet XIX *The Poems of John Milton*, 2nd edn. New York: The Ronald Press Company, 1953, p. 185.

even with a Jet Pass. My only option is to walk to each office to make an appointment to see them later, knowing each time that the person I wished to see or the receptionist will give me a hard time for not calling first.

A few times I tried to explain my circumstances, but that only made matters worse. Arrogance. Disdain. Contempt. Scorn. It wasn't worth that. Tough patutti! That's all that I can afford to be able to do to maintain the necessary contact they require. I could have skipped this hassle. I am in effect being berated for failure to have a private phone.

Since most of these agencies deal with clientele in poverty on a daily basis, I know I am not the only client in this situation. Calls to social service agencies should be free calls, like 911 calls, but should have a code which designates that it is a client's call, not a 911-emergency call. Street People should have access to telephones during business hours, even when they are locked out of the shelter. Perhaps several central locations, like shelters, could have voicemail, so a Street Person could call in or pick up messages during the day. This certainly would assist the able-bodied Street Person in securing employment. It is not unreasonable to think that the telephone company, the United Way, or even a bank could pay for such a phone line in return for some kind of Community Reinvestment Act credit.[45,46,47]

---

[45] In early 1996, US*West* announced that it would donate six voicemail lines for such use.

[46] A regional consortium of churches now has such a service center in North Minneapolis providing work readiness help, phones, messaging, resume service and child care to homeless women with children to help them reenter the work force and find permanent housing.

[47] In early May, 1996, on the "News Night" Program which aired on KTCA-TV Channel 2, Ms. Suddereth, founder of Twin Cities Community Voicemail, said,
"This Minnesota nonprofit organization has been in business 2 years to permit voice messaging service for people who do not have telephone service to receive messages. Of the 4,700 people who have been helped, 68% were homeless and 48% were working. As of early May, 1996, their client base had risen to 5,000."
With more than 53,000 homeless persons[*Search for Shelter*, pp. 14-15] per

(continued...)

TELEPHONES AND MACRO-ECONOMICS

Figure 10. Waiting to use the phone.

The House of Charity had one pay phone in the hall. I couldn't use it during most days because I was locked out. In the evening,

---

[47](...continued)
year in the Twin Cities, it is easy to see why this is an important service. In June 1996, they reapplied for a $100,000 HUD grant.

I had to share it with about 85 other people. I was successful in getting a turn about once a month after waiting in line for it for about three hours. So I asked others what they did to get to use a phone and the word was, "Go to one of the Branches, each one has a phone you can use free for local calls." The Branches are three drop-in centers run by Catholic Charities, referred to as Branch I, II, or III. The Branches were promoted as "a livingroom, a place where Street People can gather and be in community." Although none were in the directions I had to travel for anything else I was doing, I decided to check it out.

I walked south from the Food Service past HCMC, past Metropolitan Memorial Hospital[48] down Chicago Avenue, and finally, just before the ravine created by the interstate highways I-94 and I-35W, I reached Branch I. It was closed. Street People were standing out front. "It don't open 'til noon today. Staff meeting inside," a trim Native American man said to me.

"Thanks," I said and kept walking.

It was too cold to stand still. I walked for a while, then returned to the Branch. There were more Street People waiting: some surly men and only one other woman. The men were arguing about social services, availability of jobs, and Reaganomics.

One said, "I am not willing to be a damn statistic. They are manipulating my life by deciding to make it a national value to maintain a generous percentage of unemployed people so that inflation stays down. I don't want inflation either. This shouldn't be accepted as an inevitable 'either/or' situation. It should be 'both/and'— both full employment and no inflation. They need to make it a priority to figure out how to do it. Reagan made it a priority to invent a heat-seeking missile to intercept other missiles, and they're working on smart bombs. Star Wars shouldn't be more important than constituents."

Another responded, "I don't want to be a statistic. Sometimes we ain't even a statistic. Have you noticed how often lately we are just 'a market adjustment?' Every time the stock market falls, and more of us are laid off, they say it's a slight adjustment in the market.

---

[48] Now known as Metropolitan-Mt. Sinai Medical Center.

I'm not a slight adjustment in the market, and I don't want to be dehumanized that way."

By now, they were getting pretty loud, and others were joining in with: "Yeah man, you said it."

"Fuck the mother-fucking bureaucrats."

"Fuck Reagan."

"Give Reagan this cheese for breakfast, lunch, and dinner; see how long he can take it."

"Don't knock the cheese— it's good cheddar; rap the policies, complain about the policy makers, not the cheese." Someone from the Branch staff rapped on the window to get them to be quiet.

The sun had moved, and we were now all standing in the shade and getting colder, waiting for the self-proclaimed "livingroom for Street People, their daytime home away from home" to open.

The Branch social worker yelled at us, "Get off our sidewalk and clear out. We're not opening for half-an-hour! No loitering!" Where were we supposed to go for that half-an-hour? I didn't wait to use their phone.[49]

✳

JUDGMENTAL ATTITUDES

Dear Journal,

All people are entitled to be treated decently and applications for government services "processed" promptly. I am treated as if this would be a revolutionary concept. Many who are in positions of authority, with a responsibility to make it possible for others to have access to entitled services, approach it from the vantage point

---

[49] In March, 1996, to verify material for this book, I did go back to the Branch on Chicago Avenue, Minneapolis. Inside the front doorway, a uniformed guard in glassed-in cage screened each person seeking admittance. Another staff person maintained a sign-up sheet for use of the telephone which was in a lockbox. Use of the telephone was free and orderly. The staff was professional, cordial, and relaxed. Free coffee and donuts were available. Padre Johnson and I visited with some of the Street People and we had an enjoyable time. The facility had been renovated, was sparkling clean, and had bathrooms designed for accessibility.

of how to keep the entitled from getting these services, rather than how to make the system work as it should to confirm eligibility and to obtain the necessary social services to which people are entitled. Maybe a plastic eligibility confirmation card the size of a credit card could be arranged.[50]

There seems to be an undercurrent of unspoken judgment concerning recipients: *that they (we) deserve the misery of their (our) lot and should have the decency to remain invisible.*

I've been frosted so many times this week by public servants that I could build a Frosty the Snowman (snow-person) in each of their offices.

*

POSSESSIONS

Dear Journal,

For those who have a room for one night only, what they own has to be carried all day every day. This assumes they have a change of clothing, but then even owning a change of clothes becomes a problem. It can either be worn over what else is being worn or carried. You know how heavy some things get when you have to carry them for hours.

In some cities, Street People hide their blankets during the day. In Los Angeles, the pressure of the number of the Homeless population is so great that others rummaging for castoffs usually discover anything hidden. In Minneapolis, because the Skyway is the winter path, there is no place to stash belongings.

I saw one bag lady whose bag gave out, so she replaced the tote bag with a man's vinyl jacket. She stuffed her belongings in the jacket, pinned the base and neck shut, pinned the cuffs together, and put the jacket arms around her neck. She lugged this torso all over town. Many Street People solved the problem by not having a change of clothing. They just wore one set until it disintegrated. Then they obtained another set from the Free Store and put the first set in the trash. The clothes I saw in the trash belonged there.

---

[50] Some experiments are underway using this means for Food Stamp fund distribution.

"Pockets"[51]

Her given name was Emily,
but everyone called her "Pockets."
They called her that
because she insisted over and over again
that people shouldn't own anything
they can't carry
in their pockets.

For a while
Emily traveled light,
living her pocket philosophy to the letter.
However,
it didn't take long at all
to fill the four-and-a-half pockets
in her jeans.

A resourceful person,
Emily became a regular customer
of the local Army Surplus stores.
She bought garments with abundant pockets
designed to carry:
> K-Rations
> Bullets
> Maps
> Snake-Bite Kits
> P.X. Chocolate
> Canteens
> and
> Assorted Survival Gear.

Emily soon filled these pockets
toward her own survival.

---

[51]   Patricia M. Ryan, "Pockets" compiled by Janice Grana in *IMAGES: Women in Transition*. Winona, MN: St. Mary's College Press, 1977, pp. 54-55.

She carried:
    Money
    Canned Goods
    Rye Bread
    Instant Coffee
    Panty Hose
    Paperback Books
    A Clarinet
    24 Green and 7 Yellow Pills
    13 Pairs of Earrings
    2 Bottles of Apple Wine
    and
    An Electric Toothbrush (with
    Manual Paste.)

As time passed Emily added more and more clothes
with more and more pockets
to hold more and more things.
She was indeed proud
that she had never compromised
and used even one shopping bag.

Emily was last seen
somewhere in Southern California
standing very, very still.
She was wearing (several layers of clothing
under) a woolen Army greatcoat
on which she had sewn large pockets
to hold
her folding bicycle
a television
and
a complete set of the Great Books of the
Western World.

Since most of the clothes given to the Free Store have made it down the clothing chain from new to pre-owned, to hand-me-down, to garage sale, to unsalable, to giveaway, by the time they get to the Free Store there isn't much useful life left in them anyway. But I'd rather see donations continue than to have serviceable clothing thrown in the trash.

*

POSSESSIONS AND CONTAINERS FOR THEM

Dear Journal,
Pockets are portable storage units. They are like a safety deposit box. Because it didn't seem sensible to carry a purse, my pockets or my rucksack had to contain all my necessities. But there are limits to how much can be stuffed into pockets.

Light weight sturdy containers— flight bags, plastic bags, shopping bags, and whatever else is durable, inexpensive, and can be used in a pinch— are a necessity. One bank gave out blue plastic bags with a drawstring top. At Christmas, some of our hats and scarves were "wrapped" in these bags. Hundreds of these bags can be seen every day. For a while they were the primary storage unit of all Street People. Therefore, throughout January, the poorest of the poor in Minneapolis were walking billboards for the wealthiest banking institution.

*

HOARDING

Dear Journal,
There is a mental disorder characterized by compulsive hoarding to excess (which is not limited to Street People but is more visible with some of them). I had been in some garbage houses when working in NY and PA, where people so stuffed their homes, that there was no longer any room for them to get into or out of the house.

It is easy to understand how a person might become obsessed with hoarding— if he or she needed so much and had so few resources to get anything. For street people, however, this is in direct conflict with the necessity to travel light.

✳

GROOMING: HAIRCUTS

Dear Journal,
One evening Allen complained that he was being turned down for work because he had long hair. He wanted to get it cut because he had a job interview in the morning. The Jesus People would not be offering haircuts for another week. At that time, one of the beauty colleges provided hair trimming to Street People who had a proper voucher for it. There were only so many vouchers issued at a time. I don't believe everyone could get one.

I offered to give him a haircut if he would first wash his hair (so I could cut it wet), obtain permission from the staff, and ask the staff to lend us scissors. (This was apparently a big deal, because scissors are viewed as a potential weapon. It took one hour to get the scissors.) So I gave him a haircut. He was glad he got the job.

✳

GROOMING: SHAVING

Dear Journal,
The stereotype of the male Street Person always includes a seedy-looking beard. While this may be due to negligence sometimes, many times it is due to not having a razor with razor blades, a disposable razor, or access to scissors. You can't get a shave and a hair cut for a quarter anymore.

✳

TRANSPORTATION

Dear Journal,
Walking and using buses in non-peak times on a Jet Pass are the primary means of transportation. (Few Street People have cars, due in part to the aggressive tow-away policy enforced in Minneapolis in snowy winters: most view an automobile as a costly liability.)

I suffer from environmental sensitivities, among them reacting to diesel fumes, so I find it difficult to be around buses even if I'm only on the sidewalk when a bus passes. So for me, having to depend on buses again is a big deal. I haven't ridden buses since I worked on Capitol Hill in D.C. (before the Metro). This evening, on the way back from the hospital, I asked the bus driver for information about transferring. "Where do I transfer to get to the 500 block of South 8th Street?"

He said, "I have no idea. When I got the bus-driver job, they taught me this one route and never changed it. The streets along this route are the only streets in the city I ever drive on."

"A graduate of Bob Newhart's School of Bus Driving, no doubt," I thought.

Unfortunately I missed my bus stop while listening to his explanation. I wouldn't have minded the extra six-block walk back if it weren't for the wind chill of 64 degrees below zero. On the way back, I stepped inside a church to get out of the wind and get warm. They asked me to leave because it was time to lock the church.

✳

AVAILABILITY TO WORK

Dear Journal,

I need low-stress work to occupy my mind but not fry it. I am so deeply in debt and under such monumental stress that working 40 hours or more a week for wages would be a futile gesture while I am only here temporarily. If I were not in this situation perhaps I could collapse in the total exhaustion I actually feel. But even by keeping on keeping on I still have not earned enough to meet basic necessities. My goal is clear: to pursue the needs of my children and me, and tough it out while the case moves through the court system. I will pay the debts later.

✳

ABILITY TO WORK

On the days and nights that I worked, I stepped through a time warp. When I was working and dressed up as presentably as I could be under the circumstances, I walked faster, stood straighter, and had slightly less back pain. To give you some sense of the degree of distress I felt physically, the longer I was on the street, the harder it was to do any math in my head. Apparently higher-level mathematical functions get damped down when a person is under extreme stress. I was thankful that no one assigned me to make change or to balance a checkbook. I could, however, still perform mechanical skills such as word-processing and operating a ten-key. At TCF bank and a Marquette Bank, I put social security numbers into the computer and updated lists of addresses. Most fortunate of all was the ATM job that I mentioned earlier, because when the ATM machines were not acting up, I was free to do what I wanted— to write the journals which later generated this book. There it was only really busy at 8 p.m., around midnight, and on Fridays. In between times I was usually free to read and write. The journaling and capturing the stories cleared my mind, grounded me, and freed my spirit.

✷

PART V: DIFFERENT NEEDS, PERSPECTIVES, AND EXPECTATIONS

For decades, the efforts of churches, charities, nonprofits, and volunteers have carried the majority of responsibility for delivery of social services to The Homeless.

Church-affiliated programs such as Catholic Social Services, Lutheran Social Services, the Salvation Army, the American Rescue Mission, the Mennonite Relief, and others, provide a significant percentage of the social services to which the poor and homeless have access in Minneapolis. And much of the difficult work is by volunteers as well as staff. In recent years, there has been some divvying up of turf. Some only serve alcoholics. Others serve only drug-users. Some are for battered women. Some are for women with children. This is a step toward meeting better the needs of well-identified groups. It is however and invitation for smaller groups and individuals to be excluded because they do not fit one of the well-defined categories. For example, at that time, the House of Charity excluded only persons actively abusing alcohol or drugs, and persons who had been evicted previously from the House of Charity for behavior that was threatening to staff or other guests.[52]

*

---

[52] After some turned-away drunks froze to death, the House of Charity received lots of negative press about this policy.

The helping community sought a creative solution which lead to an equally creative design. In 1991, a different type of shelter was proposed to provide pods of congregate housing for homeless chronic (terminal) inebriates who were not necessarily desirous of giving up alcohol abuse. The site selected is located within reasonable proximity to one of the larger and better "soup kitchens."

UNREALISTIC EXPECTATIONS AND MUTUAL DISCOMFORT

Dear Journal,

Many attitudes that church people, social service workers, and street people have about each other are full of faulty assumptions and misconceptions. Church people, government, social workers, volunteers, the media, the public often view The Homeless with disdain, often through faulty assumptions, and with what comes across as self-righteous judgmentalism. Often these perceptions:

(1) affect the type of services delivered,

(2) result in improper assessments of the problems, and

(3) produce inappropriate or inadequate remedies.

Street People and Church People both are guilty of stereotyping each other and of faulty assumptions. Street People have high expectations of Church People. Church People expect Street People to be models of perfect kindness, compassion, fairness, honesty, and sincerity. These unrealistic expectations are often disappointed. There is a perception that Church People working with the poor care deeply about the poor. There may be an expectation that all Church People will therefore have empathy, kindness, compassion, patience, and unlimited resources. This is unrealistic too. Disappointed expectations can trigger anger and defensiveness on both sides.

On this afternoon, an ever-expanding group was forming at a table in the far corner of the Skyway level of Harvest House Cafeteria, watching out the window at the pile drivers three levels below grade driving steel deep below the 42" frost line to support a new skyscraper on the site of the old Norwest Bank, which had burned beyond repair. The dump trucks driving up and down on the ice-covered dirt ramps looked like little Matchbox trucks. Dennis said, "Church People have faulty assumptions and unrealistic expectations of Street People. Church People expect Street People to accept God on the giver's terms, to have only simple problems and simple needs that are easily remedied, to gush with enthusiastic gratefulness, to make drastic changes in our lives quickly and permanently, to get our acts together within a few days and get a high-enough-paying job to enable us to get off the street forever." He continued, "The perception of the poor and of poverty varies greatly among denominations, and also among individual church members. One factor is that a lot of us don't like to go to certain shelters because we feel used by the volunteers, who seem to be there to meet their own agenda. What I'm talking about is, if you go to certain shelters, you have to listen to a sermon for one hour for every 15 minutes you get to eat. They don't care about your body. They are after your soul, so they can keep score of how many derelicts they have saved. Some only seem to care about chalking up some 'saves' for credit toward their 'bus-ticket-out' to heaven."

Three-coats joined in, "Now, a lot of people on the street are no angels. For some it's their own damn fault. They pickled their brains in alcohol. But nowadays most of the Street People are decent people who never done anything wrong. They may be physically disabled, schizophrenic or otherwise mentally ill, or unable to find a dependable job, or recently unemployed, or displaced by a plant closing. This big batch of people are not what I would call 'the Sinners.' But the sermons before the meals always assume we are all thieves, drunks, or druggies, and try to shame us, dumping a shit-load of guilt on us, and get us 'to repent and be saved'."

Henry responded, "I wish they would look at what our skills, talents, and gifts are instead of viewing us only as 'having deficiencies'."

Three-coats replied, "But it's an absolute truth that everyone can improve somehow. And it's certain druggies and the bums need to bottom out and change."

"Well, it seems damn crazy that if you are in one shelter you are 'The Damned,' but in the other, you are the 'saintly Blessed Poor.' The truth is, nobody is all damned or all saint," Michael concluded.

Dennis said, "But for a lot of us, needing to improve doesn't mean we are worthless. It doesn't mean we are self-destructive. And it doesn't give someone else the right to rub our noses in our own misfortune."

John added, "A lot either can't work anymore, never were able to work (because of mental illness or disabilities), or can't keep a job for any long period (what with corporations getting bought out, and reductions in force and all that.)"

"For many it's the economy and government policies pushing 'em farther down and keeping 'em there. Therefore, I think the economy should repent and be saved," Dennis said. Then turning to Harry, he said, "Har, go buy something— it's your turn— so we don't get throwed out."

Michael said, "Certain churches view poverty as a sin in itself— as if it is *always* something under your control. Like if you are good for God, you're rich. Sometimes poverty does result from bad choices, and there are bad consequences. But more often it's from falling dominoes, or catastrophic and/or chronic illness. And many people work hard their whole lives and never get ahead."

"What about the self-righteous, who view poverty as a sin in and of itself— like the ones responsible for making the law that being on a public sidewalk or The Skyway without cash in your pocket and without PROOF of a fixed address is 'commitin' the sin of vagrancy'— which is against the law here: if you are from out-of-state, without a local fixed address, and without cash in hand— Whoa! it's increased to the mortal sin of Vagrancy. You can betcha that many so of the suits walking through The Skyway— so-called middle-class folks who depend on credit cards— or kiting credit cards— are probably, in fact often technically, in a state of vagrancy themselves." There were grunts and nods of general agreement around the table.

"You said it, man."

Dennis went back to grinding his axe about the churches. He continued, "Then there are other churches which have a view that there is something holy about being The Poor. They believe if they help us a little, they will get a little holy themselves. Does our holiness rub off? So, them well-off church ladies volunteer one day a month and then retreat to their well-appointed homes feeling smugly righteous about all their self-sacrifice of two hours a month to 'help feed the needy, those poor unfortunates.' They get off on tellin' their friends how valiant they are to 'mingle with the derelicts' when in fact they've helped prepare or serve the food, but didn't get to know any of the poor people there in any meaningful way. Probably wouldn't be caught dead sitting next to one or having a real conversation."

"My reaction to the volunteers doing this to get brownie points in heaven is partly anger, a little humiliation, and even some outrage about the unfairness of it all," Jackson said. "Then I feel bad about feeling angry because without them, these 'feeding' programs wouldn't work. Most of the meal programs are set up this way, with a different well-to-do church sending volunteers one day a month to take a turn providing a meal. At least by seein' us go through the line and watchin' us eat, they become more aware and more sensitized than if they didn't. Don't get me wrong. Lord knows, I'm glad for the food. I just get uncomfortable thinking what I think they might be assuming when they're watchin' us eatin'."

Harry sauntered back to the table with a newly purchased banana, swung past the coffee maker to bring another free pot of fresh coffee back to the table for the rest of us, "Yeah, I can feel them looking at me, looking through me. I know I don't present an attractive picture. It's like they think I dress this way and smell this way because this is the way I want to be. They think the reason I don't shave is because I'm lazy. It takes a lot of snow-shoveling for me to be able to afford deodorant, razors, dry cleaners, and any cheap new clothes. I need boots and a coat long before that."

"I mean about the unfairness of it all: She might think— it wouldn't be this way, my being on the street, if I just might work as hard as her husband or something like that. I worked hard all my life. I worked construction. Then my knees and back gave out, and there have been a lot of recessions which depressed housing construction. My balance wasn't good enough. I'm well past 50 and now the only work I'm offered is shoveling snow. That don't help my back and knees at all. I never intended to end up as a charity case."

"Jeeez, did you see that dump truck slide backwards down the ramp?" Max pointed. We all craned our necks to watch the truck spinning its wheels flailing its way back up the ramp. "Oofdah! I wouldn't want to be the one to have to get out and push that big mother."

"We aren't the only ones," Dennis said, "Some of them church ladies is only a paycheck away from homelessness themselves. If their man loses his job, or gets violent, or the lady gets a divorce, wouldn't be long before she'd be knockin' on the door of some long-lost relation or comin' to an emergency charity shelter, too."

"Them guys at the construction site down there is grabbing their lunch buckets and heading out. Must be past 3:30 p.m. Guess we guests can start headin' back to the House— they oughta be unlocking the door soon enough."[53]

*

TOLERANCE AND INTOLERANCE

Dear Journal,

Today, as I sat on the bench in the lobby at St. Olaf's church, I was aware that I was not sitting straight. My head had been sinking toward my knees. I tried again to sit up straight. *How can trouble, which is transparent, feel so heavy?*

I selected a *New Covenant* magazine, hoping the news of the Spirit would lift my spirit. I perused an article about "gentle Jesus." How many men can really accept Jesus as a role-model? I wondered how any of this fit the Street People.

A young man entered the vestibule. He was extremely clean for a Street Person with long, wavy golden hair that was clean, combed, and cut to an even length. Few Street People could keep hair looking like that— unless he'd just come from the Jesus People hair stylist. He was wearing an outdoor vest, a short suede jacket, and heavy boots. Over his vest he had a military fatigue jacket with lots of pockets. It said FRYE in black lettering above the left pocket flap. He paced the length of the room. From one end to the other he paced. He lit a cigarette. As he paced, he matched the draws on his cigarettes with his measured steps. The ash grew longer and longer. With the next pass, he flicked his ashes discreetly into the peculiar brass ash tray mounted on the wall— it had water to quell the ashes.

A Street Person entered the back area. He noticed a poster on the bulletin board that read "Care for the Spirit in one another so that the Spirit in all of us is strengthened in His Spirit." This man

---

[53] See Part IX: That Was Then, This Is Now for information on a video for volunteer preparation and training.

put down his large bag of life's treasures— probably some old toast, an apple, a newspaper and a change of socks. At the bulletin board, he struggled to re-pin the four corners of the poster so the sides weren't falling down.

Another Street Person walked over to him. Quietly, in gentle tones, he said, "It isn't supposed to have pins in the corners. It's put up that way to be like a scroll. Do you remember seeing scroll pictures when you were a kid? You know, they rolled up scroll letters, back when they didn't know about envelopes. They rolled this poster to look like a scroll."

"Oh. I didn't know that. I'm so sorry. I was trying to make it right. I didn't know it was already right."

"I know you were. Why don't we walk over here so we can chat, while we are waiting."

Ladies with fox-heads draped over the shoulders of their woolen tweed suits and men in gray or camelhair topcoats, filtered in. Other ladies took positions at the inner doors; sentry-like, they passed out bulletins to those leaving and to those coming for the next service. Clumps of gray and fur began forming all around that back room. A little hum of greetings and "How-are-you's" vibrated among the groups.

The golden-haired Frye paced the length again. It was harder to pace in a straight line now, with all the clumps. This pace was at the end of his cigarette, so he extinguished it in the water. A gray-woolen church man strode across the room with authoritative steps. Loudly, harshly, he said, "You can't do that here. That's a terrible thing." Emphasizing every word, he said, "You can't desecrate the Holy Water!"

Weakly, golden-haired Mr. Frye said, "I'm sorry. I meant no harm. I thought it was an ash tray. It's the only thing here like an ash tray." His humiliation shown brighter than his shiny hair.

The woman posted at the door, waving bulletins, said in a purposely loud voice, "Who is he, anyway? What's he doing here? Why doesn't he go where he belongs?"

The church man glared at him. The man who had adjusted the scroll and the other friend moved closer to Frye. I put down the magazine and glared at her. She went back to greeting people and passing out bulletins— but not to Street People.

I thought about her question, and asked myself: *Where do The Homeless belong? Isn't a church the last sanctuary? Haven't we even fallen through the Safety Net— which is the last sanctuary offered by government? Aren't we the ones who have fallen through the cracks in the pavement? Don't we qualify as the outcasts that Jesus spoke of?*

Meager possessions should meet Jesus' qualification to be able to pass through the eye of a needle. Certainly many days, we are the poor in Spirit: the discouraged, the dissociate, the down-hearted. True, the well-to-do patrons pay the heating bills and upkeep on the building but we Street People are here more than they are— we have to pray to survive each day. A lot of Street People attend Mass here every day, not just sit there while Mass is going on.

Msgr. Fleming has shown a special mercy toward the Street People because he allows the church doors to be open and the church to be heated every day of the week. Any Street People who are not disruptive and not panhandling (begging) are at least tolerated here.

Dear Journal,

At a Sunday Mass at St. Olaf's, the sermon was on "Finding Ways To Be Generous." Msgr. Fleming announced, "Please all stay for the 'Coffee Social.' All are welcome." So we did. There were fresh, tender donuts, only a few hours out of the oven. The mink and the misshapen all moved through this food line.

The emaciated old man in front of me was so thin he looked like he might expire any day. He and the heavy-set man behind me each took three donuts. Everyone else I observed took only one. The men who took three were from among a group from the House of Charity. Most had not eaten since sometime early Saturday afternoon. We were especially glad to get a donut that was weeks ahead of its expiration date.

The serving lady behind the table stared at the three-donut men and grumbled, "Greed. Lack of manners. It's sheer piggishness, stuffing oneself like that!"

When we reached the end of the line, there was a donation basket, but you cannot donate what you don't have, so we Street People walked past it.

The lady glared, then squinted at us. Some ushers grumbled at us. Soon their voices faded away as we filtered out of the line and found seats on the far edge of the room. I was so annoyed that I even wished somehow they would HAVE TO spend a week as a bag lady or a destitute man. Maybe then they'd understand.

I guess they hadn't paid attention to the sermon today "Finding Ways To Be Generous." But someone else did. A cheery lady brought pitchers of hot coffee, refilling cups, and her warmth helped cover over the bad vibes we had from the other church lady and the ushers.

✳

COMPARISON OF URBAN & RURAL POVERTY

Dear Journal,

It seems harder to be poor in the city than in a rural area. For example, there is homogeneity in Appalachia, where in 1984 (e.g. in rural central Pennsylvania), one in four persons is unemployed. People dress alike— the rich dress down, and the poor make do— and the discrepancy isn't very noticeable. People look out for one another, and there's barter, even barter clubs, generosity, sharing, and overflowing gardens. In the Twin Cities area, on the other hand, while there is extensive "corporate generosity" which sustains these social programs, to be poor feels like being judged inferior and being rejectable. If one's poor, but doesn't look poor here, perhaps more than elsewhere, it behooves one to keep one's mouth shut about it.

✳

JUDGING OTHERS

Dear Journal,

After my venting in my journal about self-righteous judgmentalism, I found myself being judgmental today. Is this another lesson for me in God's classroom?

When I saw the elderly, well-dressed couple steal three bags of groceries from the church food-for-the-poor collection basket, I was upset. I still am, perhaps because I personally don't know if they "needed" the food or not. To me, it didn't seem proper that they would steal it before it was officially distributed to the poor. It seemed sleazy. Maybe there is too much red tape for this particular elderly couple to get needed food by going through the system. Was it their pride leading them to believing it is better to take than to ask? It certainly is harder to ask, because it hurts inside, and there is probably a line to stand in to ask and another line to stand in to receive.

*

UPSTAGING THE PASTOR

Dear Journal,

Yesterday, the middle-aged woman who whines, wails, and mutters was in church. She had long, stringy hair and a long, stringy fake-fur coat. Her ski cap went up into a sharp point. She was short, with a crouching posture, hooked nose, and claw-like fingers which drooped from noticeably bent wrists. During Mass she wailed, "Do you people like me? You people are supposed to like me. You're Christians, aren't you?" She interrupted the flow of the service with her high-pitched whines. She stood when the congregation sat down. She knelt when everyone else stood up.

Msgr. Fleming of St. Olaf's Church is a firm pastor, with a veneer of gentleness. He looks as if he is nearing retirement age. He has a good sense of humor, but this strange lady had caused a disturbance at his Masses (and probably the day's other four, too) every day for two weeks. Msgr. Fleming's reservoir of patience was running out. As he began the sermon this morning on the importance and function of guilt, she stood up. He motioned for her to sit down, and she began to wail. He began, "Some modern psychologies have put emphasis on guilt-free living— a philosophy of 'It's okay to do whatever you want to do; just don't feel guilty about it, no matter what'." Father went on, "God gave us guilt as a sure-fire indicator that we have done something wrong, and we'd better not do something like that again." He said, "If you've done something wrong, it is right for the guilt to be in proportion to the wrong. A good strong load of guilt could be a therapeutic dose."

"On the other hand, guilt-free living, when you should feel guilt, deadens feelings that need to be felt. Deadening feelings is living in an unreality, and it can make you sick. Such unfeelingness is not the compassionate, sensitive way that Jesus taught." It was a pretty good sermon except that the lady interrupted it part way: "I'm guilty! He says 'I'm guilty!'. . . Am I the only one? Aren't all of you sinners? . . . You're sinners, aren't you? Don't you feel anything? Doesn't sin hurt you too?" Her words were right on, but the tone of her voice mocked her own words, and her voice did not seem to fit her body.

The congregation tried to ignore her, to pretend she wasn't there, but that was hard to do. Msgr. Fleming tried to ignore her. But she went on, louder and louder, making it impossible for him to continue the sermon. Finally, out of exasperation, he looked directly at her and said firmly, "Pipe down! Sit down! And pipe down!" It worked for a while.

I wished Msgr. Fleming had a gift of healing. Obviously the mental health professionals had not been able to cure this lady. Her inner turmoil must be a private hell for her. If only someone could "Lay Hands" on her and heal her mind and tongue. She must find some kind of spiritual relief here, since she comes to church every day. She follows the sermons— out loud. She doesn't own the tongue in her own head. That's true for a lot of people, but with her it's more apparent. The New Testament says the tongue is the hardest part of the body to cure. Certainly I believe that!

Soon Mass was over. I left the church. She was behind me, and walking in the same direction but initially at some distance. The early morning hustle of people heading to work surrounded us. I walked past the Midwest Federal building toward TCF and crossed over to the IDS Tower, to go get a coffee at Woolworth's Harvest House Cafeteria. By this time she was right behind me.

At the Marquette Street corner, a crowd gathered at each the four corners as we waited for the "Walk" lights. As my corner of people moved en masse across the street, a similar group came toward us. The cold air on my face was bracing, after being sleepy in the warm church. I opened my mouth in a big yawn, and I heard an unmistakable voice right behind me wail, "Hear, everybody! I've been judged guilty of being a sinner! I'm guilty. You're guilty. Where are you?"

Her small body was directly behind me, hidden by my huge parka. The people coming toward me across the street stared at me. A well-dressed lady stopped abruptly in front of me, glared at me, and exclaimed, "Really! Harrump!"

I stood still in the street, embarrassed. The wailing lady passed by, lost in the crowd. The prim lady stared at me, looking back over her shoulder all the way across the street as I watched her go. Her mouth was still agape. I guess I have been misjudged again. . .

✳

PEACE OF CHRIST HANDSHAKE[54]

"And now let us offer one another the sign of Peace." In many churches, at one point during the Mass, worshipers face one another, shake hands and say, "May the Peace of Christ be with you," or "Peace be to you."

"And with you also."

After Vatican II this was revolutionary for Catholics who used to put more emphasis on silence than on socializing at Mass.

In these difficult financial and emotional times, that simple greeting and smile from total strangers has given me a tremendous boost, a symbolic offering of warmth and caring. When I am traveling in a town where I know no one, it helps me know more than ever that I can be welcome in church wherever it may be. There have been some times when I have noticed that not everyone gets the same lift as I did, nor conducts the ritual in the same way. On Long Island, when the Peace of Christ is offered in a Catholic church, there is joyful hugging, kissing, and greetings as well as the hand-clasping. Sometimes people there cross, clear across the church, to reach a special someone to hug. Even alone and far from home, I cannot help but be lifted by that joy and enthusiasm.

In many places in central Pennsylvania, where a rigid Germanic tradition keeps emotions restrained, some churches have not yet been touched by such joy of the Spirit, and the ritual peace

---

[54] This vignette was previously published as "Peace of Christ Handshake," by Patricia McDonough, *The Catholic Bulletin*, St. Paul, MN: April 12, 1984 vol. 74, no. 15, p. 3B.

offering is treated with restricted and rigid conformity. No one may touch hands until the priest shakes hands with each usher, and then the usher goes row by row and shakes hands only with the person in each the center aisle seat who then passes the formal handshake and greeting down the row. There is no touching other than of hands, and no smiling. Not knowing this custom, I started extending my hand to my neighbor as soon as the priest announced, "Let us offer one another the sign of peace." She sternly rebuffed me with "Not now! It's not allowed. Only at the right time!" Where was the spontaneity and joy that could uplift the spirit and warm the church?

In another church, where street people of Minneapolis are scattered in the back pews and the mink-coated are wrapped in the front, the twain often, by necessity, "mix and mingle" in the middle pews of the church— even more so on Sundays, when the ushers reserve the back pews for themselves. When we are mixed together in the middle (all kinds and classes), human nature is sometimes at its most obvious. I have seen (unemployed?) bedraggled men with hair matted and sticking out in points and scraggly beards prickling out of pale, despairing faces. When it is time for the Peace of Christ to be shared, the warmth of caring handshakes has brought new hope and color to their bland faces— sometimes even a light to their sad eyes.

Other times, I have seen people's hands shrink and wither when they discover their "neighbor" is one of the poor in Spirit. I even saw one lady, after shaking hands, try to wring her hand off her wrist lest the hand contaminate the rest of her body. Because of the possibility of this type of reaction, I know one misguided person who was so concerned about whether or not he would be rebuffed at this part of the service that he decided consistency was better than uncertainty, even if it was consistent rejection. So when he went to church, his hair looked like John the Baptist's and he wore his favorite down jacket, a hand-me-down held together with green plastic tape. It was so full of holes that the feathers sticking out all over the jacket made him look like a poorly-plucked chicken. He said whenever he wears this coat, he is always greeted with a look of panic as well as a reluctant handshake. He says, he "enjoys having them confronted by their own attitudes."

The saddest thing I saw was a lady dressed in an elfin hat and scraggly coat that matched her scraggly hair. She had a dead look, a sad look, a look of confusion in her eyes. She muttered frequently during the service and often flailed her arms with wrists bent downward. She was obviously not at home in her own head. At Mass, she often called out, in a wailing small voice, "What's the matter, don't you like me? You are supposed to like me. Doesn't anyone here like me?" But when I offered the Handshake of Peace, her self would not permit her hand to shake with mine. I felt mocked, but I knew she was no longer responsible for her self. She "knows not what she does." And during the handshake, I am often reminded of my mother, who was so conscious of germs (sometimes, I muse, even before Pasteur's findings became widely accepted) that when someone in church would sneeze or cough, she would duck. She has never been quite comfortable shaking hands with hands that have not been washed within the last ten minutes. I thought I was free of her fetish, until just before the handshake, when the man beside me sneezed a big "Atchoo" and shielded his mouth politely with his right hand. (*Oh, Mother, in this way I am like you.*) I wanted to leave. I turned to everyone else around me to avoid the inevitable, when I must shake that hand. He saved me though: he offered his left hand. I blessed him many times over. In the book *Blessings: An Autobiographical Fragment,*[55] Mary Craig writing about her son Nicky, a child with Down's syndrome (children with Down's Syndrome are known for their exuberant love) that in church when it is time for the handshake, that was the part of the Mass her son could relate to. With joy and enthusiasm, he would go to all the aisles near them and shake every hand, emoting joy and enthusiasm, giving greetings such as "'Peace be to you, Mr. Happy . . . or Mr. Sneezey . . . .' Her friend remarked, 'He understands this part better than any one else here.'" Near the end of the Mass when the priest said "Go the Mass is ended," Nicky quipped "That's it. That's all folks," Bugs Bunny style.

---

[55] Mary Craig, *Blessings: An Autobiographical Fragment* 1st US edn. New York: Morrow Publishers, 1979, pp. 114-115.

It is unfortunate that attending Mass, giving the Sign of Peace is no guarantee of inner peace or of being in community. Inner peace, calm, contentment, and harmony sometimes seem so hard to achieve and maintain. I do get a sense of warmth and caring from this Sign of Peace handshake. I would be wonderful if that handshake could restore us all to a deep Inner Peace as well.

*

VISIT THE SICK

Dear Journal,

I went to visit Aeneas in the hospital again. He just had a second surgery and was in the intensive care unit (ICU). He was feeling lousy. As I was leaving, I ran into Father Red who filled in at St. Olaf's Church, who was making his rounds, and I recalled our dialogue of last week, the night before Aeneas' first surgery. Aeneas was fearful that he would not be able to make it through such extensive surgery, and he asked Dolly to invite the priest, who was out in the hall, to come in to talk to him.

Dolly is about 52 years old, but her mental age is about nine. She walked up to Father Red and asked, just as she would have asked for anything when she was nine years old, "Father? Aeneas has surgery tomorrow. Will you come in his room and say a few prayers with him?"

"Oh, yes. Yes, I'll be with you in a few minutes," Father Red said absently, tuning her out.

Dolly went into Aeneas room and said to him, "Father says he will pray with you in a few minutes. Isn't that good!"

"Yes. I need that. I would like him to come in." His voice was raspy from the tracheotomy tube.

I said, "I guess he'll be here in a few minutes. I can see him outside the door." But Father continued his small talk, as he walked down the hall and got on the elevator. He did not come in to see Aeneas that night.

This day as I stepped into the hall while they put Aeneas in a chair in the ICU, Father Red was again at the elevator. I approached him and asked, "Father Red, will you pray with my friend Aeneas in the ICU #2? He's in a lot of pain and asked for prayers."

"Oh, yes. I certainly will," he said, but he kept edging toward the elevator.

I took note and said, "Father, it will only take a minute. As soon as he is sitting up, we can go in."

He replied, "Oh, I'm sorry, not today. I have to be going. Another chaplain has been seeing him, I'm sure."

I was beginning to get annoyed. "That would be good, too, but he also needs some prayers now, right now. I remember your excellent sermon on healing on Saint Blaise Day. He needs that now. He has throat cancer."

"Well, do you know what denomination he is?" he asked. ("*Oh shit*," I thought, "*More red tape.*") I tried one more time. "I don't know his denomination. I do know he has a strong belief in God and the power of prayer, is battling terminal caner, and he would like you to pray with him in person."

Ignoring my reply, Father Red said, "Well, do you know where he goes to church? They would have chaplains."

"No. I don't know. I'm sure he has no firm ties here, because I think he is from out of town." That was a goof. I should know by now not to use the magic door-closing phrase "out-of-town," but I forgot.

"Well, it must say somewhere on his card what religion he is. They ask, when a patient is admitted. I'll tell the visiting chaplain to stop by. He never had any ties with me, you see."

"Father, it is all one God. Won't you please pray with him? He is one of yours, in a way: he is staying at Catholic Charities in St. Olaf's Catholic Church parish. I've seen you say mass there. Aeneas' wife asked you to pray the other night; you agreed; then you walked away. Does he have to die to get your attention? He is living in your parish. He is in the hospital in your parish, only four blocks from your church— right in that ICU room, right there in pain, and asking for you to pray with him."

"I gotta run. You're right about God, of course." Father Red was noticeably uneasy now. With the time we had spent in this unpleasant conversation, he could have prayed Aeneas directly into heaven. As he stepped on the elevator, Father Red said, "I'll tell them to be sure to see him, now that I know a little more." I doubt if he did.

I was careful to ask him to pray with him, not pray for him, and he still didn't come. I went back in to Aeneas.

Figure 11. House of Charity lobby during the flu epidemic.

"Then you pray with me," he said. Although I had experienced people praying with me and for me, I was not accustomed to praying with them, meaning leading the prayer (out loud). I, too, started to squirm. I reached into my pocket. It was torn, so my hand went into the lining, where it came in contact with a little aluminum cross a friend had given me to take on this journey. She had said, "Keep it in your pocket. Use it like a worry stone. The cross has more power. You will need it." So I dug it out of my pocket and put it on Aeneas' chest. We were sort of alone inside one of those little hospital cloth partitions.

So I started to pray out loud so that he could hear me, but quiet enough not to disturb others in the room. He put his hand on the cross and held it tight. A look of calm and repose came over him as his body relaxed. The prayer seemed to soothe him. Then he said he felt a warmth flowing through his body and it felt good. I started to say to him softly that "I've been told that there is often a sensation of warmth when the Holy Spirit comes into the body to heal." But before I could finish, the heat and the change in his body, set off his heart-monitor and whatever else he was connected to, and a bevy of nurses flooded around his bed, pushing and shoving past me. A big one grabbed me by the coatsleeve and literally threw me out: "Get out of here. Can't you see he's in the ICU. Get going and don't come back." She didn't ask me what had happened either. Frankly, I was a bit startled. I knew God could heal, but I never saw healing set off bells and whistles before.

✳

NEED FOR FAMILY CONNECTION

Dear Journal,

Eric told me part of his story today. He said, "I have a brother. We were so close. We were alike. We don't look alike anymore. He has no hair, like Kojak," Eric said. "My brother lives in Edina."

"Sometimes the lonely of the streets gets too deep. I needed family to talk to— just to have a real talk with someone from yesterday. I didn't want to stay there at their house or anything, just to have a real talk with family, to talk feelings. Before I called him, I got clean. As clean or cleaner than on Christmas day. My clothes were clean. Got my hair and beard trimmed, combed and neat, even my coat washed. I was clean all over, every inch, inside and out."

"I called my brother. 'Let's get together and talk, really talk.' He agreed. I thought it would be great to see him again. He offered to pick me up at the entrance of the "Y". We went to his home in Edina. I was so glad to see him, my own twin brother."

"But he wasn't. He could hardly talk. His wife broke into tears. She said, 'You have wrecked your life, and you embarrass us.' The saddest thing was, I could tell she was speaking for my own brother. She said, 'We don't want your type in our neighborhood, much less in our own home.' It seemed to me their life was dull and unauthentic."

Jackson added, "Sounds like a high yellow trying to be white on rice but really only bein' Minute Rice."

"Right on," Eric responded, "Only I'm white. Look at me, I look like Santa Claus on the old Coke Cola advertisement."

"Yeah, brother." Jackson added, "But I'm not so sure your twin brother is."

Eric continued his story, "My brother was so uptight inside himself he couldn't even open his mouth to really say, 'How are you? What's it like out there?' As soon as the meal was over— more like they fed me than that we broke bread together— they called their church for information. He didn't tell them I was his twin brother. They didn't even consult me to see if I had a room in town," Eric said.

"On the advice of their church, he took me to a church in Plymouth, which is nowhere near Edina. It had hundreds of cots on the floor, almost no heat— a dirty place. At breakfast they gave you a little tiny box of cereal— the kind where you put the milk in the box, only there was no milk. And you got one piece of dry toast," Eric put up his index finger to emphasize the point.

"I was still hungry. There were extra pieces of toast in a pile in the middle of the table, so I reached for a piece. A church worker hit me one on the knuckles with a long-handled spatula. 'Keep your hands off that toast. You already had a piece.' This was the loving care of my rich brother and a rich suburban church. It hurts."

✳

THE END OF THE LINE: FRYE

Frye was spending more and more time in the back of St. Olaf's church during the day. Sometimes he paced. Sometimes knelt in anguished prayer. I never saw him doze off. He was actively dealing with something. He was taking on a gaunt and hungry look. I never had a chance to chat with him as when he was in church he was very focused on something. I never saw him attend Mass in the chapel. Mostly he spent his time in the back pew of the church on his knees.

Later in the day after hearing Eric's story, I stopped in at St. Olaf's (to use the bathroom). I came in the side entrance. When I reached the main vestibule, there was clanking and commotion. The HCMC ambulance was there, and someone was on a gurney being rolled out. I strained to see who it might be. I saw the golden hair, and above the jacket pocket the name FRYE was lettered. He didn't look good.

The following morning in chapel, Father said, "We offer our prayers today for the repose of the soul of Mr. Frye, who died here yesterday."

Does Hennepin County have a potter's field, a Golgotha, for burial of the impoverished?

✳

DOUBLE STANDARDS AND HIDDEN AGENDAS

Dear Journal,

Some Street People resent that so much media hype is directed toward them at Christmas or Thanksgiving. One said, "It's always TV with the same old slant: 'Ain't we wonderful to turn out here and feed the bums and watch them eat. Doesn't it just make you feel real good inside?' It's not that we feel ungrateful for the exceptional generosity at Christmas and Thanksgiving, it's more that this type of superficial attention on camera is embarrassing and stereotyping— perhaps because it looks at the appearances, perhaps because it is distancing and uncomfortable to be the object of pity. When people want to do good works at these holidays, why do they feel the need to do it on camera? If it's to fill that need, who is it really for?"

Another said, "What bothers me is that we have to face this every day, but some act like that one day a year takes care it all."

"Well, guys. Face it. It ain't their problem."

✳

Dear Journal,

There are double standards and unwritten rules built into some social programs that provide care for The Homeless. I think some of these hidden agendas might be: "Feed the hungry, but not too much . . . . Help him/her get on his feet, but don't let him/her get too comfortable or s/he will become too dependent . . . . Don't let them stay long, we might get taken advantage of."

✻

MEDIA MISPERCEPTIONS, MISINFORMATION, AND PERSONAL SAFETY

Dear Journal,

After breakfast today, Fr. Blue was upset. He turned to me and said, "Say, I wanted to ask you a question. What do you think? Does appearance alone constitute a basis for a person being labeled a Street Person?"

"Why do you ask?" I said.

He replied, "An acquaintance of mine— more than an acquaintance really, I was for a time his parish priest— he was in the news yesterday, because he was injured by a transit bus. The TV called him a Street Person. I know the man who was injured is a wealthy man: he just didn't care to dress up. He has a hobby farm, likes to dress the farmer look. He makes it a practice to live simply, even though he has means."

"According to the news, when he stepped off the bus, his arm caught, and he was dragged three blocks to the next bus stop. He is in HCMC, so I went over to see him. He said his hospital bill was $500 a day, and he would pay cash. But the TV and newspaper reporters said he was a bum, and implied that it was no great loss that the bus had hurt him."

The story sent deep fears into all of us. The corner of 8th Street and 2nd Avenue was especially dangerous. We had all witnessed Express buses swerve toward the sidewalk whenever ragged (Street) people were there. We had all seen it frequently. The buses came right up over the curb. We had to jump back to protect our feet—

like a sci-fi nightmare where the bus has turned into a carnivorous people-eater.[56]

*

ATTITUDES: SHELTERS LOCKOUT POLICY

Dear Journal,

The-Lady-Who-Sews was standing outside the Public Library at Nicollet Mall. She was squinting, trying to read a piece of paper. "*She might need glasses,*" I thought to myself. She had on three skirts, moon-boots, a greatcoat, and a scarf around her head. At her feet she was surrounded by plastic bags of her stuff.

A perky senior citizen in a gray tweedy suit and sensible walking shoes trotted past. She turned toward the bag lady. "Disgusting. Disgusting!"

"Disgusting?" I questioned.

"Pitiful, then. Pathetic. There are places for people like that. Why don't they stay there? Why do they have to come here? Disgusting!"

Trying to keep my cool, I replied, "Because they are locked out."

"Locked up? Yes, locked up. The perfect answer. They should be locked up!"

"No. They come here because the shelters are locked during the day."

"Yes. Yes. Lock them in shelters!"

"No," I said more firmly. "Street people are in the street during the day because they are locked out of the shelter all day."

"Shelters. Yes. Places for people like that," she said.

I repeated the message slowly and clearly: "Street people come here to the public library because they are locked out of the shelters during the day. This is one of the few places they can be. There are no places during the day. Really."

---

[56] Several years later, one of the TV stations did a "hidden camera" sequence and caught the buses purposely veering toward the sidewalk when street people were there. After that, it improved (somewhat).

"Oh, I didn't understand. I had no idea. No place to go? Oh, that's terrible."

＊

Dear Journal,

It bothers me that people want Street People to be invisible, but they keep the shelters locked in the daytime. It bothers me that people think most Street People are chemical-abusers when most of the Street People are the mentally ill who got dumped out of their hospital rooms.

＊

Dear Journal

Shame is defined as being inherently defective, regardless of behavior. *Guilt* is feeling remorse about having committed some "bad" behavior.

＊

A CLOSING SOCIETY

Dear Journal,

I become impatient because the mythology, backed by the media, is that Minnesota is superior in all ways to all other places. Elsewhere is always inferior. Putting it kindly, Garrison Keillor says, "Minnesota, where the women are strong, the men are handsome, and all the children are above average." The attitude perpetuated is that Minnesota is always the best— just keep everyone else out and it will stay perfect. Often this attitude is a smokescreen to obscure the need to see and do things more humanely.

I continue to be offended that Minnesota treats persons from out-of-state as if we are all here intentionally to rip off Minnesota. Minnesotans believe it is a great place and that the benefits are outstanding. It is true that Minnesota leads the nation in some areas such as mental health care and chemical dependency treatment. It is also true that Minnesota and the Twin Cities in particular offer a high standard of living— if you already have a lot of money. The diversified industry insulates its economy from the severity of recessions that impact the rest of the nation to a greater degree. The community and the cities pay high premiums to promote amateur and professional sports teams year around. There are many cultural events here— apparently more per capita than in New York City. Most cultural events here are also very costly. So what many Minnesotans believe about the Twin Cities often assumes that one has a tremendous disposable income to start with. This isn't too relevant to the financial position of a Street Person or even to the average working parent, or single parent household, or households of one, often elderly or sick.

Frequently when I mentioned that I was here temporarily from Pennsylvania, people would make a snide remark such as: *"Yes, it's a problem, having so many people come here for jobs and welfare. We wish people would stop competing with us for the jobs here. Couldn't you get a job back East?"* . . . *"We ought to cut off in-migration. If you're not from here (Minnesota), don't come here— that would be the end of it. All these Street People came here from somewhere else just to bleed us dry."*[57]

*

---

[57] When I was seeking shelter, I wasn't trying to get welfare, or to move to Minnesota for welfare benefits. I was only seeking a place to stay short-term during a family emergency. But just being from out of state was enough to place this onus on my application. By 1991, this bias against persons from out of state had become even stronger. The residency requirement for eligibility to apply for AFDC and other social services is now longer. In 1996, the Legislature considered yet another bill to extended residency requirement for General Assistance and medical assistance.

It seems as if a growing number of states are moving toward establishment of border-crossings and by piecemeal legislation creating such indirect domestic immigration laws, as if each were a separate nation. Soon the unlanded class may need social service visas to be able to cross state lines. I believe this further points up the need for a national Comprehensive Bill of Rights to insure rights from state to state, and the need for a national standard for more equitable treatment of persons who must, for whatever reason, relocate to another state.

LINES

One of the biggest problems The System could solve would be to rearrange access to services so a person would not have to stand in line 22 hours a week. It would seem better to have some coordination and "one-stop shopping" centers for social services, so that people don't have to go so many places and wait in so many lines every day of the week. Unfortunately, that would also create an incredible opportunity for The System to abuse power and do more harm. As it was, little people with a little power, with little pieces of the pie, made little acts of abuse all the time.

JUNG "ON SELF-CRITICISM"[58]

In actual life it requires the greatest discipline to be simple, and the acceptance of oneself is the essence of the moral problem and epitome of a whole outlook upon life. That I feed the hungry, that I forgive an insult, that I love my enemy in the name of Christ— all these are undoubtedly great virtues. What I do unto the least of my brethren, that I do unto Christ. But what if I should discover that the least among them all, the poorest of all the beggars, the most impudent of all the offenders, the very enemy himself— that these are within me, and that I myself stand in need of the alms of my own kindness, that I myself am the enemy who must be loved— What then? As a rule the Christian's attitude is then reversed; there is no longer any question of love or long suffering; we say to the brother within us "Revenge!" and condemn and rage against ourselves. We hide it from the world; we refuse to admit ever having met this least among the lowly in ourselves. Had it been God himself who drew near to us in this despicable form, we would have denied him a thousand times before a single cock had crowed.

---

[58] Quotation attributed to Carl Jung. I received this handout somewhere in my travels and do not have a complete citation. If the reader knows, please write or e-mail the author.

REPRESSED REPROACHMENT: DEALING WITH DIFFICULT NEEDY PEOPLE

I have heard student volunteers working with homeless people complain that Street People do not seem very grateful. My experience was that some were, some weren't, some were overacting, and some didn't know how to behave at all. Some Street People I met were hostile, verbally aggressive, and sharp to every social service person they had to deal with. This *Defensive Anger* had become ingrained. Feeling uncomfortable, feeling powerless, they overreacted in such a way as to maintain control of the situation— by being angry and hostile first, before the other person could. I saw the opposite dynamic take place, too. Some are so emotionally needy, due to long privation, that when one finally receives that which is really needed, the recipient dumps on the person who just gave the praise or validation the needy one had so long sought. What has happened is that this new kindness has broken through the emotional defenses, tapping the well-spring of accumulated but suppressed disappointment, anger, and frustration. The recipient of validation, is overtaken by this surfacing flood of repression, responds uncontrollably to all this unexpected, unplanned release flowing from their own ancient hurts and horrors, instead of reacting with appreciation to the action of the current moment. In that instant with emotions swirling over them, out of control, this sometimes results in:

(1) an angry outburst— as if the anger could override this stampede and rein it in, or

(2) feelings of grief and sadness for all the other times when this need went without acknowledgement, or

(3) an unwelcome flashback of "old tapes" which had an outcome that was not what was needed or wanted;

(4) humiliation and even shame at having had such deeply repressed emotions now "made naked" to the casual observer— and; any or all of these feelings.

Now the victim's original need finally gets some long-suppressed recognition and perhaps even fulfillment, but at the same time the recipient— and the benefactor, too— is dumped on by the recipient's own suppressed flood of feelings and further victimized by that. Thus the well-intended person who wanted to do the right thing (and may have,) in order to be genuinely helpful is flabbergasted and at a loss to understand what is happening. This *Repressed Reproachment* dynamic can be extremely confusing for everyone concerned. (Even understanding this dynamic as I do, I want to be clear that I am not advocating that social workers should have to take being dumped on verbally, physically assaulted, or otherwise abused, to do their job.)

The opposite reaction also occurs. A repressed flood of hurt, anger, rage, or grief doesn't always happen. Some Street People have become too shut-down to feel or express anything that when a kindness is done on their behalf, they just accept it mutely.

*

Another source of frustration for social workers is that because Street People generally must put seeking solutions for short-term survival ahead of seeking longer-term solutions, they are apt to behave in what appears to be the social service provider as unpredictable ways. For example, if the Street Person is preoccupied with finding shelter for herself and her children for that night, and she learns that a particular social service program cannot offer a placement for two weeks, the applicant may leave the meeting before all the paperwork is complete, or skip the appointment altogether, in favor of going to a different appointment that might be able to provide housing for that night. Choosing the short-term solution is a necessity but it might pre-empt a more permanent solution from being established.

*

Dear Journal,
The System really sucks. I have seen social service workers dump on clients, and clients dump on social workers. Some days I think everybody is fried or brain-dead.

*

Dear Journal,

Today, little Sally went over to the Hennepin County Medical Center and got her arm caught in the elevator door by the Emergency Room. Her arm was broken near the elbow and is now in a cast. I was feeling a lot of compassion for her. It could have happened to any of us. Then she started bragging about having an uncle who was a personal injury attorney and that she had gotten some really big settlements before. I was really ticked off. Some people will go to any extreme to work The System.

✻

APPROPRIATE HUMILITY

Dear Journal,

The "helping system" does a lot of harm, even when it is helping. How the professional on the "front line" treats the client makes a big difference. There is an ocean of difference between giving and receiving humbly, compared to giving out (and taking in) humiliation. The people in authority seem to need recipients to appear humble. The people in authority dish out humiliations as if this would produce the "appropriate humility" in the recipient. Think about it for a few minutes: it becomes clear that this is craziness. Humiliation produces strong deep response because it cuts at the core of a person's innate dignity and self-worth. In the movie "Popeye," when the men in the bar remind Popeye that he was abandoned in infancy by his father and the barmates ridiculed him for this, at first Popeye (played by Robin Williams) blinked back tears, but not wanting to be seen as vulnerable, he immediately switched into an aggressive posture and said, "I've a strong sense of 'humiligration' in this place."

It is obvious that humiliating people does not make them humble; it hurts them. When it cuts deep enough, it can make them hate you.

✻

HUMILIATION

Dear Journal,
   The System wants recipients to be humble, but it tries to accomplish this by humiliation. Can't anyone understand the difference? After yesterday's journal entry, I looked for books that covered the topic of humility and humiliation. I came across this:

> But humility is not humiliation. To be humble enough to accept the human condition and its complications and limitations is one of the most valuable human assets. Despite cultural confusion, feeling truly humble produces great strength and freedom from fear of falling off illusory peaks.[59]

> In a state of grace with ourselves, we immediately, as part of the human condition, contribute to a more compassionate culture. Compassionate self-acceptance invariably makes for better relating to ourselves and [others]. Inner peace makes peace with others a possibility. Once the struggle for a compassionate life is engaged, it continues all our days. This is the essence of healthy human growth. This is the stuff that enables us to feel like people, real people who are able to dignify and enjoy the richness of daily possibility.[60]

✳

SOCIAL SERVICE PERSONNEL BURN-OUT

Edelwich wrote,

> We can use the term *Burn-out* to refer to a progressive loss of idealism, energy, and purpose experienced by people in the helping professions as a result of the conditions of their work. These conditions range from insufficient training to client overload, from too many hours at too little pay, from inadequate funding to ungrateful clients, from bureaucratic or political

---

[59] Theodore I. Rubin with Eleanor Rubin, *Compassion & Self Hate: An Alternative to Despair.* New York: David McKay Co., Inc., 1975, p. 262.

[60] *Ibid.*, p. 295.

constraints, to the inherent gap between aspiration and accomp lishment.[61]

I believe the following quote refers to social service workers just as well as to the parents for whom it was originally written:

> Generally, we are better parents to our children as we are able to be better parents to ourselves. Self-nourishment leads to a healthier relationship with them. Self-neglect and chronic self-sacrifice produces much repressed hostility toward them and sicker relating to them.[62]

> It is important that the therapist's [substitute social service worker's or volunteer's] caring be nonpossessive. If the caring stems from their own needs to be liked and appreciated, constructive change in the client is inhibited . . . . One implication of this emphasis on acceptance of the client is that therapists who have little respect for their clients or an active dislike or disgust can anticipate that their work will not be fruitful. Clients will sense the lack of regard and become increasingly defensive.[63]

*

It is rugged on the social workers and other paid staff. They arrived, bright-eyed, with dreams of "helping people," "being needed," and "making a difference." They soon found out that they could not solve many problems because the problems were fluid, not static, and because most people had a lot of problems; even more discouraging (as in industry), solving one problem often creates a new problem. It is hard for a new social worker to accept that s/he can probably only help a little, but cannot alone "cure" the whole gamut of problems.

---

[61] Edelwich, Jerry, and Brodsky, Archie, *Burn-out: Stages of Disillusionment in the Helping Professions.* New York: Human Services Press, 1980. p. 14.

[62] *Ibid.*, p. 285.

[63] Corey, Gerald, *Theory and Practice of Counseling and Psychotherapy*, 3rd edn. Monterey, CA: Brooks/Cole Publishing Co., 1977, pp. 108-109.

The social workers soon learned that they could not control anything. But they could make a difference in some ways. One way was to listen with compassion and without being judgemental. Another was to work on one or two problems instead of being overwhelmed by all of them. If each social worker with whom Street People came in contact could solve one or two problems, eventually some people would be helped a lot, and they, in turn, could help others.

> Helpers spend most of their time 'downstream' dealing with people who are already in trouble . . . . This is hard work. As time goes by, it can also become discouraging work. More and more people in the helping professions are becoming concerned about what can be called helper 'burn-out',[64] Newman and Newman give a brief description of this syndrome [as follows]
>
> > In daily work interactions, human service professionals often encounter situations that are emotionally arousing, frustrating, and perhaps personally threatening. In response to these intense experiences some people begin to take a very cynical, derogatory view of the people they are hired to help. They become callous, claiming that the clients deserve their fate. They begin to experience physical symptoms, increased use of drugs, marital conflict, and needs for solitude or detachment from all social contacts. They come to see themselves as bad people and their clients as deserving of bad treatment. In this and other examples of stagnation, the person loses sight of the potential for nurturing, educating, or guiding others and becomes trapped in the struggle to protect or maintain the self.[65]
>
> Edelwich probes the causes of burn-out, describes four stages of "progressive disillusionment— enthusiasm, stagnation, frustration, and apathy" and suggests interventions to break the cycle as

---

[64] Gerard Egan, *The Skilled Helper: Model, Skills, and Methods for Effective Helping*, 2nd edn. Monterey CA: Brooks/Cole Publishing Co., 1982, p. 301 making reference to the term "Burn-out" as described in Edelwich's book, as cited earlier.

[65] Egan, pp. 301-302, using quotation from: Newman, B. M., & Newman, P. R., *Development Through Life: A Psychosocial Approach* (rev. edn.). Homewood, IL: Dorsey Press, 1979, p. 430.

remedies for both individuals and institutions because enthusiasm and apathy are both contagious to clients, co-workers, and the institutions.[66]

Corey has listed some causes of burn-out.

Recognizing the causes of burn-out can be one step in dealing with it. A few of them are:

- doing the same type of work with little variation, especially if this work seems meaningless

- giving a great deal personally and not getting back much in the way of appreciation or other positive responses

- being under constant and strong pressure to produce, perform, and meet deadlines— many of which may be unrealistic

- working with a difficult population— those who are highly resistant, who are involuntary clients, or who show very little progress or change

- conflict and tension among staff; an absence of support from colleagues and an abundance of criticism

- lack of trust between supervisors and mental-health workers— a condition in which they are working against each other instead of toward commonly valued goals

- not having opportunities for personal expression or for taking initiative in trying new approaches— a situation in which experimentation, change, and innovations not only are not rewarded but are actively discouraged

- having jobs that are both personally and professionally taxing without much opportunity for supervision, continuing education, or other forms of in-service training

---

[66] Edelwich, Jerry, pp. 29-30.

■ unresolved personal conflicts beyond the job situation, such as marital tensions, chronic health problems, financial problems, and so on . . . . I see acceptance of *personal responsibility* as one of the most critical factors . . . . It has almost become standard to hear mental-health workers blame the system and other external factors for their condition; the more they look outside themselves for reasons why they feel dead, the greater becomes their sense of impotence and hopelessness. . . .[67] What I see as critical is that counselors recognize that, even though there are external realities that exert a toll on personal energy, they are playing a role in allowing themselves to remain passive. For example, although there are bureaucratic obstacles that make it difficult to function effectively, it is possible to learn ways to survive with dignity within an institution and to engage in meaningful work. This means that counselors will have to become active and stop blaming the system for all that they *cannot do.* Instead, as a place to begin, they can focus on what they *can do* to bring about *some* changes and to create a climate in which they can do work which has meaning to them.[68]

✳

Dear Journal,

It is really important that the social service workers at the front desk get better personal and professional support and reinforcement. There probably needs to be better screening and placement of personnel, too. Much in-service training could be added to help sustain them physically, spiritually, and emotionally. It seems as if The System now cares as little about the social workers in the front lines as it does about the Street People. Perhaps The System sees the social workers as another paycheck to dole out. It doesn't seem to care how many workers get used up and burnt out.

✳

---

[67] *Ibid.*, p. 384.

[68] *Ibid.*, p. 385.

Dear Journal,

The social service delivery system is very important to the lives of the recipients and to society in general. It is a difficult and yet essential service. But, as presently constituted, the experience itself is generally dehumanizing.

How any individual caseworker has managed or practiced his/her own self care— to prevent burn-out— and how well the supervisor has kept the case-load manageable for an individual caseworker, makes an enormous difference how the recipient experiences The System; the recipient's caseworker is agent of The System for the delivery of the voucher, service, or authorization, as well as for a reconnection with (mainstream) humanity. Therefore it is essential that The System care for the caseworker as well as the recipient.

I would like to see instituted a series of mandatory continuing education in-service days for social workers covering:

- Sane self-care,

- Stress management,

- Listening skills,

- How to avoid burn-out,

- Codependency recovery,

- Boundaries— how to say enough is enough,

- How to identify and avoid passive-aggressive anger in yourself and others,

- Applying the Myers-Briggs Personality Inventory to communication and needs in the workplace, with clients, and in private life,

- Take a Plunge Week— experience the social service delivery system from the recipient's viewpoint,

- How to identify and respond to a client's unleashing "Repressed Reproachment",

- How to deal with difficult people,

- Methods of restoring and maintaining inner calm,

- Learning to do things differently,

- How to make changes within The System,

- Accepting feedback positively,

- Change is part of life,

- Dealing with clients who have experienced long-term trauma or post-traumatic stress,

- Death is part of life, and

- Flexibility doesn't mean surrendering values.

As Corey points out on preventing burn-out:

> Learning to look within ourselves to determine what choices we are making and not making to keep ourselves alive can go a long way in preventing what some people consider as an inevitable condition associated with the helping professions. There are other ways that we can prevent professional burn-out, most of which include assuming the responsibility to actively nourish ourselves:

- finding other interests besides work,

- thinking of ways to bring variety into work,

- taking the initiative to start new projects that have personal meaning and not waiting for the system to sanction this initiative,

- attending to our health through adequate sleep, an exercise program, proper diet, and some meditation,

- developing a few friendships that are characterized by a mutuality of giving *and* receiving,

- learning how to ask for what we want, though not expecting to always get it,

- learning how to work for self-confirmation and for self-rewards, as opposed to looking externally for validation and rewards,

- playing, traveling, or seeking new experiences,

- taking the time to evaluate the meaningfulness of our projects to determine where personal investment and time will continue to be spent,

- avoiding assuming the burden of responsibility that is properly the responsibility of others— for example, worrying more about clients than they are seeming to worry about themselves,

- reading, both professional literature and books for fun,

- taking new classes or workshops or attending conferences and conventions to get new perspectives on old issues,

- exchanging jobs with a colleague for a short period or asking a colleague to join forces in a common work project,

- taking the initiative to form a support group with colleagues to openly share feelings of frustration and to find better ways of approaching the reality of certain job situations, and

- cultivating some hobbies that bring pleasure.[69]

✳

---

[69] Corey, pp. 385-386.

Figure 12. Evelyn, social worker.

PART VI: Public Policy

ECONOMIC POLICY

Dear Journal,

I recently learned that there is an economic model called The Phillips Curve that relates the unemployment rate with the inflation rate in a series of graphs pairing the national unemployment rate with the national rate of inflation. Over the last 40 years, the tradeoffs between the inflation rate and the unemployment rate have periodically worsened. The national unemployment rate has ranged from a low in 3½% in 1969 to 11% in 1982. The inflation rate has varied from 1% in 1959 to 12% in 1980.[70]

According to the Phillips Curve model *if government permitted real full employment, runaway inflation would occur; therefore a certain percentage of unemployment must be accepted (maintained).*[71] So, to limit inflation, the government's economic policy can set an "acceptable level of unemployment" and treat that as if it were "full employment." Some administrations have also manipulated the number by redefining "unemployment" to count only persons receiving and reporting for unemployment compensation and not counting those whose benefits have been exhausted but who were unable to find a job.

While the Phillips Curve graphs may only affect perceptions of reality, when those perceptions are believed and acted upon, it also affects in painful financial ways, the day-to-day reality of working and employable unemployed people. Frequently "the market" and

---

[70] Ralph T. Byrns and Gerald W. Stone, *Economics*, 5th edn. New York: Harper Collins Publishers, 1992, pp. 360-367.

[71] *Full employment* is now generally considered to mean that about 5 to 5½% are still "unemployed, and being reported as unemployed, still receiving unemployment compensation, and seeking work."

"a slow economy" are blamed for generating too few jobs, when, in truth, it may be a consequence of restrictive economic policies by The Fed, by the Congress, and/or by the Executive Branch. When The Fed chooses to overly tighten interest rates, it spawns unemployment and underemployment, and that displacement can result in our people (pawns) becoming homeless— most likely more persons than who might become homeless as a result of the inflation.   The blame is placed on "The Market" as if it "just happened."   Shouldn't the Executive Branch, the Legislative Branch, and The Fed carry some responsibility for their policies or lack thereof?   Shouldn't we, the citizens of this country, also carry responsibility for the policies which we directly or indirectly allow?

The inflation rate is tied to U.S. Treasury bonds and debt financing. Shifts can make a negative impact the following year. Increasing taxes to generate new revenues and fiscally responsible measures (limiting government spending) would, in theory, make more money available for interest payments, debt reduction, and other transfer payments and that should, in the long, run create a better financial climate for business and job creation. There is no simple solution.[72]

While these are not easy choices, there must be some responsibility for the most vulnerable segments of our population, and for those who are made vulnerable temporarily by these temporary or permanent shifts in national priorities to some extent.

*

Today many white-collar and blue-collar men and women are being dislocated by economic factors such as the closing of factories, decline in military spending, shifts in spending and saving, shifts in priorities as a nation, and the transplanting of factories of

---

[72]   In polls taken after the 1992 election, a majority of the American people indicated a willingness to tighten their belts, reduce spending and increase taxes if the increased tax burden were equitable for all, without loopholes for the most privileged, and if it would result in dissolving the national debt (not just the deficit) over a prescribed number of years and limit inappropriate government spending.

US corporations to locations outside of the United States. There are major shifts in government spending that affect jobs, government services, and providers of government services. When people become unemployed and subsequently often become homeless, this is viewed by the economists as a "market adjustment" or a "restructuring." Many of yesterday's working poor and middle-class people may be tomorrow's Street People.

✳

Most people at the shelter had multiple problems of major proportions. I don't believe people end up in a shelter or other housing for The Homeless because they have a problem. They get there because they have so many problems. One problem doesn't break down a whole system. One problem doesn't break a family, and it doesn't break a person. But a constellation of problems can bring a person down in a hurry— way down.

For some, the problems were separate instances occurring coincidentally; for others it was like a set of rapidly-falling dominoes. I heard over and over, "It hit all at once. If it had just been this one thing, I could have handled it, but the troubles came one after another all in a short time. I lost my wife in a car accident, then my daughter died of cancer, then I lost my job to a reduction in force."

There was the recurrent theme of too many calamitous things happening too quickly. One young girl told me, "If there had just been one problem, I would have been all right. But as soon as I lost my job, then I lost my apartment, my car, everything. In a month I went from being set, to being out with no money, no car, no place to go, and no future. It's been a year now. A hard year. The best I've been able to do is to get day-work here and there. Nothing steady."

"It was just too much. I couldn't get back up from one problem before another hit. I couldn't keep up."

For whatever reason, they no longer have enough of the usual support system— no family, no friends who are in a position to help, no job network, no close ties to church or community. For the most part, they are completely on their own resources and on those resources they can uncover through the bureaucracy or through church-sponsored charities.

The system helps. It helps a lot. But even so, it is not enough, because each agency or charity could only help in one or two ways, but the problems confronting the people are very complicated and usually arrive in multiples.

✳

FEDERAL POLICY: ELECTIONS/POVERTIZATION OF WOMEN

Dear Journal,
Unequal pay for women, unfair and unequal enforcement of the law contributes to the povertization of women and children. And on and on. Government policies are creating poverty and continuing poverty. Government needs to take responsibility to mend its ways. I wish when we voted there was a lever marked "None of the Above." If "None of the Above" wins, we get a new slate of candidates with fresh platforms until acceptable candidates are elected.[73]

✳

FEDERAL POLICY AND HOUSING

Dear Journal,
While I don't want to increase the deficit or the national debt, I do believe that Federal government's policy has a long-term effect on how well and how many people are housed. As early as the 1950s, the country knew it was not building enough houses. Then, in the 1960s, it again issued a report saying there would be widespread homelessness in the '80s and '90s if action wasn't taken in the '60s to increase the number of affordable units. While there were a number of rental housing programs established, the urban removal of SROs and other low-cost housing progressed at a rate faster than replacement units were created.

Many actions that were taken were regressive: creation of permissible levels of unemployment, of urban removal programs, high interest rates, drops in construction, regressive taxes, and

---

[73] "None of the Above" is apparently already a choice on the Russian ballot now.

worse yet, corruption at HUD, which robbed eligible applicants of proper decent, safe, and sanitary housing— and, in fact, promoted blight— the very thing it was established to fight against.

These policies affected not only my housing selection but also my ability to produce income, because most aspects of my work have been in one area of housing or another at various times. Especially during the 1980s, the federal government's policy and the financial market impact on the development of affordable housing, construction of housing in general, rehabilitation of housing, depressed real estate sales, high interest rates, and inspection of housing— and all affected my ability to earn dollars to support my family. These areas of the economy are negatively impacted when there is inflation, recession, fear of recession, or a depression.

During the Reagan years, the federal government:

■　allowed housing shortages to increase,

■　allowed government programs in housing to be cut back,

■　at times tolerated corruption in spending housing-program dollars,

■　for a long time, pretended that the Street People are not a national population needing national as well as local attention,

■　minimized figures on inflation, recession, and depression by altering the method of calculating the figures,

■　allowed unemployment to remain at an unnecessarily high level,

■　minimized some depressions by calling them "just a temporary recession",

■　for a long time, prevented citizens with no(official) fixed address ("NFA") from registering to vote,

- made only token efforts to count Homeless people in the Decennial Census and initially refused to consider counting suburban and rural Homeless people at all,

- allowed the minimum wage to remain artificially low, and

- even now, prevents a person with no fixed address from renting a Post Office box.

The Legislature and the Court system together

- have prevented persons with no fixed address from equal access to state welfare payments,

- are just beginning to recognize that homeless families, mentally ill, youth, and homeless veterans are distinct homeless populations that need special services and separate facilities.[74]

*

---

[74] The Friday open sessions of the Hennepin County Commissioners are broadcast on radio station KSJN 88.5. In the October, 1995, I listened as the county staff reported to the Commissioners that 21 categories of homeless persons and families had been identified as regularly applying for shelter placements. The 21 categories were to be used to *triage* the decision making process to prioritize who would get placement in shelters. Highest ranking were women accompanied by minor children. The lowest ranking were single men.

About 6 months later on another broadcast of the meeting of county commissioners, it was mentioned that with this method, only the first three categories typically were able to be accommodated. Nevertheless they were touting this as a model for the nation.

While I believe this is a much saner approach than assuming that all homeless people have identical needs and capacities, it is clear that I would have been turned away since I was unaccompanied by my children, had this system been in place when I needed the help. I and many other homeless people would fall through the eligibility cracks.

HOUSING IN THE SHELTERS

All housing options were expensive. There was a shortage of inexpensive housing. As is the practice throughout the country, "Urban Removal" was systematically blowing up and knocking down inexpensive lodging in the downtown area of Minneapolis to make room for additional office space and parking ramps. The result has been that the number of displaced people is increasing, and once in the shelter system, many of the same people circulate from shelter to shelter like a merry-go-round. To be able to get off, a person has to have a lot of money and skills (accumulated over a long period of time— sometimes years). A week of housing and meals will keep a person from freezing that week, but it will not solve the long-term problems of affordable housing, emotional support, sheltered jobs, a sufficient number of jobs or sufficient wages, appropriate access to government checks, and to have such government checks be sufficient to meet costs of the minimum of necessities and lodging.

✻

MISTAKING THE HOMELESS AS A SINGLE CATEGORY

Dear Journal,

Before I was on the street, I think I thought of the Homeless as lumps of humanity globbed in each major city. But that thinking is obviously wrong. It doesn't work. When assessing the problem of housing the homeless, it is important to recognize that the only thing the homeless have in common with one another is that they are homeless. For example, those who are mentally ill and on medically prescribed maintenance doses of anti-psychotic drugs need different congregate housing than do chemically dependent youths seeking a safe, chemically-free environment for aftercare, or than do people of advanced years. The "problem of homelessness" is less overwhelming to analyze when the population groups that constitute Street People are recognized and identified, and then equitable but different creative solutions are derived to meet the diverse needs of each group.

✻

Dear Journal,

Most people assume that most Street People are chemical abusers and therefore brought about their own downward mobility. As in "tough love," leaving chemical abusers alone to hit bottom may be the best course.[75] This type of tough love can sometimes work with chemical abusers. But it doesn't fit today's diverse Homeless population. For example, the addictive personality's goal is pain avoidance. Neurotic people, on the other hand, seek to discover and to confront their own problems often to the extent of total enmeshment inside their own process or too much confrontation indiscriminately, all over the place. A problem arises because there are many other people who constitute the "new" homeless population who are not chemical abusers or mentally ill, such as women and youth fleeing unsafe conditions at home, economically dislocated, and so forth. I believe that recognition of the diverse origins of Street People needs to happen so that remedies relevant to these populations can be implemented.

*

ALTERNATIVE SHELTERS

When I talk about my experience on the street, people generally ask why I was in a shelter with men. At that time in the Twin Cities, there were a few shelters for women with children and women in transition, such as St. Joseph's Home and the Dorothy Day Center. I called Chrysalis, The Red Cross, Dorothy Day Center, St. Joseph's

---

[75] "Tough love" is *letting him hurt enough to want to get well.* It means letting all his crises happen to him without erasing the painful consequences for him anymore. It means that when he's hurting very badly, you don't raise a finger to help–otherwise, he won't have the incentive to reach for *real* help. The crisis you didn't allow to happen may have been the one he needed to make him reach for the phone and call A.A. He'll never make that phone call for help if he doesn't hurt. *No alcoholic ever woke up one fine morning and stretched and smiled and said, 'I think I'll get sober today!'* People don't seek help if they don't hurt.
Toby Rice Drews, *Getting Them Sober: A Guide for Those Who Live With an Alcoholic.* vol. I, Bridge Publishing, Inc., South Plainfield, New Jersey 07080, 1980, pp. 41-42.

Home, and Harriet Tubman Shelter to make application for myself at the time, but was told that "Because you are from out of state, not a Minnesota resident, and unaccompanied by your children, you are not eligible." Several did say I could call back when my children were with me or my situation changed in a substantive way.

At the time ago the term "battered women" was not common parlance. A short time later, the term was originated in Minnetonka, Minnesota, by a women's shelter staff who noticed that most of the women seeking shelter (then called runaway wives) were also bruised and otherwise injured on arrival. (Minnetonka is an affluent western suburb of Minneapolis.) Today, the standard of eligibility might include a question about "Are you being battered today? Right now?" to determine eligibility for women's shelter services.

WILDER SHELTER SURVEY: "Where are they from?"[76]

Where are they from? The Wilder shelter survey estimates that nearly 50% of youth in the metro area shelters were raised in the Minneapolis St. Paul area . . . . Runaway youth serving agencies in Minneapolis (The Bridge) have recognized for years that for a large percentage of homeless youth, reunification with the family is not possible. The U.S. Department of Health and Human Services estimates that 25% of youth served by runaway services cannot safely return home. Many of the homeless youth have left home to escape physical abuse, sexual abuse, neglect or alcoholism. Many others have been evicted because they are gay or lesbian. Others have "aged out" of the foster care or welfare system.

HOUSING: SROs

It was a sunny morning with no wind. I decided to walk in a new area. I crossed over the Interstate, near the Social Security Office,

---

[76] Minnesota Act Up and Out of Poverty: "Facts on Homeless Youth in Minnesota," (a handout) 7/10/91.

and the [then] Chicago Avenue Detox Center. Nearby were some row houses, and some had Apartment For Rent signs. I went into one and spoke with the caretaker.

These were SROs. The term SRO refers to Single Room Occupancy and generally means a private sleeping room, sometimes with a kitchenette, and always a shared bathroom way down the hall. The hallway in this one was long, narrow, and lit by a single 60-watt bulb dangling from the ceiling. The apartment itself was old but not shabby. The big windows let in a lot of daylight but were also thick with many layers of paint, probably lead paint. The kitchen was furnished with one sink, one cabinet, and one Roach Motel. Here, unfurnished means bring your own furniture *and* appliances. That was better than some rural areas of southern Minnesota, where in 1969, the Postmaster of Good Thunder, Minnesota told me "unfurnished" can also mean bring your own furniture, appliances *and furnace*.

I thought a while about this type of housing. Besides a boarding house, the SRO was the next step above a shelter. But to get into this SRO, a person needed rent and a security deposit of $500 up front and $215 per month. That sounds routine, but to those with only about $15 to spend per week, there is no way to save the money. In the interim, those who save a little money are considered to "have money" and thus are no longer eligible for most shelter situations. And those who don't save money, can't get out of the shelter system.

After looking at the SRO, I knew couldn't afford it, and I didn't want it. Besides that, I still have my lovely apartment in central Pennsylvania— that's a two-story townhouse with 2,000 sq. ft. of living space— and from every window the most exquisite view of the mountains and a patchwork pattern of farmland. (Our home had been sold as part of the court-ordered property settlement of the divorce.)

It was hard to understand why the Court believed that my children and I ought to want to live in Minneapolis, Minnesota, where I was now on the bottom of the heap, when we could be living at home in Pennsylvania and be comfortable middle-class, and living near the top.

I left the SRO. It was too depressing.

Cathy and Dennis had decided to pair up and were planning to rent an SRO when they got enough money together for a security deposit, rent, utilities hookup fees, and utilities. They encouraged me to take a look at the place they hoped to move into. It was awful. The bathroom was in the cubbyhole under the stairs and had a low, slanted ceiling. The shower was the smallest I'd ever seen. I went down the dark hall to the apartment they wanted to rent. It was one room, with a cooking unit (stove/refrigerator/ counter all in one). The walls were partitions of wood paneling, without proper studding. It was apparent that the landlord had installed these little partitions to make more apartment units than the building had been designed for. It was really dingy.

*

LACK OF A COHERENT AFFORDABLE HOUSING POLICY

Complicating this already difficult housing problem is the number of mentally ill who were dumped out onto the street because of the "least restrictive setting" rule, pursuant to the 1963 Mental Retardation and Community Mental Health Centers Construction Act.

"Only 700 of what was originally planned to be 2,500 community mental health centers were opened in the 1960s and 1970s, and these often wound up serving a more affluent and less severely disturbed clientele than the population previously confined to state mental hospitals."[77]

It seems clear to me that the street isn't the appropriate "setting of least restriction" for persons with severe, chronic mental illness. The terminology seems to be interpreted to put the emphasis on provision of the least.

---

[77] Fantasia, Rick, and Isserman, Maurice, *Homelessness: A Sourcebook.* New York: Facts on File®, 1994, p. 66.

Figure 13. Harry, retired construction worker.

NEED FOR LOW RENT HOUSING[78]

Although it may not be widely recognized, there is not a single "safety net" providing assistance to the poor throughout the United States. Instead, there are separate and differing safety nets in each state and the District of Columbia . . . .

As the reports indicate, the gaps in the safety nets in many states remain larger than many Americans realize. Narrowing these gaps can serve to help alleviate the effects of poverty and to diminish the ranks of the poor.

Under federal regulations, 'low income' households are those whose incomes are less than 80% of the median household income in their area. 'Very low income' households are those whose incomes fall below the 50% of the median income in their area . . . . Housing is not an entitlement program. This means that benefits are not automatically provided to all households that apply and are found eligible . . . . Other measures of unmet needs for low-income housing, including the huge number of homeless individuals in some areas of the country, also indicate the large gap between low-income housing availability and the need for such housing. The Low Income Housing Information Service has issued a 'Rental Housing Crisis Index,' which uses Census data to compare the number of very low-income renter households in each state to the number of very low rent housing units in the state. The Rental Housing Crisis Index shows that the number of very low income renter households substantially exceeds the number of very low-rent units in most states. In Minnesota: the Rental Housing Crisis Index indicates that in 1985 the number of very low-income renter households substantially exceeds the number of very low-rent units by 110%. This represents a shortage of 61,125 very low-rent units.

Unfortunately, the already large gap between the number of very low-income households and the number of rental units available at a low rental cost is expected to grow even wider for the duration of this century. In June, 1987, the Neighborhood Reinvestment Corporation, a Congressionally-chartered institution, issued a major report stating that nationwide, if recent trends continue, by the year 2003 there will

[78] Shapiro, Isaac, and Greenstein, Robert, *Holes in the Safety Nets: Poverty Programs and Policies in the States: Minnesota, a State Analysis.* Washington, D.C.:Center on Budget and Priorities, Spring, 1988, pp. iii, 1, 15-16.

be 8.8 million more low-income households unable to find low rent units than there were in 1983. The causes of this gap include an expected increase in the need for low-rent housing, the expiration of many current federal low-income housing contracts, and the dearth of production of low-rent housing by the private market.[79]

The number of women and children, even whole families, who are homeless is increasing. There are still insufficient affordable housing opportunities for rental and for first-time home ownership. Obviously, whenever there are dips in the economy or discontinued social programs, even more people are displaced and many become homeless as a result.

Willingness to work is not the key issue. Today, even those who work may not be able to afford adequate housing. Because minimum wage is so far below the need, two persons earning at minimum wage level do not earn sufficient to meet one payment of rent and monthly living expenses for a family of four in a major metropolitan area. It is not uncommon for a family of four to have both adults working two full-time jobs each, just to maintain the family and obtain minimum basic necessities. If the children are of high school age, they also may be working 15 hours or more a week after school and on weekends. According to the 1990 Census data, there are 90,000 single-parent households in Minnesota. Only 17,000 of these are headed by men.[80]

*

---

[79] Recently the impact of downtown development is becoming recognized as another contributor to the pressure for housing units. A study in Los Angeles in the early 1990s, concerning the problem of the impact of office construction on housing, determined that creation of office space creates a demand for affordable housing, and suggested that new office developments be taxed a one-time fee of $6/office, to be used for creation of affordable housing.

[80] In 1984, the country still had a strong middle class. By 1991, this had substantially eroded, and poverty has become more widespread. On a housing tour of their core service neighborhoods, officials of the Los Angeles Neighborhood Housing Services told me that in 1991, there were 40,000 people known to be living there in garages, without running water or toilet facilities.

HOUSING: "ST. JOSEPH AND THE SYSTEM"

Dear Journal,
I often wonder if the Holy Family would have gotten by in this economy. Could you see them applying for Rent Assistance so they could move out of the stable? I think it would go like this:

"I am sorry Joseph, the House of David has too many assets. You have a late model donkey, and your work history shows no consistency— a pattern of frequent relocations. But if you were to move out, your wife would be eligible for Aid to Dependent Children, Food Stamps, and other food and nutrition supplements under the Women, Infant, and Children program."

"The stable, however, does not meet Section 8 Guidelines for a 'decent, safe, and sanitary' dwelling unit. It is an illegal conversion of non-residential space to residential use, without Plan and Zoning Reviews, and without a Certificate of Occupancy. Now that we know about the stable arrangement, we will have to have you all evicted. It's in the best interest of the child, you know. It will be up to you to find suitable affordable housing. We can't help with that. As you know, there is a shortage of rental property for low income families in Bethlehem."

"We could perhaps provide you with a caravan ticket out of town. We discourage welfare transients— anyone who has no long-established residence here— because we don't want word to get back to Nazareth and other places that the benefits are better here. We would be flooded with seasonally unemployed carpenters and other such riff-raff. I would recommend you apply at the Temple, but their benefit programs are restricted to contributing members, especially families related to Pharisees and Sadducees. Maybe if you passed them some pigeons or a fatted calf under the table they'd make an exception. I know things will work out for you and your family. Perhaps you could relocate to Egypt. I have heard there

Figure 14. Temporarily homeless family.

is a shortage of laborers there for public works type construction jobs— pyramids and such. Good luck."

✳

THE STANFORD FAMILY: TEMPORARILY HOMELESS

"I came from a big family and I entered the Army when I was just a kid. My folks signed for me to enlist. I got sent to Germany and was really living it up and having a great time. Then the Army decided we all had to have swine flu injections— you heard about that, I guess. I got one of the bad ones and I've had trouble ever since," Stanford told the older Black lady sitting beside him. It was almost time for the door keys to be released so people could go into the sleeping room assigned for the night.

"After I got out of the Army," he continued, " I've had trouble keeping steady work with the fatigue and all that. But I met Ruth and we got married. We sorta had a business house sitting for people and did pretty good with that for a number of years. But when we had our first child, people didn't want us to house sit anymore; so we ended up homeless and jobless as well. We're trying to get some job skills training and some money saved up for a security deposit and first month's rent."

✳

CONTRIBUTING FACTORS

The U.S. Conference of Mayors listed several reasons why people are homeless, in order of frequency:

(1)   a lack of affordable housing as well as other housing problems;

(2)   mental illness and a shortage of adequate services for the mentally ill;

(3)   substance abuse and lack of services for abusers;

(4)   unemployment;

(5)   poverty and lack of income;

(6)   inadequate levels in benefit assistance programs, and

(7)   family problems.[81]

The Federal government passed enabling legislation for transitional housing programs to assist The Homeless. But the appropriations to fund such programs for The Homeless have had their ups and downs.

> In 1983, the Department of Housing and Urban Development (HUD) decreed that Community Development Block Grant (CDBG) funds could be spent to buy and fix up buildings to be used as shelters for low-income and homeless people . . . . In 1986, Congress passed the Homeless Housing Act of 1986 (PL99-591) which provided HUD with money for emergency shelters and transitional housing . . . . In 1986 Congress enacted the Homeless Eligibility Clarification Act (PL 99-570) which provided for the delivery of benefits such as food stamps, Medicaid, Aid to Families with Dependent Children (AFDC), and Supplemental Security Income (SSI) to persons with no fixed address.

In 1987 Congress passed the Stewart B. McKinney Homeless Assistance Act (PL 100-77) which was made up of several programs including

(1)   health care,

(2)   community-based mental health service for homeless individuals who are chronically mentally ill,

(3)   emergency shelters,

---

[81] U.S. Conference of Mayors. *A Status Report on Hunger and Homelessness in American Cities: 1990.* Washington, D.C.: US Conference of Mayors, 1990 quoted in Binford, Shari M., Siegel, Mark A., and Landes, Alison (eds.), *Homeless: Struggling to Survive.* Wylie TX: Information Plus, 1991, p. 6.

(4)   transitional housing especially for the elderly and homeless families with children,

(5)   community services to provide follow-up and long-term services,

(6)   job and literacy (reading and writing) training,

(7)   permanent housing for handicapped homeless persons, and

(8)   grants for groups to fix up, convert, purchase, lease, or construct buildings . . . .

The Act has tried to focus government help and to develop some long-term solutions for homelessness rather than only reacting to emergency situations . . . .[82]

From this, six federal programs provided money to state and local governments, charitable organizations, community action agencies and homelessness prevention: Emergency Food and Shelter (EFS), Emergency Assistance (EA), Low Income Home Energy Assistance Program (LIHEAP), Emergency Shelter Grants (ESG), Emergency Community Services Homeless Grant Program, Housing Counseling.[83]

The General Accounting Office (GAO) in *Homelessness: Too Early to Tell What Kinds of Prevention Assistance Work Best*[84] measured the effectiveness of some of these programs. . . .

Although many organizations said they did not have enough funds to serve all those in need, officials did believe that prevention aid had kept some people from becoming homeless. However only a few of the 42 agencies actually kept track of their clients to find out if the assistance truly prevented them from losing their homes.

✳

---

[82]   Binford, pp. 6, 10-11.

[83]   *Ibid.*, pp. 11-12.

[84]   General Accounting Office (GAO), *Homelessness: Too Early to Tell What Kinds of Prevention Assistance Work Best*, Washington, DC: Government Printing Office, 1990 quoted in Binford, pp. 10-12.

CAREGIVING, AND DISTRESS ON THE FAMILY SYSTEM

Dear Journal,

The largest population of persons on the street are the mentally ill. In the book *Families in Pain*, Phyllis Vine discusses aspects of how having a mentally ill family member impacts the entire family. Some family systems can be reorganized to provide care for a mentally ill member. Other family systems disintegrate, and the member with mental illness is left to fend alone.

> Some families believe that mental illness is a blemish which cannot be erased, and that it contaminates all who are associated with the patient.
>
> When mental illness was thought to be an instrument of the devil, many avoided the person whose faith was so tenuous that he or she allowed nefarious influences to dominate. Nobody wanted to be associated with that individual . . . . Yet there are many, psychiatrists among them, who argue that the mentally disabled are not 'sick' but simply different, for which reason they are ill-served by being called 'psychotic' or 'schizophrenic,' a label as ostracizing as was the earlier one of 'witch.'[85]

> Studies have indicated that when patients are discharged and return home to cope with many of the same tensions which produced stressful situations before, the problems are exacerbated and there is a high incidence of readmission. Some of the tensions are perpetuated by family members who have been neglected or ignored while their relative was the focus of attention. Other sources of difficulty may stem from idiosyncratic communication within a family which produced turbulence and frustration for all, particularly the individual who ended up in the hospital. Frequently there is a residue of hostility which surfaces only when a person is in a hospital and no longer making unreasonable demands that cannot be met. Whatever patterns occurred prior to someone's hospitalization, mental health professionals believe that the entire family needs attention, help, support . . . .

---

[85] Phyllis Vine, *Families in Pain: Children, Siblings, Spouses, and Parents of Mentally Ill Speak Out.* New York: Random House, Inc., 1982, p. 63.

Recognizing that it does little good to ignore the family while salvaging the patient, many programs try to provide a forum for releasing the emotional turmoil that parents or children have sustained.

For whatever reasons, these recommendations have not been implemented for mentally ill Street People, who have been released to fend for themselves with no support system.[86]

*

HOUSING THE MENTALLY ILL

Dear Journal,

Many of these social programs attend only to bodily needs and ignore the alienation that a Street Person or a poor person feels— and ignore the pain of separation, the isolation, the lack of even family connectedness.

They are estranged for whatever reasons from their family, which may have been a support system at one time, but now no longer can provide emotional, physical, or monetary support— maybe it never did. Maybe it never could adequately offer the essential, unconditional love of being valued for one's own unique person-hood. Ideally, family should be a place where, while they do not have to agree with you, offers some ties of relationship, of connectedness, that still function. Robert Frost in "The Death of the Hired Man" penned, "Home is the place where, when you have to go there, they have to take you in."[87]

"I always thought of a family as some place you could go and be welcome, no matter what. But I found out differently," Eric said. "A family should be a source of emotional support— not necessarily approval and nor of pity, but maybe recognition of how much hardship you have had to endure. But I found out that my family was the first to turn against me."

---

[86] *Ibid.*, pp. 80-81.

[87] Robert Frost, "On the Death of the Hired Man", *A Pocket Book of Robert Frost's Poems: With an Introduction and Commentary by Louis Untermeyer*. New York: Washington Square Press, 1960, pp. 165-166.

Ted, the young man who had developed a brain disorder from previous chemical abuse, said, "I love my family, and I know they love me, but my nervousness, my pacing, my inability to sit still, and my inability to hold down a job drive them up a wall. It's best for them and for me if I find someplace else to live. I have lived sometimes in group homes for former mental patients, and that seems to work out best, but there are waiting lists and many cities don't have them."

These perplexities have been addressed by some studies:

> The problem of where he or she will live after discharge is among the most important questions a family will have to face.
>
> In some instances families [of persons with mental illness] can sustain a relative's chronic demands only when the person does not live with them . . . . Relatives are fully aware of what the mental health professional can only guess: Living with that particular individual would drive others crazy.[88]

> Halfway houses [for the mentally ill] vary in quality as well as in the services they provide. Many are no more than boarding houses with expensive rents, managed with little orientation toward the needs of their residents. Others require residents to participate in housekeeping duties as a form of rehabilitation. Still other are connected with counseling services, job rehabilitation programs, or psychotherapeutic agencies.
>
> While a social worker is supposed to arrange for aftercare, he or she can only rely upon what is available.[89]

Street People frequently have been cut off from their family because they didn't measure up: they were "Black Sheep," they were too much trouble. They created too much havoc, or had "bad habits." Many of the younger people were "fired" from their families, disowned. If the family needed to cease being enablers, I could understand it. But many minors were abandoned by parents

---

[88] Vine, p. 93.

[89] *Ibid.,* pp. 91, 93.

who preferred "to do their own thing" without the encumbrance of children, or who had recoupled with someone who did not like the children or was even harmful to them. Most runaway children leave for good reason, usually to protect themselves from sexual abuse by a relative or step-parent.

The breakdown of the nuclear and the extended family systems, partly occasioned by the necessity of needing two wage-earners to maintain a household financially and thus losing a fulltime homemaker and caregiver, has displaced from family life those with chronic physical or mental illness. There is no longer anyone at home to provide care. The phrase "There is no place like home" has a different meaning for them. There is no place. There is no place.

✶

INTERDEPENDENT COUPLES

Dear Journal,

On the street, I see many instances of dependent pairs, such as Aeneas and Dolly. They appear to be better off together than apart. Many would not have been able to manage alone due to physical or mental disability, but their disabilities somehow seem complementary— so that they are able to compensate for one another.

✶

METROPOLITAN AREA SUMMARY ON THE HOMELESS[90]

The Minnesota State Planning Agency Metropolitan Area Summary on Homelessness reports that *the majority of the homeless are not continually homeless.* During a six month period, 76% of homeless individuals interviewed had gotten off the streets at least once[:]

"Subpopulations of the homeless in the metropolitan area include: individuals with chronic health problems (38%); veterans (37% homeless men): individuals having left corrections (36%); chemically dependent (30%); mentally ill (24%); and the unemployed (90%). Individuals may fall into more than one category. (Wilder Foundation data.)

The number of homeless in the state has increased from 1,165 in August 1985 to 2,425 in August, 1987. *Children made up 23% of the homeless.*

---

[90] Minnesota State Planning Agency: *Homelessness in Minnesota.* St. Paul: Minnesota State Planning Agency, February, 1988, pp. v-vi.

PART VII: Feelings, Frustration, Fatigue, and Distress

EMOTIONAL BAGGAGE AREA

Dear God,
What negative emotions am I inappropriately bringing into this situation? What might be weighing me down unnecessarily? What can I clarify to lighten my load?

I am a very strong person and I can endure hardship if I have too. But I don't want to go looking for hardship, chaos, pain, turmoil, or a myriad of other miseries. And I don't want to hold onto stuff I can resolve and release.

*

Dear Journal,
Living at the House of Charity under any circumstance is difficult. Like the others, I didn't arrive unscathed. I am carrying heavy emotional baggage from my failed marriage, the abduction of my children, the failure of the Courts to be timely, just, and fair.

Despite the load, I am mentally clear, perhaps the way one becomes when a building is burning: *keep one's wits or perish.*

*

SOMATIC PAINS

Dear Journal,
The situation feels like a baseball lodged in my stomach. My shoulders feel like there are cinder blocks on the back of my neck.

*

ELIGIBILITY FITNESS

Dear Journal,

It seems that the social service personnel don't know what to do about me because I am here as a mother, but they don't see my children.

*

FAMILY BURN-OUT

Dear Journal,

Although sometimes my mother sends postage stamps and cash, our personal relationship remains distant. I finally told her I was in a shelter and eating at soup kitchens but she didn't seem to hear or to want to hear. I always expect and want some connection, some emotional support. It seems I am only acceptable to her when I am within her notion of perfection.

*

REGIONAL LANGUAGE

Dear Journal,

I know winter is not on my list of priorities or values. When I said to a Minnesotan that "I don't want to live in Minnesota. I do not like the severe climate." The reply is generally "We are strong and rugged people out here. If you were like us, you could take it." That really wasn't the point. I'm no wimp, but I prefer a temperate climate.

*

FRIENDSHIP BURN-OUT

Dear Journal,

Another reason I feel so cut off, when my (middle class) friends listen to my story, they become devastated by the overwhelming complexity of the situation. Within two years I have gone from a typical middle-class housewife with a family and career, to being without assets, and having a very restricted income. If it could happen to me and so fast, it could happen to them too. That thought is more than most of my friends can deal with. It is as if destitution is contagious. That reality is threatening some, resulting in social distance between us.

*

RECEIVING

Dear Journal,

After reviewing what I vented in my journal yesterday, I have to say that at that time, sometimes when emotional support was offered, I probably didn't know how to receive it and take it in. This is not uncommon for people experiencing such trauma. I must learn to recognize the good stuff so I don't miss out.

*

INDOOR AIR QUALITY

Dear Journal,

I have always disliked cigarette smoke. It makes it hard for me to breathe and swallow. Now living at the House of Charity with the coughing and wheezing, I have a total aversion to tobacco smoke.

Some of the coughing and wheezing I am exposed to may not just be because many Street People are heavy smokers. The television news broadcast warned that there is an outbreak of tuberculosis spreading through some Twin Cities shelters now.

*

FATIGUE

Dear Lord,

Today I am bone tired. I am tired of being needy. I am tired of having to poor mouth to get even necessities. I am tired of no money. I am tired of standing in lines, boring lines, day after day.

*

Dear Journal,

The longer I am on the street the shorter my patience and the sharper my tongue. I am impatient with the unavoidable conflicts in schedule. As a recipient of the system, I am impatient with my powerlessness to make even simple changes that would have expedited the process. I am also well aware that I'd best not "bite the hand that feeds me."

✳

COURT

Dear Journal,

I kept believing that "the court, in its wisdom" was a real thing. I really believed that courts would make decisions. I was waiting for wise decisions to correct what had happened. More and more I am beginning to feel that court is not a place of wisdom: it is a place where dreams are shattered.

✳

CANCER OF ATTITUDE

Dear Journal,

I feel a build-up of non-specific generalized resentment, about the way Street People are treated, the red tape, and the way the whole system is set up. I am discouraged and fed up with the injustice of it all. It's infecting me like a cancer— a Cancer of Attitude. I don't have proper remedies or appropriate channels in which dissipate my annoyance with The System. My irritability is growing deeper and more generalized, entrenching itself as a deep-seated anger. I have noticed that the more exasperated I am about this whole mess, the more back pain I experience. My lymphatic system has formed hard nodes up and down my back and in my neck. They feel like bruises under the skin. The more frustrated I feel, the more my back hurts. [See Appendix for further information.]

✳

SHARED TRIBULATIONS

Dear Journal,

Everyone at the House of Charity is going through a private hell. No one person feels like he/she is "the only one" in misery. We all have miseries— and that, in itself, is the bond.

Sometimes the fact that we're all suffering makes it easier for me to relate with Street People than with people who otherwise would have been my "peers." Because all the Street People have complicated problems, sharing mine is not particularly threatening or distressing to them.

✳

NON-VERBAL COMMUNICATION: JUDGMENTAL LOOKS

Dear Journal,

I notice that Street People don't talk much, except when hanging out in restaurants or waiting in the House of Charity living room during a long blizzard. Most other talk is restricted to trading survival information. Almost all carry an extensive phone-book of numbers for caseworkers, agencies, and listing eligibility criteria. But past that, human contact is most often limited to experiencing the scorn and derision that one receives for just being alive and walking through the Skyway, or for walking on the sidewalk minding one's own business— which business is generally to find a phone, a bathroom, or a warm place to exist for a while until the shelter opens up. Looks give messages. Every day, all day, Street People are affronted by the feedback of negative judgmental looks.

And then when we actually use our vocal cords to converse with another human being, more often than not, that person is an irritable, burned-out government worker. To apply for social services, a person must be vulnerable, and willing and able to tell enormous quantities of the most private information, over and over, to strangers. Some say this is why many fall through the cracks before they even apply.

✳

I saw a copy of the *Catholic Worker* woodcut print "Jesus of the Breadline"[91] hanging on the wall at Catholic Social Services, and it inspired me to shape a prayer to go with The Lord's Prayer about it.

OUR FATHER OF THE STREET[92]

Our Father, who art in heaven . . .
Show us a little heaven in this hell.
Hallowed be Thy Name,
Your Special Name. We don't use names much anymore on the street.
Thy kingdom come . . .
Being with you would be a lot easier than being here,
Thy will be done . . .
Do You really will us to live life this way?
Or did we mess up all by ourselves?
Are you really closer to the poor and homeless, You, who had no place to lay your head?
On earth as it is in heaven . . .
There isn't any fairness down here. Will it get any better?
Give us this day our daily bread . . .
At the soup line, and give us a warm place to sleep tonight.
And forgive us our trespasses . . .
Lord, You know all about where we have been.
You know all about what we have and have not done.
As we forgive those who trespass against us . . .
We can forgive those yesterdays that went wrong,
But it is hard today to forgive the people
Who despise our clothing, or who pretend we are invisible,
Or who flee when we say, "Hello"?

---

[91] Eichenberg, Fritz, "Jesus of the Breadline" *The Catholic Worker*, v. 18, no. 11, June, 1952, p.1

[92] *The Lord's Prayer* by Jesus Christ. Interior monologue by Pat McDonough.
©1984 by Patricia A. McDonough/*Our Father of the Street.*

> *We will try to forgive those who deride us because*
> *They don't understand how it feels out here on the street.*
> *We will try to forget the red tape, and the long lines,*
> *We will try to forgive the daily humiliations that*
>   *we endure to stay alive.*

Lead us not into temptation . . .

> *We don't want no more trouble.*
> *We got too much troubles already.*

But deliver us from evil . . .

> *We need help from you on the delivering.*
> *If it don't come soon and strong, we fear*
>   *we may all be delivered of our health and sanity.*
> *Hold us up a little longer: our troubles weigh heavy, so heavy,*
>   *Lord. We are a small problem in your bigness,*
> *But to us, it is a big problem to our smallness.*
> *Be all you can be for us, God.*

For Thine is the kingdom, power, and the glory now and forever . . .

> *We mean no offense, Lord, but you have it all.*
> *You have the full deck.*
> *You have the power, the glory, the security, the eternity.*
> *We ain't got nothin' but today and some days we can't be sure of*
>   *that.*
> *Thanks for listening, Lord.*
> *We don't want to take up much of your Time. But, Lord,*
> *Don't forget the bread.*

AMEN.

THE SHIELD

Under the circumstances I was not different from others at the House of Charity except that— this would never be a permanent way of life for me, yet for some there it might be.

I was embarrassed to be on the street. But I was not embarrassed because of the people I was with on the street. What hurt was not my embarrassment: it was feeling Judgment. Generally, if I were walking with a street person, or known to be staying at the House of Charity, then it was assumed, *de facto*, that I had done something rotten to deserve my fate. But I did not have reason to be ashamed of my circumstances. I did not accept the shame: I had done nothing to deserve this shame, but nonetheless, I felt it come at me. I am reminded of John Harry Griffin's *Black Like Me*— in which the author noted the devastating effect that scornful looks burned into one's self-concept, and how necessary it was to shield one's self from the message of such disapproving glares and the see-through-you looks.

The paradox was that even though I tried to shield myself from the shame projected toward me, some of it seeped into my being.[93]

The shield concept is basically that when something undesirable is projected toward you, you don't have to catch it, assimilate it, and take it in as a piece of your identity. You can mentally shield yourself from unwelcome verbal projectiles.[94] Another version of it is at the end of the Book of Ephesians in the New Testament.

✳

THE STRAIN OF TELLING/RETELLING

To be human is to experience our thoughts, feelings, physical presence, perceptions, intuitions, and gut reactions— to fully experience the moments of our life. To be able to function in extremely painful circumstances, I sometimes had to become alienated from my own story. Eventually I became able to say it without any feeling, to say it superficially— as if I were a tape recorder giving "the facts, nothing but the facts." To become separated in this way from one's story is to become detached from one's own life, to be less alive. It was depersonalizing. To tell my story, I had to keep the feelings somewhere else, or the pain in my gut would be so bad I couldn't stand it. I would choke up: my throat would constrict. I couldn't get words out.

---

[93] For about two years after the street experience, I was still trying to get over the disturbing reality that I had been, in a way, a bag lady. It took closer to eight years to heal the "social phobia" that resulted and to be free of flash-backs whenever I went into The Government Center or the Skyway.

[94] I later learned more about this skill from Fae Moog, who researches and teaches a class on dealing with passive-aggressive people. She adapted it from the works of Anne Wilson Schaef of Colorado.

Some people have said, "Well, this applied to your situation, but not to The Homeless." I believe that is wrong, because each of them has a unique and painful story to tell. And the fact that it has to be told over and over, impersonally, to get access to what the system controls is depersonalizing to them just as it was for me.

When I had to tell my story to someone, there was always the initial problem of the denial, minimizing, misunderstanding, or trying to fix it with the *"Why don't you? Why haven't you?"*. I know they meant to be helpful and were trying to assimilate the pieces, but I was by this time quite fragile. It hurt just to be there. It hurt to tell the story. I hurt all over. And the process seemed to prolong the agony. The only way I could do it was to shut down and tell it as if I weren't living it.

On the occasions when I had contact with a really integrated, compassionate social worker, when I told my story the social worker was frequently blown away— while I had to stay *disconnected* to tell the facts I had to tell. I am sure some identified with me, which made it harder for them. It was necessary to go through the pain of telling and retelling, because each one had control over some one part of The System.

*

RECONNECT

I had to learn to shut down my feelings to be able to relate my story. I also had to learn to reconnect with my feelings to be human. For a long time, I could only reconnect with my feelings for short periods of time and only in certain settings. I could reconnect through certain music, through scriptural passages, and writing and journaling.

Music and lyrics of such songs as "Be Not Afraid," "On Eagle's Wings," "Hosea," and "Here I Am, Lord" triggered my long-repressed tears. These songs opened the flood gates. My friend Phyllis told me tears are a gift of the Holy Spirit that allows healing to begin.

I also reconnected to my feelings in church, in prayer, or in praying the Mass. In prayer, I said what I couldn't say to anyone else— whether it was praise, supplication, or a venting of my frustration. At daily Mass, I listened to the Scriptural readings of the day for a passage which might have meaning for that day.   It was uncanny how often it was relevant.

I also stayed connected with my attitudes and feelings during journaling. Writing is for me, even if my brain cannot quite form the concepts, a way my hands can express something for me; as if my writing fingers know what I think and feel and want to express more than other parts of me may be able to conceptualize or say.

After the street experience, it took me two years of processing for my whole self successfully to begin to reintegrate my thoughts, physical body, and feelings with my spoken words, and took many years before the process felt completed. Having to shut down and then having to reintegrate is what survivors of catastrophic trauma have to relearn how to do. To fail to do this work is to experience the rest of life as a spiritual amputee.

*

MY MOTIVATION

I knew that being on the street was a temporary necessity: I had to attend to needs of my children and repair the breech in my finances later. Since the court for reasons never made clear did not permit my children to leave Minnesota for care, I had to stay in Minnesota. So I was clear about purpose for being in Minneapolis. I am very grateful to the House of Charity and Catholic Social Services for permitting me to stay there for three months and for assigning me the luxury of a private room.

*

As I entered the fifth or sixth week on the street, I noticed I was growing more introspective. In my journaling I became both a participant and an observer of my own process. What skills did I bring into this situation that could be significant coping tools? What different skills was I acquiring? What insights could I draw from this experience? Aside from the obvious, what things were different for Street People and people in the middle class? What was working in my favor? What were stumbling blocks?

*

COMMUNICATING

Dear Journal,

It's a good thing I have worked with diversity in many contexts: (economic; ethnic; professions; subject areas; regional and geographic cultures; and a diversity of races) in the United States. While I do not speak any "foreign" language fluently, having grown up in Washington, D.C., an international capital, I already had developed skills in the use of cross-cultural language and behavior. This made it easier to listen, be open, and communicate with differing populations. Growing up in the Nation's capitol area, I have had to speak many of this country's "cultural languages" with competence in my work and private life; without a doubt, learning to speak and understand Minnesotan has been the most difficult. But, for some reason, I have a hard time speaking to most (middle class) Minnesotans. I guess I assumed that it should be the easiest group to communicate with. However, this is a different geographical region; the division between the rich and the poor is more clearly delineated; there are many differences in how time is viewed and used here; and the speech norms and taboos are different. For most Minnesotans, there is a distinct language of polite understatement. As someone from "Out East," I am accustomed to being as direct as possible. The result has been a lot of communicational misfires.

Minnesotans as a rule do not say directly what they mean. Everything is so tempered. Apparently it is the practice to grossly understate everything and then remove all potential feeling perspective from it, so that the speech is often flattened with words like "a bit," "a tad," "sorta," "fairly," "kinda."

On TV KARE-11 today, I wrote down what the weather forecaster said. He said,

> Don't be surprised if you see more than a few before morning of, you know, that's the S-word. Right now, there is a little bitty bit of rain falling in higher elevations in the sky but already it's not coming down to the ground. There will be some fairly chilly air and fairly widespread cold.

That's all he said. When the cards came up showing the weather synopsis, it said,

Expect six inches of snow tonight in the Twin Cities. Deeper accumulations in outlying areas. Blowing and drifting possible. Severe cold conditions tomorrow. Possible windchill temperature of 14 degrees below zero. Stockmen's advisories are posted.

I have heard a Minnesotan say, "I think I could eat a little something," and proceed to consume four plates full of spaghetti and meatballs.

At the beach at Shady Oak Lake several youngsters were throwing rocks at the other swimmers in the water when I heard the lifeguard on the megaphone say "Kids, I want to ask you to do me a favor. Please don't throw rocks at the swimmers."

It is not just how Minnesotans speak; it includes how they listen. It is a technically oriented society. For many Minnesotans, all statements are taken literally, and thinking is quantitative. For example to an exclamation "Statements like that raise my blood pressure!" An appropriate Minnesota response would be: "Oh? Just how high is your blood pressure?"

If a person were to use hyperbole to emphasize a point, some Minnesotans would be apt to focus on the quantitative aspect but miss the point entirely. For example, "I would have to live to be a million before I would do that— that's how long it would take!" Many Minnesotans would begin the calculations to figure out when that would be, to see when he could count on the job being completed, and ask "Do most people in your family live to be a million?"

I have always gone to the other extreme, to try to say everything with a directness and honesty but not necessarily in numerically quantifiable terms and allow an occasional exaggeration or embellishment. That is not how to speak Minnesotan.[95]

Before I caught on to what was happening, here is a typical communicational misfire:

I would say what I meant with as much forthrightness as I could muster. A Minnesotan listening to me would then assumed that in the spoken word everyone tempers down and understates, so whatever I said, would be assumed to be politely vague— therefore

---

[95] A book on this subject by Howard Mohr came later.

it obviously meant a great deal more than what was actually spoken. The Minnesota listener knows it is up to him/her to fill in the gaps, make the assumptions, and take the great leap to arrive at what was implied by my (assumed) understatement. So with this setup, if I say exactly what I mean, the meaning is certain to be inflated by the hearer to mean something entirely different. We have had an exchange but not communication, not comprehension of the message; what I said is not what the other person registered.

It misfires in the other direction, also. If a Minnesotan makes a statement to me, it sounds like a vague, unspecific hint, and I often haven't the slightest idea what they really mean. In most instances, I expect a person to say honestly and clearly what they need and want.[96]

Now I have developed the habit of saying "What does it mean when you say . . ." For example, "What does it mean when you say it might be a little cooler tonight?"

The worst time this language gap affected me was when a Minnesota court official called me in Pennsylvania and said, "You'd better prepare to come out here. Court will be (such and such) date." So I flew out, prepared to spend an extra day. Years later, I learned that what was meant by the statement was "We expect you to be moved out here and have an established household before that date." [In addition, the court and social workers never allowed that I might not want to move "out here." then]

*

---

[96]   Another example: several years after my Street People experience, my Minnesota neighbor called to say "Hello." We talked about the weather, the price of groceries, my kids, and her grandchildren. Then she said that the neighbor on her other side had to fix her fence. She asked me "You know, the lumber yard doesn't deliver any more?" I said "No, I didn't know." The conversation ended. We said "Goodbye." Several days later my kids told me that these two neighbors were angry with me for refusing to offer my pickup truck to help get their lumber order for the repairs to their fence. As far as I was concerned, I didn't refuse anything. No one asked me. Had I been asked or known I was being asked, I would have been glad to help.

TIME

Dear Journal,

Generally in Minnesota, if you set a meeting between an Easterner and a Minnesotan and the time is set for 7:00, the Minnesotan will show up at 7:00 a.m. and the Easterner will show up at 7:00 p.m. So I have learned to clarify what time the person really prefers to meet and negotiate from there.

I am discovering that the meaning of Time is not the same for all people. I discovered that "time" is a viewpoint. It has different cultural meanings to people in different circumstances. I thought about it a lot tonight while monitoring the ATM machines. A conceptual framework concerning Time affects a person's behavior, outlook, and treatment of other people. How I discovered this was that when I stepped back and forth between my role as a Street Person and my role as a Bank Worker, I felt almost dizzy. On a very deep level, I felt like I was stepping through a time-warp when I shifted from one scene to the other.

It was disorienting. Some of it was a little like getting out of a car after a long journey, but continuing to experience the sensation of the movement of the car. Or like jet lag. Or like shifting from Standard Time to Daylight Savings Time. I knew that this shift was nothing superficial. Once I realized the differences in perception of Time, I could prepare myself to deal with it and treat it like a process of re-entry. The relative value of Time for me then depended less on which domestic culture I was in and more on my ability to recognize it and shift gears accordingly.

People who live within the strictures of Time often have certain attitudes which flow from that. For example, if *Time is of the Essence,* a person will be more interested in getting a thing accomplished by a certain time. If there is a "Time Schedule," there is an expectation that certain tasks will be accomplished within the allotted Time, whether the schedule is reasonable or not. Then it follows that some Times will be rushed to fit it all in, and once in a while there will be extra time, whatever that means. But most of the time, there isn't enough Time to fit in all the tasks. It's planned that way so that no one can "waste" Time. But what really happens is that the "Time Schedule," the "Production Schedule" within a "Time Schedule," and accomplishing the tasks within the "Time Schedule" take priority over all else— especially over the needs of the participants. [This also pressures and discourages workers who take pride in their work quality, and it discourages perfectionists, to the point where they say, "*I quit, I've had it. I'm outta' here.*"] The tasks, the time schedule, the production schedule based on deadlines, all take priority over the needs of people. Keeping the production schedule becomes more important than recipients of a service, for example— in this case serving Street People. And it becomes more important than the deliverers of the service— in this case social service workers. So the Time Schedule is often recorded by numbers: production numbers or case numbers.

It all becomes more important than the social service workers. That's one way The System burns out social service workers, too, as if they are an expendable cog in the Time machine of The System. Some think that without this rigid view of time, the Industrial Revolution could not have taken place.

In most of the world, except the most industrialized nations, Time is viewed differently: Time there is at the service of the people. There is always more time— an eternity of it— but people are precious. So the needs of the people are more important than Time. Schedules are readily adjusted, as often as needed, to meet and respect the present needs of the people. For example, in some cultures, if a person must leave a meeting early, the entire meeting adjourns so that a proper goodbye can take place before that person must depart, rather than making do with a casual wave goodbye and a continued meeting. If some people need more attention, the agenda can readily be extended to accommodate their need. People are more important than the task and are given the amount of time it requires to attend to their needs adequately. For example, is your view that when you meet with someone, does he/she *take* time, or are you *giving* time, or is time not part of it at all?

I had already recognized that there were time differences among certain groups— fast-paced urban as opposed to agrarian rural communities— but while on the street I noticed that there were time differences between various groups within the city. I developed a new awareness of the relative value of Time in differing cultures within the U.S.

How often have we heard that "Time is Money." How much is structured around "Pay Periods." For example, general contractors generally get paid in thirds according to the percentage of completion of a job. Think how difficult this makes it to be "on time." making monthly car or mortgage payments on a set due date.

When I had to get to the bank job in the morning, my attitude, behavior, and pace were different than they were on the days, such as Sunday, when there was no opportunity for purposeful activity in my life. But the issue wasn't whether the activity was purposeful or not. I did a lot of purposeful activity on the Street, to meet the needs of the court case, the medical situation, and so forth. What was different was the view of Time itself. It soon became apparent that what Time meant, as a value, was different depending on one's station in life at the moment. Time was relative.

People who are professionals or employees generally believe Time is a limited commodity. They believe that if I give you some of this time, I have to give up some of that time. People who are professionals or employees, when walking, are almost always walking to something and have a set amount of Time in which to complete this task. They will generally return to a sit-down job. So when they race through the Skyway, weaving, pushing, and passing, that requires a spurt to get somewhere quickly, to exercise, to alleviate fanny-fatigue, or as a diversion before returning to their perception of "real activity", which is "the work." Such people rarely looked around, and in thought they usually seemed someplace else, perhaps preoccupied with what had to be done in Time for tomorrow, or next week, or some other Time that wasn't relevant to surviving the present moment. In the Skyway, they were predominantly lean, fit, healthy, high-energy, and were easily identified because they didn't have to wear their coat in the Skyway. (Many Street People wear their coats everywhere winter and summer.)

As I walked through the Skyway during the work week, distortions of Time were readily apparent to me. For Street People, Time was a liability. There was always more time, too much more time, days and days and days of Time to get through, hours and hours and hours of Time before it was possible to go back to the shelter and get warm. For most, there was no job to go to, no one who needed them to be around— or even allowed them to be around. The Street People either had too much Time or, what Time they had was used up by other people, such as people in authority who required Street People to stand in long lines and to wait for a long Time. Time was filled with waiting for something needed that someone else had control of. Time was a liability, except for the hectic schedule of getting to and reporting to all the social workers, which in itself was more difficult to schedule and manage than matriculating at a university. There is typically continuous pressure from the professional people, employers, and employees to be on time. The pressure to be on time began to seem almost irrelevant when the body was aching, tired, and suffering from malnutrition and eventually infections, disease, parasites, pneumonia, and fungi, especially since "being on time" meant waiting a long time in yet another line. Moreover, the professional people, employers, and employees arrogantly believe they are *doing the Street Person a service by demanding that they be on time to instill good work habits.*

Street People walk for endurance, not speed. They have to walk in every kind of weather. They have to walk and keep walking on a minimal caloric intake. Street People have to walk all day most of every day, seven days a week. One has to be able to last, to endure. In some combination, they have to walk or stand for eight to twelve hours, seven days a week. Walking might be for five to 25 miles or more in eight hours. As I mentioned earlier, they are generally also carrying everything they own at the time.

Each day what a Street Person had to look forward to was Nothing. What you had to do was "Wait" and "Stand in a Line" for each and every basic human need, or to "kill Time."

On the weekend, professional people and employees usually get to go somewhere else. On the weekend, they may often get to play. On Sundays they can be inside or could choose to be outside doing recreational activities for a certain amount of Time, or select activities to do in the home environment— a visually and geographically different place from the work environment.

On the weekend, Street People have to stay in the same place and in a similar routine to that during the week. For the Street People, Time on Sundays was the reality of total alienation. There is no home, no place to be inside, and no money to do activities; one can only walk, drink coffee, and walk some more, in winter, spring, summer, fall— just walk all day Sunday, usually carrying everything with you. On the weekend and during the week there is no opportunity for anything that might be considered play. There is no real difference in weekend activity from activities on another day except that it is harder to find a bathroom and there are fewer lines. For "Street People," there are no outside or inside recreational athletics. There were no jigsaw puzzles to pass the Time. No card games or board games are allowed in the shelter because of the past history that games had been taken so seriously that tempers flared and violence had often ensued. In the shelter, there was no VCR or movies to rent. Going to a movie matinee was usually not recreational: it was done to buy a place to sit and sleep for a few hours when the shelter was closed. The minimal TV viewing was restricted and only in evening hours. There was no respite from the stress of real life. There was no music, no song. There was no way to get away from it for those who did not abuse drugs or alcohol, or take a geographic. A geographic was no real solution, because as Ernie Larson says, "Where ever you go, there you are." Street People need wholesome recreation as respite from their burdens, too.[97]

---

[97] Sister Rose Tillemans' Peace House, while not targeted to Street People per se, is a drop-in center on Franklin Avenue in Minneapolis which opened in the late 1980s. On Tuesday afternoons after meditation and lunch, there is a sing-a-long. The "guests" have recorded a cassette tape of their vocals and instrumentals entitled **Courtin' for Peace** and a **Peace House Songbook** to provide the words to the songs on the tape. Many songs are on theme's relevant to the life of the Homeless: *Housing Now, Jerusalem Slim* (a Hobo slang for Jesus Christ)

> I was an outcast the same as him,
> He was the rebel called Jerusalem Slim.
> He was a preacher who roamed a lot.
> I was the man sleeping near your cot.
> I was a tramp who walked all day.
> He was a boy who slept in the hay. . . .

My point of mentioning it here is that this singing was valuable recreation and an opportunity to be in community. It is affirming, recognizing each person has a unique talent, contribution, and potential.

It almost goes without saying that very few engaged in sexual activity with a partner, or had a place in which to share sex with a partner, or the energy— somewhat like having fouled spark plugs. While in this book I relate a few stories of people who paired or who were lecherous leerers soon after the Valentine's Day decorations were put up, the vast percentage seemed oblivious to this and most displayed no "courtship readiness" body language.

✳

THE PACE OF TIME

Dear Journal,

For a Street Person, weighted down with heavy clothing, fatigue, malnutrition, and emotional depletion, it is nearly impossible to walk fast. The dimension of time is very different. Other people are responding to clocks that run faster, and they have the energy to run with those clocks. Having eaten few vegetables, little protein, and an assortment of rotten food donated "to help the poor," the bodies of Street People are often very run-down. When other people walk or jog for 25 miles, they wear high-tech shoes and special lightweight attire, and they choose to do it for health and fitness. They could choose to be doing something else. A Street Person wears heavy clothes and carries everything s/he owns as well. To make this more equitable, maybe others should try carrying everything they own for seven hours or more, day after day.

✳

EXHAUSTION TIME

Dear Journal,

When I was in the Skyway today and feeling so rotten and being pressured to make all the appointments but having little stamina left, I recalled the painting of the clock in Salvadore Dali's painting. I felt like one of the limp, melted clocks draped limply across the trees and the landscape when I was trying to adjust to these diverse Time zones.

✳

MEETING TIME

Dear Journal,
No one asks a Street Person if a meeting-time is convenient or if a schedule is workable. They just order them to "Be at so-and-so at such-and-such a time." It's a power thing. I wished I could say I'll be there "If the Good Lord is willing and the creeks don't rise," or "I'll do it when the Spirit moves me." When I tried, it didn't work. They got indignant.

I would have preferred to set my appointments to begin within a window of time, not at a specific moment in time, especially since it seemed that none of them began precisely on time at all. I wanted to say, "I'll get there sometime between 9 a.m. and 9:30 a.m." It didn't ever work. I only tried that a few times. They didn't understand what I meant. They interpreted it to mean, "the meeting should last from 9:00 a.m. to 9:30 a.m." So, arriving any time after 9:00 a.m. was labeled "being late" and then interpreted to mean "You were late because you don't care." Our language would benefit us by having/inventing some new words because the old ones can lead to so much confusion. But the real problem isn't with language itself, it's with listening and assuming.

Some Minnesotans brag about using "Vince Lombardi Time": for example, a person might say "I'll meet you at 7," (as I mentioned earlier 7 would most likely mean 7 a.m.), but if the person says, "I'll meet you at 7, Vince Lombardi time" that really meant "I'd like both of us to be there by 6:40 a.m. and we'll get started right away." In other words, with this person, if you arrive on time, you're late.

*

SENSE OF PLACE

My understanding of a sense of place started when I was 3 or 4 years old. In the Walt Disney movie when Jimminy Cricket told Pinocchio that everyone needs to have a Laughing Place, I took that suggestion seriously. When I was little, each afternoon we would pass through a long dim underpass (tunnel) in downtown Washington, DC, I would get the giggles: That was my "Laughing Place." Later, this concept somehow I expanded to include "a place to restore my spirit" (Sense of Place) and/or "a place to laugh" (Laughing Place). To have a place to laugh, I had to find and to store up things to laugh about. This stories in this book are my expression of finding some things to laugh about despite unfavorable circumstances.

In normal times, my Sense of Place to restore my spirit had to have spectacular scenic beauty to breathe in its restorative powers. When I had free time, I could in memory revisit these beautiful spots to help refresh me. Shirley McLaine calls such visual refreshment an open-eyed meditation.

*

CAMPING AND RELOCATION SKILLS

Two other things also helped. Since my teen years, I had also been a frequent camper. So my tent and my van were also special places too. I spent so much time driving locally and on long trips, and camping with it, that my customized van seemed more like home than my residence.

My camping skills served me well in this new situation too. In my married life, we had moved frequently for job promotions, reductions in force, and job-and-wage freezes, so I was accustomed to living with uncertainty. For those years, I had become accustomed to living in temporary housing, frequent moves, frequent packing and unpacking.

*

CREATING A PLACE

After a while, on the street, I began to need defenses against feeling homeless and placeless. I purposely began a few rituals, to provide a semblance of routine and security. Since Street People have No Place like Home, I decided I needed to create a Sense of Place for myself. Nothing in the city gave me a feeling of being protected, the way the view of the mountains did. I found it a struggle to find any places of spectacular scenic beauty in the dead of winter in and around the House of Charity. I could find no natural beauty in the wintry, mostly treeless, downtown streets. At that time, there were only about ten leafless trees in the entire downtown. The city lakes and parks were not accessible to me.

While the new architecture was exciting, most of the new skyscrapers were under construction and obscured by scaffolding. Another big restriction of visibility was the 60" snowfall, graying and mounded and piled everywhere.

My primary sense of place became a certain well-lighted pew in the back of St. Olaf's Church, where it was warm. In this way I managed to stay grounded and frequently serene, despite living through the insanities of The System. When I went to the library, although I selected reading material from almost every section of the library, I tried to sit in one sunny corner of the second floor. These spots lacked spectacular natural beauty; I had to make do. I now know that sunlight is an antidepressant through the gray days of winter, by seeking the sunniest corner of the library and the brightest pew in the church, my instincts were true to what I needed.

✻

RITUAL

I had been a person who thrived on diversity, challenge, and adventure, and adjusted readily to change. But during my street experience, I was over-saturated with changes and adjustments. I was tired. I began to appreciate ritual and predictability where formerly I had abhorred it. Predictability was one reason why I wanted the Post Office Box so much. Going to the Post Office to pickup the mail is a carryover from childhood delights walking to the Post Office/General Store with friends to get the mail in Garrett Park, MD— where the mail sack was thrown from a postal rail car pulled by a glistening-black, Baltimore and Ohio steam locomotive.

Having a Post Office Box and its key became symbolically important to me, especially after Robert spoke to me about Keys. The Post Office Box represented a place that was mine and a link to other places that mattered to me. Walking to a Post Office Box to collect the mail had all my life been a special time out to collect myself as well.

✻

JOURNALING

I believe journaling too was emerging as an important survival skill which helped me to keep things in perspective. As an adult, I had not used journaling as a tool. In fact, I started this journal as a way to hone my writing skills by copying down what people actually said and how speech varied from speaker to speaker. So much was happening around me that I was eager to capture it in writing. I was delighted to discover the other powerful benefits that journaling offered: as a way to gain insights, to diffuse some of the internal distress of past and present events, to lighten my emotional baggage, and ultimately as a way to pray. It was useful to name and write about the good and bad things that had happened, and helped me to keep on keeping on, day to day. It also gave me an organized place to note down information and observations while at the library. The writing energized me.

In addition to "Dear Journal" letters, I began to use "Dear God" letters to help me think through problems and strive for solutions.

*

HUNGER FOR LAUGHTER

For the most part, I felt isolation. I craved opportunities to laugh, as if laughter and humor could somehow heal my woundedness. Laughter for balance. I didn't find many opportunities to laugh at things that are really funny, mostly the humor of this situation was in the ironies and absurdities. I delighted in some of the stories I gathered. Even writing them down gave me a second time to enjoy their humor. I was almost celebrating that in this situation I was still maintaining a sense of humor, a sense of the ridiculous, a sense of the absurd, a sense of humor and my sanity. The writing energized me.

I can't define a sense of the ridiculous but this entire experience is about it. It is like the humor on the TV show "MASH." It is a way to refine the absurdities of life into a compact kernel of wisdom, to point out how inane certain rigidities can become. In this book I call some of them "legalisms." I think it is like Gandhi's position that absurdities have to be pointed out to a wider audience by the living out of them: e.g. how some regulations, which may seem perfectly sensible on the books, in practice in real life can be totally inappropriate and harmful. Until this discrepancy can be elaborated in the arena of life, changes don't or can't come about to remedy the injustice. My sense of the ridiculous is my attempt to arrive at the essence of "What is the nature of the underlying problem? Will the real problem please state your name?"

*

BELONGING AND IDENTITY

Dear Journal,

Insofar as I am on the street and have the same dilemmas as many other Street People, I am a Street Person. But my identity does not flow from being a Street Person. My personal identity remains distinct. It does not flow from having or not having a job either. It never has.

I prefer to work on projects rather than to administer programs. A "Project" is something which has a beginning, a middle, and an end, as opposed to a "Program," which is ongoing and must be administered to perpetuate itself. Projects may have independent contractors or employees. Programs generally have employees. I have preferred to work as an independent contractor. Typically, the projects I have completed were generally for a set period of time, usually one to three years; the terms of my work were spelled out in a contract. The contract specified each person's role, responsibility, authority, tasks, and task schedule. I am a good innovator, a good coordinator, a good manager of a project, a good problem solver.

If I allowed my identity to be determined by "my job," I might have to schedule an identity crisis every time one contract is completed and another begins. My identity remains separate from "what company I am working for" or "what position or role I am filling" for them at that point in time. My identity is not dependent on a job title. My experience on the street did not add to or diminish my identity. I use similar skills and a similar approach for most projects, even though the subject areas and the tasks change. I have learned to keep my "Self" separate from my project. In other words, my identity does not flow from a specific employment, role, or position the way it usually does for an employee on a career-track in a large corporation. Work is what I do, it is not who I am. This longstanding practice of keeping my "Self" apart from my employment helped me keep my "Self" intact on the street.

✳

IDENTITY AND WORK

It is a necessary inconvenience that occasionally there is a gap between one project's ending and another's beginning. It's a great time to catch up at home or to take a vacation. But if the length of time between projects extended too long, I took work as a temporary ("Temp") or as an employee. The benefit to doing Temp work is that it is a way to add new skills.

Since I did not expect to be in Minneapolis more than two weeks, I took Temp work as opposed to seeking permanent employment. (Without an established network, it is difficult for me to get established in contract work. Even when you know all the players, it may take a lead time of twelve months or more for discussions, preparation, and negotiations before a contract can be signed.) A disadvantage of contracted work is that medical insurance and retirement payments are rarely included. The independent contractor is responsible for paying his/her benefits, and for paying withholding tax and social security.

✳

PART VIII: IN GOD'S REFINERY

Dear Journal,

I am frustrated by the limited range of choices I have and had each step of the way regardless of how diligently I have tried to uncover better options. I have learned that the unfortunate reality about making decisions is that each time I have to make a choice I can only select from among the options I can identify. Once a choice is made, the next set of choices is conditioned by those already made. Ernie Larson says, "We can only play from the hand we are dealt. Each play, we select the best card in our hand."

I have been working for many months now on learning to be a less controlling person and I know I am making progress. I know I cannot make anything happen faster, so wanting to control it, to control the progress, to control the schedule, is only underscoring my powerlessness so that rather than alleviating anxiety and restoring calm, which is what controlling behavior desires, it is in fact creating more turmoil, and chaos and disharmony. Trying to control what cannot be controlled becomes intolerable. I need to bring closure to this court mess. But I cannot "bring" it, I can only hope for it, move toward it, wait for it. It is interesting that the word *ponder*, which should be in the judicial process, has been replaced by *ponderous*. I need more words for what I am feeling. Mad, sad, glad, and bad just don't cut it when the trauma is this deep.

I seem to be drained by an apprehension that all of this will never get resolved. I tried to find a word for it. Most everyone who has tried to console me has said, "Don't worry." But my track record for predicting the next worst turn of events has been incredibly good.

I don't think I'm worried, in the sense they mean. I looked up a lot of feeling words in the Thesaurus and decided I may be anxious. I looked up the words *anxiety* and *worry* in some psych books. I read somewhere that *anxiety* means concern about the future; *worry*, on the other hand, is concern about the past. If that is so, there is no doubt about it: I'm not worried, I'm anxious. I have been suffering from unremitting anxiety about the well-being of my children because of what they have been suffering.

∗

THINKING IN CIRCLES AND PROCRASTINATION

Dear Journal,

I am beginning to think that we can put our selves under extra stress by thinking in circles, especially when bad things are happening. I am aware now when I am thinking in circles. I named it an *Anxiety Loop*. Somehow I will learn to intercept my thought processes before I get caught in the paralysis of an anxiety loop. It is okay to be productive, even if anxious; but it does no good to feed anxiety, escalating it, and thereby stay mired in unproductive circles.

What might the relationship be between the paralysis of an anxiety loop and the paralysis of procrastination? An *anxiety loop* keeps me from focussing on anything else, generates tension and energy, but it is not useful, because it, too, feeds back into the loop. *Procrastination*, on the other hand, drains energy away from availability. It drains tension, and allows me to be distracted by almost anything else. When I procrastinate, my conscious mind is drained of energy while my subconscious mind, and even my dreams, use all their capacities to try to resolve the problem. If I can catch myself procrastinating, it is usually about something I don't have enough information about, or it may be something where the choices seem equally bad. Now, when I catch myself in procrastination, I ask: What additional information do I need? Where can I find it? Who might have it or know where I can get it? If I have a lot of information but no clearly discernible best option, I can decide to:

(1) delay a decision for events to catch up (putting on hold),

(2) analyze the problem from a different perspective,

(3) see if the impasse is a result of "stinkin' thinkin',"— obsolete or inappropriate beliefs, or other faulty logic,

(4) identify other resources

(5)   seek advice,

(6)   pray briefly for clear discernment

(7)   weigh pros and cons to see if that changes the desirability of one option over another,

(8)   make a decision on the spot, knowing that I have a 50% chance of making a good decision; or decide not to do it at all. Even choosing not to do anything feels clear, because it is in the realm of decision-making, not in the obscurity of the procrastination-storage area. At least choosing is an active state.

✳

Dear Journal,

I have heard that Japanese executives, when faced by a decision to make but no clear solution, play golf to allow their subconscious mind time to sort out the issues and a possible solution to float up into their conscious mind. Viewed this way, some procrastination has its productivity.

✳

GRIEF

Dear Journal,

After I had processed the dynamics of my worry, anxiety, and procrastination, another feeling came to the forefront. At first I didn't know what it was. I was intermittently angry and sad. What surprised me was that I was not at all depressed— this was different. What was I feeling? Reading an account of a mother in Europe at the end of after World War II learning her child had Downs Syndrome, I came to understand that grief is not confined to the experience of someone's death. Grief has to do with loss.

I am dealing with loss. Is what I feel grief?

Foremost was loss my children, then the forced sale of our home and some acres of mountain land. To heal and move past it, I need to put into words the losses I have endured (before I arrived at the House of Charity). Before I got to Minnesota, to raise funds I had to sell the few possessions I had salvaged in the divorce— which were the possessions I had brought into the marriage: family heirlooms, antiques, books, and furniture. Although I am not materialistic, I have been grieving their loss because this was part of my personal family history and cultural heritage. [See Appendix.]

Now that I recognize that I am grieving, I feel uneasy about my grief about my children because, thank God, they are alive and coping. I am pleased that my children are alive and resourceful. But because it is still in courts and the length of time this has gone on, and even because there was no death as others experience it, there could be no sense of closure. It took me some time to understand that I am grieving and what grief is. It's no wonder other people don't seem to relate to this difficult form of bereavement I'm experiencing. Our society does not handle grief well. It is most often relegated to a 3-day leave and business as usual.

The most typical reaction, if I mention the situation with my children being taken by their father, has been "I've heard about this kind of thing on TV. *That kind of thing doesn't happen around here.* You're the first person I've met in real life who had *that sort of thing* happen." I know how awkward it is to speak to a grieving person. I know people mean well but saying "You're the only one" is treating me like I am some oddity and is not consoling at all. It just increases my sense of isolation.

In addition, even compassionate empathetic listeners had little understanding of *the symptoms of grief* I was experiencing, and I didn't understand it well myself, but I knew I had to find things that worked for me. To survive I had to recognize and to acknowledge that I was grieving over my children and some losses, and be willing to experience that pain despite having to keep on with the tasks that had to be accomplished in the present. One major recognition was that *I must be gentle with myself, allow for diminished energy, and take extra steps to be self-caring.* [See Appendices for useful information regarding symptoms and handling grief and loss.]

*

It is normal in anticipation of grief to experience pre-grief. For example, when caring for someone who is dying a caregiver often anticipates with grief the grief they will actually feel later when the death occurs. After a death, it is also normal for the survivor's grief to take about 1½ years to 2 years to be completed, and for the person then to be able to resume "normal life" by the 3rd year— but with a new concept of what is normal. Some people need even longer. Non-custodial parents and parents of an abducted child (or children), however, have a unique circumstance. Non-custodial parents grieve when they are apart from their children. Even when they are happy to be together, they experience pre-grief in anticipation of yet another separation. The children experience this too.

When a child is abducted, this is a complicated bereavement for the parents because (having no body to bury, no ritual ceremony to bring support and transition, and holding on to the hope that the child survives) there is no closure. Every day is a life in suspended animation. Such a parent may try to live normally, go through the actions of normal life, but it isn't what normal is supposed to be like. The grief is similar to that of families who have someone Missing in Action.

For persons in grief, holidays can be especially painful. Although I was with my younger son on Christmas Day, and saw my other son for a hour or two over the Christmas holidays, it was a bittersweet experience for us. We were so happy to be together but it was like a different kind of being together: it was simultaneously joy and sorrow. We were elated to be together but anticipating the pain of yet another separation. We were in a great deal of pain about having all the accoutrements of a "normal life" stripped away even though we were in agreement that being together was the important part. I was staying at the House of Charity and without funds, so I couldn't lavish presents on them or cook a meal. It was not an old-fashioned Christmas.[98] [Someone commented, "Baby Jesus didn't have an old-fashioned Christmas either."]

✳

PEELING THE ONION

Dear Journal,

After allowing myself time to recognize and deal with the feelings of grief, I am moving out of that sorrow. Now it is different. Now I want to imitate the movie and yell out the window, "I'm mad as hell, and I won't take it anymore." But I have to take it, and I have to find a way to protect my children. I have to get myself out from

---

[98] In later years, we three valued being together on Christmas and Thanksgiving far above any set menu or gift giving.

this pit underneath the safety net. I don't think I can any longer do that in Minneapolis. Despite my desire to continue to live in Pennsylvania, I have sent out resumes here for appropriate middle management positions in housing— positions for which I am fully qualified, but the response has been fruitless. I have made follow up calls to see why I was not selected even for an interview, and while the responses vary, the theme seems to be that "You must know someone" and "You must be from here." Not encouraging.

*

REFRAMING

I am trying to use more sophisticated ways of thinking through my options by analyzing my options from every perspective. *Reframing* is to take the facts of a situation and look at them in a new view. Mother Teresa tells people to substitute the word "Gift" for the word "Problem." To maintain my integrity with myself, however, I could not just tell myself to "think positive," because for me that was denial of current reality. Denial would be a "false positive." I found an extension of that idea on a CELESTIAL SEASONINGS™ tea box:[99]

> If you will call your 'troubles' 'experiences' and remember that every experience develops some latent force within you, you will grow vigorous and happy, however adverse your circumstances may seem to be.

*

ADVICE

Dear Journal,
This week, I think three different well-intentioned people told me, "That which doesn't kill you, will make you a stronger person,"

---

[99] CELESTIAL SEASONINGS™ Tea Box Number 891221/6B.

which is a adapted from the writings of Neitzsche.[100]   I think I groaned every time I heard it. At this point, I don't want any more tests to make me a stronger person. Right now for a while I want nice, easy, routine things that I don't have to be strong to survive. All my life I have loved change and challenge. I must be incredibly exhausted to desire nice, easy routine things.

*

RESOLVE

Dear Journal,

After pondering when I am anxious, I discovered that a lot of it was fretting about: *"How will I be able to pay my bills?"* It's really been stressing me out. For my own survival, I have decided to be rather cold-blooded about it for now: *If incurring bills is what I have to do to protect my children and survive this ordeal, that's what I have to do. Somehow I will pay the debts. I keep my word.*

That's a far sight better than Scarlet O'Hara's resolve which was "If I have to lie, cheat, steal, so help me, I'll never go hungry

---

[100]   In *The Portable Neitzsche* the passage is as follows:

I have often asked myself whether I am not more heavily obligated to the hardest years of my life than to any others. As my inmost nature teaches me, whatever is necessary— as seen from the heights and in the sense of a *great* economy— is also the useful par excellence: one should not only bear it, one should *love* it. *Amor fati*: that is my inmost nature. And as for my long sickness, do I not owe it indescribably more than I owe to my health? I owe it a *higher* health— one which is made stronger by whatever does not kill it. *I also owe my philosophy to it.* Only great pain is the ultimate liberator of the spirit . . . . pain which takes time— only this forces us philosophers to descent into our ultimate depths and to put away all trust, all good-naturedness, all that would veil, all mildness, all that is medium— things in which formerly we may have found our humanity. I doubt that such a pain makes us "better", but I know that it makes us more *profound*.

Epilogue 1. *The Portable Neitzsche.* Friedrich Nietzsche, pp. 680-681.

again." Her resolve isn't within my values and my integrity, and I'm no longer afraid of being hungry.

✳

FAITHS, CHURCHES, AND BELIEF SYSTEMS

Although I have had a spiritual basis in my life for as long as I can remember, I spent many years investigating various systems of faith. I explored not only Catholicism but also Protestantism (Baptist, Methodist, Presbyterian, Assembly of God, Church of Christ, Full Gospel, and Church of God), as well as the Unitarian Universalist Society, Buddhism, Hinduism, Islam, Church of Jesus Christ of the Latter Day Saints, Christian Science, and agnosticism. It did not seem to me that any of them had all the answers: all were made up of imperfect human beings. Obviously, not all of the rules or beliefs are compatible. Within each system, I found sincere seekers of God; people who were living simply, making God a priority in their daily lives.

In my opinion, there are many ways to worship God. The important thing is to make the spiritual journey and find God for yourself. Not everyone climbs the mountain by the same path. With this in mind, I began to ask myself *"Where can I best be outfitted for the journey."*

In the spring of 1982, I began to experience a reentry into the Catholic Church, and a reintegration of my belief system with the teachings of the Catholic Church. I have no delusions that the institutional Catholic Church is perfect. I especially disagree with the institutional church's attitude toward and treatment of women in the United States and throughout the world. I think the rules against married clergy in the Roman Rite and allowing married clergy in the Maronite Rite show how inconsistent it can be. I think the Pope's Catholic policy against married clergy is a political, economic, and administrative decision. Originally, it seems that it came about because the church didn't want to have to pay the cost of upkeep of a family and as a way to resolve the issues surrounding inheritance of land in the cases where a secular prince was also clergy (e.g. a bishop), so that the land would pass into ownership of the church rather than to any heirs of that prince (and thereby out of the church control.)

So while I am not particularly espousing that everyone rush out and join the Catholic Church, I am relating how it has been unfolding for me.

Over the course of 1982 through 1983, I had an unfolding of a "conversion experience" (an experience of Jesus, the Holy Spirit, and our Creator God in a deeper, more meaningful way.) At that time, I read and studied the Bible, cover to cover. Initially I used the Good News Bible, because it was readily understandable. Then I compared it with the New International Bible, which seemed somewhat dry, and with the Jerusalem Bible, which is like an epic poem. By the time I had to live with the Street People, I had read scripture and was familiar with it even if, like most Catholics, I "didn't have the numbers down." My life of faith was deep and strong. If I hadn't brought that with me "Through [the] many dangers, toils, and snares I have already come,"[101] I know that sticking it out those three months would have been much more difficult for me.

My personal program then was strictly one of personal growth through faith, introspection, reading the writings of the great mystics and spiritual doctors such as Theresa of Avila, St. John of the Cross, *The Cloud of Unknowing*, Fenelon, Clarence Engler, and contemporary popular Christian writers like the Sherrills, Wilkerson, ten Boom, Thomas Merton, Henri J. M. Nouwen, and Gabrielle Bossis.[102]

*

Dear Journal,

Perhaps because I have time to think and write, I am more in touch with what is working and is not working in my life. How certain federal policies and city and county and court policies directly impacted on my life and that of my children. For example, if Judge Wilson had been appropriate and effective in the beginning, I believe none of these falling dominoes would have

---

[101] Newton, John: "Amazing Grace." Ascribed to Sir John Ries.

[102] Later I would also discover the self-help concepts through books and classes dealing with topics such as "codependency," "boundaries," "family systems theory," which brought me improved interpersonal skills.

toppled over. I believe my life and my children's lives would be a lot different.

Although for me being on the street is appropriate for now, I feel a nonspecific shame about it. Most of the people I meet on the street are decent people, broken people, fragile people, who are trying to take responsibility for their lives and make changes but are deeply enmeshed in a system that works to perpetuate their dependency.

But I am absolutely certain that I won't be on the street even one day more than absolutely necessary. I have had enough. I am getting lonely, isolated, alienated, and ill. I needed to move on and to heal.

Unfortunately, moving on isn't an option.

*

Dear Journal,

While I was making the loss list to acknowledge the losses, I realized that I do not count the end of my 13-year marriage as a loss, only as a beginning. The real loss was the amount of time we had spent trying to make it work.

*

GRACE

Dear Journal,

I have been reading a series of Anne Morrow Lindbergh books that I found on the bookcase beside the plaster Jesus statue. She was another wife connected by marriage to Minnesota. She suffered that horrible kidnaping and murder of her son. I can learn from her. How did she handle grief?

I have been trying to achieve what Anne Morrow Lindbergh discussed in *Gift from the Sea*:

> But I want first of all— in fact, as an end to these other desires— to be at peace with myself. I want a singleness of eye, a purity of intentions, a central core to my life that will enable me to carry out these obligations and activities as well as I can. I want, in fact— to borrow from the language of the saints— to live "in grace" as much of the time as possible .... By grace, I mean an inner harmony, essentially spiritual, which can be translated into

outward harmony. I am seeking perhaps what Socrates asked for in prayer . . . when he said, "May the outward and inward man [person] be at one." I would like to achieve a state of inner spiritual grace from which I could function and give as I was meant to give in the eye of God.[103]

*

ISSUES OF MEANING AND REDEMPTIVE SUFFERING

Dear God,

I thought a lot about why bad things happen to good people, and why Job got all that grief for so long, and all the miseries the prophets had to endure for doing their prophet thing. And I don't have good answers. I am struggling to understand what might be the purpose of suffering. I think suffering must mean something entirely different from Your perspective, God, than from ours. Maybe You are looking at the top of the woven fabric, and we only see the knots on the underside.

I know You said somewhere in scripture that the people You don't care about can run amuck; but those You love, You chastise and prune. I guess You love me a lot. Right now, I don't feel thankful for this pain if that's how You show your love. St. Theresa of Avila said, "No wonder you don't have many friends: look how You treat them."[104] I take that one step further. I am terrified about being considered a "child of God"— look what You did to Jesus. If you do that to Your own kid, what would You do to the rest of us? Look what you did to your employees— Peter, Paul, and all the other martyred apostles and saints. And even what You allow us to do to ourselves? Why? Is it a set up? Jesus said we have to be willing to drink of the cup of suffering. Why? What is the significance? Why the cup of suffering? That's why I think You are

---

[103] Lindbergh, Anne Morrow: *Gifts from the Sea*, New York:Pantheon Books, 1975, pp. 23-24.

[104] Attributed to St. Theresa of Avila.

keeping something secret. I think suffering must be a key to something— a secret passage. I think perhaps suffering is a key to wisdom.

∗

Dear Journal,

For the past year I have been working on learning to give up being a controlling person: It was hard to do.

What works best is to try to live one day at a time. On the street that's about all I can do anyway. I keep thinking about having to live from day to day because of the uncertainty of the court schedule, my sons care and needs, and the uncertainties that court has placed on every thread of the fabric of my life. Sometimes it hard to live one day at a time. Sometimes one hour at a time. When it is really bad, at times, I have to deal with five minutes at a time.

∗

GOD'S TIME

Dear Journal,

I am learning to accept God's timing. God has always provided, so far, but when the delivery is so slow I do get concerned. I wish God really would "free me from all inappropriate anxiety and grant me peace in my day." I think anxiety is fear disguised, and fear is sometimes a lack of trust. Is anxiety a fear that God just might let me down? Or not come through soon enough? I wondered if God gets perturbed by our anxieties? I didn't want to perturb God, for heaven's sake.

All I know is that I have had a lot of troubles over the last few years and every time I have prayed intensely— even as a last resort,— I have always gotten an answer but only before the last minute. Unfortunately it was not always the answer I wanted. Sometimes the answer was "Not yet. Arrangements are not yet in place." Sometimes I didn't get what I wanted the way I wanted: Usually though, I got what I truly needed. Frequently, in trusting in God to provide, I have noticed that the provisions come only at the last minute. God doesn't seem to send anything early. It takes Time for me to get things ready, and we are supposed to be in the image and likeness of God. I guess it takes God Time to get things ready. In the Bible, an angel apologized for being three weeks late making a delivery.[105] The angel's excuse was that it had to wrestle with a force which tried to detain it from its mission. Look at how long it took Jesus to get to heaven and then to send the Holy Spirit back to the Apostles. Jesus had told them: Wait right here so that when I send the Spirit back, It will know where to find you.[106] So even 'Time Travel' must take Time.

Does God ever procrastinate? Does God have a subconscious mind? What is the meaning of Time to God? What is the function of Time for God? What is God's Time? Maybe our measure of Time isn't so important to God.

*

SUFFERING

Dear Journal,

I think suffering makes other changes in some people. At first I thought just wisdom. Now I think there are other parts of it, too. Like discernment: It's like a nonverbal understanding, deeper than words.

*

ANCHOR

Dear Journal,

It is clear that a major survival skill for me is in allowing my spirituality to become my anchor— my anchor of sanity within this crazy situation. Daily Mass and Communion are my real food— not by Danish alone does a person live. Mass and Communion are feeding my spirit, sustaining me and my love for my sons: that love for them keeps me going now.

*

---

[105]   Genesis 32:25-30, *The Bible.*

[106]   Acts 1:4-6.

Dear Journal,

Someone asked me casually, "How are you surviving the winter, the month of January?" The person was not aware that temporarily I had become a penniless Street Person. The only answer to "How are you surviving the winter?" that I could think to say was, "By courage. Sheer courage." The person seemed startled by my response. I'm sure the person had no inkling of the depth of courage it took for me to get through each day. I had to get closer to God to help me sustain that courage. Once a fortune cookie message I received read, "Happiness is a form of courage."

Most people said something like, "Winter's not that bad— just bundle up, run from the warm house to the warm car, drive with the heater on, park in the ramp, then run to the heated Skyway to go to a heated office." But, of course, that isn't my day-to-day experience just now.

✳

SPIRITUAL FOOD

Dear Journal,

Feeding my spirit is my key to surviving this ordeal. I began to live the Daily Mass and love it. Especially the prayer which follows the Our Father:

> Deliver us, Lord, from every evil,
> and grant us peace in our day.
>
> In your mercy, keep us free from sin
> and protect us from all anxiety
> as we wait in joyful hope
> for the coming of our Savior, Jesus Christ.
> For the kingdom, the power,
> and the glory are yours
> now and forever.[107]

---

[107] Catholic Book Publishing Company, *New ... Complete St. Joseph's Daily Missal: Vol I—Advent to Pentecost,* New York: Catholic Books Publishing Co., 1975, pp. 646-647.

In the Catholic tradition, the anchor symbolizes Hope. Through prayer, I can stay in what I call "an Attitude of Hope." In this way, I manage to stay grounded and become serene despite living through the insanities of the system. Once I got to that plateau the inner harmony and serenity became strong despite the outward turmoil and awkward circumstances. The prayer says "in joyful hope."

An *Attitude of Hope* is an attitude that the situation or circumstance is not *hopeless*. It is a call to action rather than apathy. It is quite different from "think positive," which can be permission to deny reality. An *Attitude of Hope* is a general and pervasive position, and is distinct from "Hope for," which is a wish for a specific, defined objective or outcome which may or may not occur. It feels different from being optimistic. Hope seems more expectant, perhaps expectant anticipation. An *Attitude of Hope*, I believe, is the forerunner of Trust. The expression of this Trust is Belief.

One radio preacher said: "Hoping is closer to wishing and it is not as strong as believing. If you hope God will do it [as in 'hope for'], you give God the option not to. But if you maintain [an Attitude of] Hope, and you trust and believe intensely enough, that's a different story."

✳

WAITING AND TRUSTING

I do not believe that "trusting in God" means just to plop down and wait for a miracle. I believe strongly in "Active Waiting." In trusting that God will provide, we must undertake the preparations to make it possible and to be ready. A marquee on a Lancaster PA Rescue Mission read, "God does everything in two steps. You take the first step. God takes the second." A friend from North Dakota said her 12-step group taught her, "Faith can move mountains; bring your shovel."

✳

DEPENDENCE ON GOD

Dear Journal,

In addition to spiritual food and scriptural inspiration, I placed my dependence on God that I would be provided with tangible necessities too. And while resources came to me through many persons, many parts of The System, and by happenstance, I thanked God each day for directly or indirectly making this possible. While, to some, total dependence on God may seem naive, it made perfect sense to me. *I now believe that coincidence is Providence.* It has provided for me in multitudinous ways. Looking at it from another perspective: since I had nothing, I had nothing else to lose, so "Why Not?" I think that's what Jesus was getting at, with the rich man getting through the eye of the needle. He had more baggage and therefore more to lose. Jesse Lair paraphrases it "Here is a splendid, abundant life for you, all you need to do is let loose of' your garbage."[108]

✻

PAT'S PRAYER 1

Dear Lord,
Send more grace, Lord, I'm leaking.
Help me God,
Help my children.
Lamb of God, help my Lambs.
Lamb of God, help me.
Lamb of God, give my Lambs and me Peace, in our day, in Your mercy and kindness.
Now, please.

✻

---

[108] Jesse Lair, *"I Ain't Well— But I Sure Am Better": Mutual Need Therapy.* Garden City, NY: Doubleday and Company, Inc., 1975, p. 188.

SUFFICIENCY

Dear Journal,

I asked God for help and promised to be satisfied with whatever God would find as a way to provide as long as it is "enough— just enough." After all, if I had asked for "more than enough" that might mean some would be wasted and maybe someone else wouldn't get enough of something because I had been greedy for more. And while on the street, the thought occurred to me, that if I got "more than enough" I might have to carry it around.[109]

✳

HOW TO 'ASK AND YOU SHALL RECEIVE'

Dear Journal,

Through all this personal turmoil, I have trusted God to provide enough and God has (directly and indirectly). God hasn't let me down once— but often it's been at the last minute. Jesus said, "Ask and you shall receive." So I decided: if He said it, He meant it. *What I learned in this experiment is that the more specific the request, the more likely it is to be provided.* For example, if I prayed, "God, I need $471 for airplane fare to fly from Williamsport to Minneapolis for Court on October 15" and continued to pray about it, a check in that amount (from a forgotten insurance claim from sometime earlier) arrived in the mail the day before I had to depart. (God must not know that Super Saver fares require advance reservations and payment!) Ah, yes, God is Timeless. On the other hand, if I prayed, "Dear God, I need to be out of court-related debt. Please help me out of debt," but didn't give all the specifics, not much happened and whatever did happen happened slowly. It isn't just money. It has been that way with whatever I asked (presuming it wasn't harmful for me).

✳

---

[109] I now think this prayer for just sufficiency discounted God's power and desire to give abundantly also.

ATTITUDE OF TRUST

Dear God,

One thing I am learning is that by totally trusting in You that "God will provide," even while I am in this struggle to provide for myself, I am able to keep concerns to a manageable level. It also gives me a better attitude most of the time, making my ordeals and tribulations seem more bearable. I am learning from Street People. Those with a good attitude also have this childlike trust despite the hardships. Things seemed to be better for those who trust in You than for either the ones who are seething with rage about anything and everything, or the ones who are passive, almost not there.

THOMAS MERTON'S PRAYER[110]

I found the Thomas Merton's prayer helpful in trying to accept all of this:

MY LORD GOD, I have no idea where I am going. I do not see the road ahead of me. I cannot know for certain where it will end. Nor do I really know myself and the fact that I think that I am following Your will does not mean that I am actually doing so. But I believe that the desire to please You does in fact please You. And I hope that I will never do anything apart from that desire. And I know that if I do this, You will lead me by the right road though I may know nothing about it. Therefore I will trust You always though I may seem to be lost in the shadow of death. I will not fear, for You are ever with me, and You will never leave me to face my perils alone.

---

[110]   Thomas Merton a/k/a Brother Louie, was, until his untimely death, a member of the Trappist order of monks at the Abbey of Gethsemani, Gethsemani, KY.

Figure 15.   Three-coats trudging through the snow.

Dear God,

What will normal be for us? God, help me face the future. Many days the past was a living hell. Sometimes I think that hell after death is a myth, that we've been in it all along. I had hoped this would be the beginning of "better." Thank you for teaching me to live one day at a time.

Please help me to temper my "take charge" attitude and my need for reassurance about income. I have wanted to know what paying job contract I will have and I want to have control over where I live. It seems I don't have freedom anymore since the Minnesota Courts took jurisdiction. It's the old "God, give me patience, and I need it now."

The mountains by our house gave me strength and assurance. Lord, if I have to stay here in this flat landscape, send me mountains of strength. I'm going to need it. You have tested my strength, over and over again, and often provided some little comforts and assurances— like in the fall, when I was feeling so alone going up the steps to court, and there was a ladybug on the step and I had the thought that the ladybug is so tiny it doesn't see me stepping around it. And I thought about how vast You must be, that I am like that little ladybug on the courthouse step unaware of what movement is taking place in the universe to protect me.

I need some more reassurances like that, now. I had hoped, prayed, Lord, that somewhere this week or this month, You or someone would say, "It's okay now. It's going to be all right. The bad time is all over. It's going to be better." But it just goes on. At least it keeps me close in touch with you, God. I need you. Help me through this terrible time. Keep me whole, Lord, in mind and body. Keep my Spirit, and your Spirit in me, strong. Hear me and help!

*

DUKING IT OUT WITH GOD

Dear God,

You know I am trying to Let Go about all of this. Being angry with You doesn't change anything. Bargaining with you doesn't get my kids back. Being infuriated by the court fiasco doesn't repair the damage. Being resentful of the built-in "adversarialness" of the divorce process doesn't change it. I really get discouraged. I can't hurry the court. I can't hurry the hospital. I can't hurry the healing. I can't even walk away— even though I was willing if that is what it would take to keep my children safe.

I used to think I could do anything I set my mind to, but not this time. This is different. Since nothing on earth seems to be working to get this case resolved, I don't think this is about my ex-husband and me any more. I don't think it is about the court any more. I think it has something to do with You. I think this battle is between You and me and I don't like it. Get real, how can I win against God? What did I do to bring this on? What is your gripe with my kids? They are good kids. What is Your gripe with me? I have been a good person. What do You get out of letting my kids be hurt and keeping me in these circumstances? Believe me, I can depend on You without being this miserable! I am putting You on notice, God, that if this is some kind of a game for You, I'm not playing. I give up. I'm crying "Quit it, I've had enough."

Oh, I get it— You want to prove to me I'm powerless. You want to show me I can't resolve it or end the case on my own. Okay. You win: I can't. But You could. But you won't, 'til You're good and ready. Well, get the message, God. I'm ready.

✻

Dear God,

I am trying to put it into words, God, but prose doesn't express my anguish. I think King David must have hit this impasse too, then he got the format down. [That night I decided to give it a try and wrote Pat's Psalm 1.]

PAT'S PSALM 1

I cry to You, my Lord,
I am burdened in this life.
I work for You each day, all day long,
And live in Your loving Presence.
Provide for me manna in many forms.
Shower me with blessings— of enough,
Of freedom from debt, from anxiety,
From unfulfilled longing, from grief.

Bless my children, whom I do not see,
Watch over and guide them as I cannot.
Help me hold up those around me, as You
Continue to hold me up, with Your loving care.
You are my security and my employer.
You are my insurance and provider.
You nurture my soul and love me, even in my weakness.
Do not drop me with unconcern.

Be real as my Savior.
Love me even in my failures. Provide some successes.
Give me true humility that crashes barriers
And opens, unfolds effectiveness.
Give me the courage to see Your leading.
Give me the strength to endure Your long testing.
"*Uncle*" I cry to You; Your tests are so hard.
I give You my difficult path.

Make me sure-footed and bold in Your ways.
Lead me to the stillness that quiets my soul.
Unfold for me the rewards of each day.
Restore joy to my inmost self.
Open my eyes to see Your miracles in action.
Open my ears to hear Your loving words.
Open my heart from scars and wounds of sadness.
Liberate my mind in Your light.

Wash me in compassion.
Clothe me in Your wisdom.
Shelter me in Your goodness.
Protect me with Your angels.
Feed my soul with Your intimate all-love.
Inspire me with Your Spirit.
Open me to Your human vulnerability
But close me to hurts that might follow.

Lift me from the pain of losses.
Surround me with vision and intuitive foresight.
Bring back my young ones (to You, and to me).
Heal the aches that beat at my soul.
Remove the barriers that impede loving kindness.
You know I am all Yours.
When will my raw ore be sufficiently melted?
When will I be molded enough?

When will the living debts to You be satisfied?
When will the suffering cease?
Do not be offended that I ask,
But perhaps I cannot bear the answer.
You have given much— I am asking.
You have offered much— I am taking.
You have hidden much— I am seeking.
I am knocking at the door of heaven.

Let me in or let some of it spill over here.
Give some answers. Create some solutions.
If suffering cannot cease, Help me and mine to grow appropriately
Through the wisdom of Your will.
I surrender, I forgive, I give.
We claim all Your love, all Your blessings.
We claim all Your nourishment, Your healing. We claim Your delight.
You are only. You are all. There is nothing else.

Dear Journal,

Again I want to clarify what was changing and what is remaining the same. What needed to change? What needed to remain the same? I am changing somehow. I think I am tougher.

Almost immediately after this series of prayer, the bureaucracy began to move with more than deliberate speed and changes happened in quick succession. My son was released from the hospital. In a complicated series of rulings, unbelievably the court ruled that Minnesota had become my children's permanent home state and they would not be permitted to return home to Pennsylvania; since I was not a Minnesota resident and Hennepin County would not permit a "home study" of our home in Pennsylvania despite the willingness of the Pennsylvania jurisdiction, my younger son was placed in a foster home until I could make arrangements to permanently move to Minnesota, thereby splitting up the family.

Almost the same day, I learned that many shelters in the Twin Cities shut down as soon as the calendar indicates that worst of the winter has probably ended: the House of Charity informed me that it would be closing for the season and all occupants (guests) must vacate on or before March 31.

＊

After filing for divorce, I have had many problems develop in rapid succession (an ugly divorce, court stress, the court-ordered visitation with their father from which my children did not return, and the failure of the court and the sheriff to enforce legal remedies, geographic relocations, oral surgeries, financial distress, changes in type and places of work).

Dear God,

I am trying to get a handle on what You are teaching me and what helps me stay together. I have been struggling to come up with a list of principles or precepts to help me stay grounded, to consolidate what I am learning, and to use later too.

＊

27 Directives for Coping

Dear God,
What would you have me learn?

1. Have clear priorities and purpose for going through this. I know why I am here (on the street) and why (for my children).

2. Keep my identity distinct from the situation I am in (now) just as I have always kept my identity distinct from what work I agree to do.

3. "Shield" myself from inappropriate looks, projections, and judgments.

4. Telling my story is so painful, I am having to shut down my feelings (dehumanize) to be able to relate it when I have to, but even more important is to somehow reconnect with those feelings afterward to stay a person, human and healthy. (I need more help with this, God.)

5. Create a sense of place even in strange surroundings. I am so yearning for familiar geography. Familiar history. Familiar surroundings. Creature comforts. A hot tea in a cozy chair beside a fireplace crackling and warm.

6. Attend to my inner process to stay grounded.

7. Make lemonade (when life sours). I must remember to ask for the sugar and lemon along with the glass of water.

8. Stay alert to the humor and absurdities going on around me.

9. Find a way to tell my story without blowing away the compassionate listener by using word skills and body language to communicate in ways appropriate and considerate of the listener so that the listener can take what is being conveyed and the information itself can cross the cultural and attitudinal chasms.

10. Apply 'active waiting.'

11. Keep asking questions.

12. Let go of Fear of Hunger.

13. Grieve and be open to what grief is and does.

14. Be aware that people are often influenced by the messages they have absorbed from faddish ideas in current pop culture, of which one may be unaware. Popular culture frequently shapes the attitudes with which people listen, then filter and reinterpret what is being said to them-- so that what you said and meant may result in a confused conclusion on their part that is not at all what you were stating. In effect popular culture is often a hidden component influencing conversations.

15. Learn to live one day at a time.

16. Accept that "time" is a perceptual viewpoint, not the same for all people or in all circumstances.

17. Learn to let go and let God.

18. Learn to accept God's timing.

19. Appreciate the significance of paradox.

20. Surrender the need to be in control.

21. Learn to live in an "attitude of spiritual dependence."

22. Learn to remain in an "attitude of hope" about any situation.

23. Reframe problems into opportunities.

24. Pray for all concerned that we may reach a reasonable, appropriate, satisfying, timely and peaceful solution.

25. Take time out frequently to write 'Dear Journal' entries and 'Dear God' letters.

26. Know that coincidence is Providence.

27. Listen to You, God, and respond to the nudges of the Spirit.

✳

Dear God,

Why didn't You give out a list like this when You passed out the 10 Commandments?

✳

Dear Journal,

I am beginning to recognize the deep personal significance of accepting a paradox. I needed to follow a 'road less traveled' in order to be on the right road for me.

I feel as if so much of my self, perhaps my more superficial self, has been melted away. What remains feels like the select metal of my being.

I think that God views suffering and uses suffering differently than our view of it. That while we do not welcome suffering, when it is unavoidable, suffering can be a teacher, can be a cruicible in which we are subjected to tremendous heat and pressure, but can leave us in the end more compassionate, purified, grounded, and with increased insight and depth.

✳

PART IX: DISENGAGING

My last full day at the House of Charity was the most bizarre of all my experiences there. The weather was warming. The six foot high glaciers formed of solid ice (snow ice) piled at the edge of the sidewalks and streets were receding, depositing a residue of glacial debris along the edges. Some people were searching for dropped coins at the bases of parking meters. With the advent of weather in the 20 to 30 degree range, the men at the shelter who were seasonal workers had left, and it was less crowded. Others were heading out to stake a claim under a bridge or in a park, because most of the shelters would shut down April 1 and not reopen until the winter set in again. With the men pulling out, the population left behind were those who couldn't take the rigors of any outdoor living and must remain at the shelter. The population at the House of Charity shifted. Those who could not head for greener pastures remained. They were the more elderly, mentally ill, physically infirmed and destitute women. This left a concentration of the remaining Street People at the House of Charity of the mentally deranged, many of whom came into prominence in my encounters on my last full day there.

✳

THE HANDBAG

I spent most of that last day on the street being attentive to what was going on around me. At Mass in St. Olaf's Chapel, there were few seats available. I found a somewhat vacant chair in a back row except a Church Lady wearing a pink Harris tweed coat had her leather handbag on the seat. I went into the row and stood there for a minute or more, but the lady made no indication that she was willing to remove her handbag so that I could sit down. I guess I looked more like a Street Person now than I realized, but I was there for Mass, and I needed a place to sit down, so I moved her handbag into her lap.

That really got her attention. She was uneasy from then on. She moved the handbag to her other side, holding it tight. She fidgeted constantly through the service and gave me dark looks from the corner of her eye. When it was time for the Peace of Christ handshake, she would not shake my hand, but stood hostilely crouched over her handbag. At Communion, she made no indication that she intended to go up front, so I stood up to pass in front of her to get out to the aisle. As soon as I took the first step, she startled, grabbed her purse and ran out of the church. I'm sure this Church Lady will tell everyone there was a purse-snatcher in St. Olaf's Chapel.

*

ANNE BEGINS TO TELL THE STORY OF CREATION

After Mass, I was at the book rack to select a book for a gift for a neighbor at home who had been watching my apartment and watering the plants. Anne was over in the corner, on the bench, talking to herself in a little-girl voice. She was rambling out loud, and I listened at a distance:

"There was a story of the beginning of the world. God made a handsome man. He called him Adam. But the translation in this country is Andrew. Some places he is called Devon. Then God made a woman Eve. He gave them a tour of the place in the garden, and he showed them all around, especially a really pretty fruit tree full of red ripe fruit. He said, 'Leave the fruit tree alone. It's mine.'"

"Along came a creature that told Adam, 'Pick the cherries. They are red luscious and ripe. Eat the cherries. They're delicious.' So Adam and Eve ate the red plump cherries. Not Eve alone. They did this together. Men who wrote the first books about it said that about Eve to keep men out of trouble."

"Adam liked the cherries, and he picked and ate a whole bunch. The cherries made him hungry for other things too. So he took Eve and roughly pushed her down and got down on her. 'Cause he said, 'I like all kinds of cherries now.'"

"Eve said, 'Adam, you're gonna be in big trouble.' She was shaking and naked and scared of what Adam had done taking the cherries and pushing down on her and all."

"The raspy voice that talked to them in the garden told them, 'Don't worry. It was okay. You did what I told you to do.'"

"Then an Angel came along and told them, 'Get out! Get out of the garden right now!'"

"'Why?' asked Adam."

"''Cause God told you not to touch THAT tree! He made those cherries for Himself on the tree. He told you they were His. Don't mess with God's stuff.'"

"Eve asked, 'Where do we go?   Is there any place else in creation?'"

"The Angel said, 'Just go. You have to find the way yourself.' For the rest of his life, Devon never asked for directions. Then Devon and Eve were leaving, and God came to say goodbye."

"God said, 'Adam. The tree was mine. Mine alone. You and Eve ate the cherries— perfect ripe luscious cherries. You are both cherries. You are cherries for each other.'"

"'But you had to go messing with my tree so I don't want you here now. You treat each other decent. You are a special fruit of my tree, not to be left to rot, but taken care of to be ripe and ready, to share cherry fruit.'"

Anne continued talking to the air, "But when I told my Doctor this story 'bout the cherries and the First People and how that man took Eve and pushed on her and scared her— when I told him all this, you know what he said to me?"

"He said, 'Anne, forget all this stuff about God's cherries. Maybe even some is right. Maybe God made some people cherries. But God didn't make you a cherry, Anne. So forget it. God made you a Walnut. And there ain't nothing you can do about it.' That's what he said. 'You're a Walnut, Anne: don't forget it.'"

Her voice was filled with rising anger, and she got up off the bench and stomped out. "He called me a walnut! A nut!"

Then I went up to Catholic Charities to complete some volunteer work I had been doing in the office. I wondered about Anne's childhood. Many of the street women I talked to had been victims of rape, usually by incest. This was even more true for the women who identified themselves as lesbians. From Anne's ramblings, it sounded like Anne been raped when she was young, and these ramblings were the way her unconscious tried to deal with the repressed memories.

I didn't talk to Anne, as I was worried about my Manpower check and had to get to their office to see if the check had arrived. If not, I needed to make arrangements to have it forwarded. It was two weeks late, and I needed the money for my trip back home. The check did not arrive.

After meeting with Manpower, I went into the lobby of the Midwest Federal bank and sat on a bench to rearrange the papers in my rucksack. In the back of the atrium, a gazebo was set up to advertise wood construction. There were potted mums among the wood chips surrounding the gazebo. Electric cords were around the circumference under the wood chips connecting spotlights to highlight the gazebo. It had a shake shingle roof, redwood lattice work panels and sides, window openings, and deck chairs.

As I sorted through my papers to decide what to keep for the trip and what to throw away. I heard a familiar voice muttering. I looked up, and there in the gazebo sat Anne. She sat in a deck chair, had her legs propped up on the railing, and was casually smoking discarded cigarette butts. There were tiny tables there, littered with empty waxed beverage cups. She was using one for an ashtray. She lit a another cigarette from the stub of the first, then flicked the first over the railing.

I turned back to my sorting until I began to smell smoke. Immediately the building smoke alarms went off and people were screaming and pointing to the wood chips. Sparks were shooting out of the electrical cord around the back of the gazebo, the cord under the wood chips. Flames began to climb up the trellis. Almost instantly, maintenance men arrived with fire extinguishers. Soon the fire department arrived with water hoses, flooding the wood chips, floodlights, and electrical wires.

No one noticed Anne spacing out in the gazebo, smoking another cigarette, muttering away. She seemed annoyed by the commotion interrupting her privacy. She got up, walked regally down the steps of the gazebo, and left the building going out through the door connected to the Foshay Tower, oblivious to the fire, the smoke, and the frantic firemen at the back of the flaming gazebo.

After the excitement of watching the gazebo turn to charcoal, I got back to the details of my life, trying to arrange to go home. I found I was eligible for the infamous "Bus Ticket Out". I obtained a bus ticket and $100 travel money. The bureaucracy called this program and ticket a Bus Ticket Home, but the Street People called it a "Bus Ticket Out," because they had no home to which to go. So even the generosity of a free bus ticket, because of its misnomer, felt like a slap in the face.

At 9 a.m., I returned to the House of Charity to see what time the social worker would be in, so that I could confirm that I would be taking a bus out.

*

LEE'S RACKET

A slender young woman was waiting outside the House of Charity. She had an intense austereness about her. She looked frantic, perplexed and somewhat disoriented. I asked, "May I help you?"

With a pleading look, the woman responded, "I need a place to stay."

I said, "House of Charity offices doesn't open for an hour. Do you want to come with me for coffee and then come back here in an hour?"

"No. No. I'll be okay."

"You could go inside and wait in the waiting room. It's like a living room. That way you can be one of the first to put your name on the housing list. Since rooms are given out 'first come, first served,' it's important to put your name on the list early." I sounded like an old-timer.

"No. No. Please. I'm not washed. They might smell me." She said, looking from side to side to see if anyone had heard.

"They'll never notice you. It's okay. Most everyone else here is the same way," I laughed.

"Oh, no. I couldn't. I might pass gas."

"Believe me, they'll never notice. Just go in and have a seat. I'll be back later, maybe I'll see you then." Two hours later, I was back. She was now inside of the storm door sitting on the lowest steps of the vestibule.

"Let me take you inside. I could introduce you at the desk. It's really important to get your name on the list because there is a lot of competition for rooms."

Figure 16. Lee.

"Oh no. I couldn't. Don't put yourself out for me. Please let me be."

"Okay, I'll be back later. Get yourself inside, though, so you can see the social worker."

I came back at 12:30. By then, I had mentally named her Lee, since I did not yet know her name. When I arrived, Lee had made her way up to the top step. But the social workers had left for their lunch hour. Lee had her reddish-blond hair neatly pulled back under a beret. She sat with her face in her lean hands. Her hands had blotchy dry skin. The wore thick wool socks in pack boots and a thin white coat that looked as if all the stuffing had gone out of it. "Oh, please. Don't bother about me. I've put you to too much trouble already. Please don't do anything more for me."

What HAD I done, I wondered? "I have to go now. You go on into the lobby and get your name on that Housing list before it's too late. You got to get on the list early if you want a room."

At 3:30 p.m. I came back. She had made it to the night desk just inside the vestibule. She was hanging back along the wall, trying to seem inconspicuous, but she still had not made it into the lobby.

"Hi. Have you been in yet? Did you get a room?"

"Oh no. I wouldn't want to put anyone to any trouble for me."

"Housing is 'first come first served.' You'd better get on the list. They will be closing in a few minutes."

"No. I'll be all right. I just want to talk to the social worker. Now please leave me alone."

I looked around the room. Aeneas and Dolly were preening in their new clothes. Max was bumming a cigarette from Domingo. The Man-in-the-Iron-Mask was sitting in the shadow of the gigantic Jesus. He had dumped the contents of his bed-roll on the floor and was carefully rearranging the stuff in a new order. Sarah was sitting next to him, looking at the ceiling, muttering.

Anne was rambling to herself, sitting on a metal chair. Beside her was an elderly woman wearing a lace bonnet under a knit skicap. The skicap was pulled down to her eyebrows, and the lace showed around the edges. She had round rosy cheeks and an angelic look about her. Lee was still in line at the reception desk.

I went into the lobby and plopped down in the main room in a chair next to Cathy and Dennis who were sitting on the love seat. They were having a disagreement about whether Cathy should be friendly with bag ladies (who mutter). Dennis was mad at Cathy for talking to the old lady called Sarah. Sarah looked so much like a man that it was a full month before I realized that this six-foot tall person in combat boots was female.

Earlier in the day, when Cathy ran into Sarah, Sarah had been muttering because she had been kicked out of the Skyway above 8th Street for muttering too loudly to the reflection of herself in the glass, and had been thrown out of the Crystal Court for panhandling cigarettes. (Legalism: it's okay to gather butts from the ashtrays or the floor, but not to ask for one.) I saw them shortly after I left the TCF Atrium where the gazebo had burned. I watched Cathy say "Hello" to Sarah and Sarah answered. Then suddenly Cathy was in a three-way conversation with two copies of Sarah, carried on within herself.

Sarah #1 said, "Who asked you to put in your 2¢?"

Sarah #2 said to Sarah #1, "Hey, I want to talk to her. You're interrupting. Bug off. Ain't it bad enough you got us kicked out of the Skyway?"

Sarah #1 answered, "Bug off yourself, or I'll give you a fist in the face!" At this point, Dennis thought Sarah #2 was threatening Cathy so he grabbed Cathy and pulled her away.

Cathy said to me, "I talk to her sometimes. No one else pays any attention to her, and she must be lonely. Sometimes we have a nice visit. But sometimes if I, or if anybody, talks to her long, she gets violently angry. Today she was angry about being evicted from the Skyway. She was angry from that, not from anything I said. Dennis didn't understand."

"I know you mean well, honey. But I think you are asking for trouble."

"Dennis doesn't like me to talk to bag ladies, but I think they are interesting people and have regular-people feelings. It seems like we should at least say 'Hello.' It's not like walking up to a complete stranger. After all, we are all living in the same house. We all have similar problems."

"Have similar problems," echoed[111] the Woman-in-the-Bonnet whose bonnet held her hair in place under the skicap. Her small features were squished tightly together, all in the middle of her face. Her jaw jutted forward, and she had no teeth. She was fat and squat.

Over in the corner, Anne was continuing the saga of Adam and Eve, now out of the garden: "And then Adam invented names for things. He looked at Eve, and he gave things names like tits, pits, twat, tummy, and pussy. Adam said, 'I like that name. I like pussy best of all'."

"I like pussy best of all," echoed the old lady loudly. Conversation in the room stopped. About 50 men turned to stare at Anne and the old lady.

Oblivious Anne continued to ramble, "Then Adam, called Devon, named things for himself— muscles, brains, hair. 'Should I call it cock or Charlie? I'll call it cock when it's sleeping, and Charlie when it's awake.'"

"'Cock when it's sleeping and Charlie when it's awake,'" echoed the lady.

Then the men made a few remarks like "Shut up, you old hags," and then went back to their conversations.

"Shut up you old hags," the Woman-in-the-Bonnet repeated.

The social workers worked late that afternoon. Soon the young woman, Lee, was the only one left who had not had a turn. She had stepped into the back corner of the room, but she still had not crossed the room to put her name on the list. Finally, as the social workers were locking the office door, she approached them. "Please, do you have a room for me for the night?"

"I'm terribly sorry. We are all filled up for tonight. You should have come here this morning," the social worker said gently.

"Should have come this morning," the lady echoed.

Lee glared at the social worker, her face distorted with rage. She shouted, "I knew it would be useless applying. Turned away again. Rejected! Always rejected! No money for bus fare. No place to go. I knew it would be this way!"

---

[111] She had a mental condition called "Echolalia" which means she had a compulsion to echo whatever was said.

"Rejected. Always rejected," echoed the Woman-in-the-Bonnet. I thought to myself "*I'll really be glad when I can go home from this loony bin. Tomorrow I can get on a bus and go home.*"

"*Go home. Go home,*" my mind echoed.

✳

Dear Journal,

Hard times. What causes hard times? Circumstances? Unemployment? Ill health? Past bad habits or crises that have left broken bodies and deadened spirits?

I have met only one Street Person who was content to be on the street. It is a life of waiting in lines, humiliation, cold, and discouragement. Occasionally Street People help one another. Mostly they are very alone.

The majority of Street People were mentally disabled.

Some Street People are trying very hard to climb out of the cracks in the pavement and back up into economic stability, security, and financial independence. Many would like to have "a job, just a job" as Leonard had mentioned. But along the way, it is a hungry path. Winter, especially winter in Minneapolis, requires more calories. Even if it is mostly donuts or Reagan cheese.

✳

LEAVE-TAKING

The following morning, I got out my luggage cart, loaded on a suitcase, a brief case, a sports bag, and my rucksack. Except for the six spiral notebooks of my journal, I left with the same amount I arrived with, minus one pair of shoes (which I had given away) and my engraved Cross pen (which had been lost.) I put on my navy-blue suit and pulled on my parka. As I left, I caught my reflection in the glass. I was horrified by my changed appearance.

My navy-blue Sierra Designs parka was now a dark brown. The top pocket was torn and dangling down. The lower two pockets were worn through at all four corners. The coat stunk of stale cigarettes and I don't smoke. No matter how much I put water on my hair to hold it down, it was thin and kept sticking out in points.

I had a broken eye-tooth dangling in my mouth, and other teeth were loose; one was abscessed.

I was weak. I was ashen. But looking at the reflection, what really scared me was my eyes: my eyes were sunken. There were heavy blue circles under my eyes. My eyelashes had fallen out. There was a stare in my eyes, like shell shock.

I had survived winter, surgery, gangrene, pneumonia, another round of court, and the pit beneath the safety net. I was still the same person. My spirit was still strong. My spiritual life was deep and rejuvenated. The House of Charity, in hindsight, seemed like a retreat center. I had accomplished a solid three months of library research, reading, and journaling. I survived with mental clarity. I had met and mingled with interesting people in a way I never would have planned.

I began the walk up 8th Street to the Loop Station Post Office where at last I received all my mail— the mail that had been crossing the country from central Pennsylvania to Minneapolis, and the same mail that was sent back to my home and returned again: my mail made two round trips from December to March while I was walking and standing in line in Minneapolis without funds. Some of the Christmas cards contained money from relatives.

Max walked a few blocks with me to the bus station, to say "Goodbye." Aeneas and Dolly came over and gave me a big hug. At the ticket counter, I presented my "Bus Ticket Out."

The trip was a mixture of numbness, relief, and a sense of failure. I had succeeded in getting medical care for one son, but no change in circumstance for the other. The medical care was not at the Children's Hospital in Pennsylvania, where arrangements had been made by my son's physician, and the care provided through the court didn't really fill his need either. I had failed in getting my children what they really needed through the court, and what this round of court had decreed in the short and long run resulted in making matters worse. The children were not permitted to testify, speak to a judge, or at any hearing during this period. I was once again having to leave without my children, and without even having a satisfactory visitation schedule established. The Minnesota court refused to cooperate with the Pennsylvania court to evaluate our homelife, perhaps believing that I really was an indigent bag lady, not just a person caught short by the court's own order.

In addition, the court case had again been scheduled on the Week Certain system, not the Day Certain system, so I would again be on standby for one week every month, to be prepared to appear in court in Minneapolis on one hour's notice— despite the fact that my home was in Pennsylvania. It is an insane scheduling system. It takes a day to fly to Minneapolis, or 26 hours to drive, but aside from saying, "It might be your turn," they only give one hour's notice. I left Minneapolis with a resolve to go home to tend to necessary matters— like the rent, banking, contacting my former clients to see what could be worked out. (I had not been able to renew my last contract when it had become necessary to leave to go find my children.) I went home to raise funds, regroup, regain my physical strength, and then return to see my kids and go to court (again and again and again). I resolved that when I returned to Minneapolis the next, I would have to have a better support system.

*

LEGALISM: BUS COMPANY BAGGAGE OR STOWAGE

Dear Journal,

On my way home, when I transferred at 2 a.m. at the bus station in Chicago, a thin young man got off a bus wearing a military greatcoat and carrying all his other clothes in a gigantic box tied with a string. He moved into the line in which I was waiting for another bus. Our bus driver kicked the box and told him, "Your box of clothes is oversized. You cannot take it on the bus." The string broke. The man's clothes and meager possessions were scattered on the pavement. His face showed the humiliation, but he said nothing to the bus driver.

Someone handed him a length of bungee cord. "Here, son. See if this helps."

"Thanks." He spread his greatcoat onto the concrete to repackaged everything from the box onto the coat, rolled all it up, and secured it with the bungee. He looked questioningly at the bus driver. We all held our breath.

"Okay, okay, you can get on the bus. Now it's considered carry on baggage. But it is not acceptable that way as stowage. Next time bring proper luggage." The bus driver pushed in front of the boarding passengers and swung himself into the drivers seat.

As the young man struggled to haul the bulky load to the back of the bus, I heard him muttering, "Nobody here but me knows how hard it is to live on the street."

I was too exhausted to say otherwise. I quickly fell asleep and slept for hours.

At a change of busses in Harrisburg, PA, I bought a cotton shirt in the gift shop. It had a GUIN DON cartoon on it of a bag lady. I reboarded the bus, pleased that I had something new. My spirits lifted when the bus made the turn to follow north along the river. I thrilled to seeing again the stately Susquehanna River and the protective mountain ridges, and felt excitement to be nearing home.

*

Figure 17. Anne.

PART X: REPERCUSSIONS AND VALUES

Despite the fact that the System was working to provide me with certain necessities, such as food, shelter, and medical care, because of the disrespect inherent in The System (e.g. obstructionistic bureaucrats, imbalance in the control of scheduling, most of each week spent standing in one line or another, locked bathrooms, inability to cut through the red tape or to secure justice, unfair regional attitude toward persons from out of state, attitude toward persons of diminished capacity [however one might define that], attitude toward persons in poverty, attitude toward persons perceived to be powerless, etc.), I frequently felt disrespected, and from being on the recipient side of this recurrent disrespect, I eventually felt violated by it and in the core of my being a deep-seated outrage took root, separate and apart from the delight I took in everyday living, of the adventure of seeing life from the perspective of a Street Person, of the role of hope, and apart from my intact and evolving spiritual self.

I didn't have a name for it then, but as a result of court trauma and somewhat of having been on the street, for 10 years I had a sort of "social phobia." Social phobia can manifest itself in many ways. For me, one way I believe it came about was because when things were very, very bad, and when I met a casual acquaintance who said conversationally, "How are you? How's it going?" I lost the interpersonal skills to not say too much— spewing out the whole awful horror of my situation, words tumbling out, my brain unable to hold back words, because my human person needed emotional support. Viktor E. Frankl mentions that persons who survived the trauma of the concentration camps had similar experience and it took many years of therapy to work it through.

So I too began to clam up because I might tell someone and not only was it embarrassing to me to say so much, it would also be more than they would want to hear. I knew it would blow them away if they heard the truth of my situation yet, I was too wounded to censor out a lot of data once I started to talk about it. On top of that, I have always been uncomfortable with the socially acceptable "white lie."

It is painful to tell people anything real and see them crumble from the impact. Then I'd feel guilty that I did not have a drop of energy to caretake or to help them process what they had just heard. It was frustrating to want to talk with a trusted friend but to be so needy to talk that I could not stop with just a casual, "As good as can be expected," or the out and out lie, "Fine, just fine. How about you?" Eventually I settled for a noncommittal answer of "I'm doing good. Good to see you. I gotta run." (And making the mental reservation "I'm doing as good as I can under the circumstances" and then dashing off in terror that I might say more.) More than once during this time, I had "spilled my guts" to a perfect stranger when I hadn't wanted or intended to share my pain. And they certainly didn't welcome the experience. It got so awkward that I didn't want to talk to anyone anymore. Eventually it became more convenient to be a hermit. The only persons who could relate were the persons who had had a lot of tragedy in their own history and had developed a lot of coping skills along the way.

I wondered if this was how so many other Street People became non-communicative.

Frequently well-meaning friends would play 20 questions, interrogating me to be sure I have left no stone unturned, or to prove and prove again to themselves that the facts were really true. It was humiliating, even shaming to be questioned so much. And they couldn't realize that I had undergone such extensive interrogation by every social worker, attorney, court person, etc., that being asked a lot of questions— especially when it was clear that the reason the questions were being asked was because the asker didn't want to get it— had a depersonalizing force to it.

Several years later, I sat breakfasting with Helen Drotning-Miller and Edwina Hershberger, comfortably munching on home fries and scrambled eggs in The Good Egg restaurant on Chicago Avenue. Edwina was conducting interviews for her doctoral dissertation. When she asked me her key question: "It has been said that many homeless people are deeply angry people. Do you think there is anything inherent in the system or the experience of homelessness that produces rage or outrage?" I'm afraid I may have given her a total melt-down from the blast that came out of me about this issue, and, as you may well imagine, I had much to say.

✳

The impact on me physically was debilitating. The impact on me emotionally was inconsistent. I came to grips with my anger and frustration with the court actions up to that time, but most was unresolved. And the residual social discomfort and flashbacks took a long time to resolve. The impact on me spiritually turned out to be strengthening. My writing skills improved. Most of my skills remained unaffected, except doing math mentally and cooking.

✳

Even after years after, I suffered "flashbacks of being on the street."[112] It most often occurred when I was in a physical location that would trigger the unwanted recollection. This was especially true when I entered the Hennepin County Government Center or whenever I had to stand in a line for any length of time. To get over it, I desensitized myself by going there every two weeks on routine business over several years time.

The personal trauma to me of the abduction of my children, the blunders of the courts in two different states, and finding myself living among the Street People, were each about 9.9 on the Richter Scale. They were not without intense pain: physically and psychologically.

In addition to the pain, other reactions also were triggered. Other examples were:

- When I stood in a line, I got miserably restless— like my fight or flight mechanism was triggered. I just wanted to leave. Now I do what I have to do in lines as little as possible. I still have a strong dislike for them.

---

[112] *Flashbacks* here means a spontaneous and unwelcome intrusive memory which flashed across my mind's eye causing the discomfort and misery to flood over me, but not so much that I would not know where I really was.

- If I were welcomed to someone's home and was greeted me with, "May I take your coat?," my instinct was to flinch, clutch it, and mentally respond, "Of course not! It's the only one I've got. I can't spare it!" I might think it, but I didn't say it— but I nevertheless felt extreme discomfort. I knew they really meant, "May I hang up your coat," but in Minnesota, to take a Street Person's winter coat would be a death sentence. Street People are so protective of their coats they don't even take them off when they are eating.

- I no longer fully enjoy frosting-covered Danish sweet rolls or cake donuts. Marie Antoinette's "Let them eat cake" has become "Let them eat donuts. Let them eat Danish (sweet rolls)."

- I now need to be aware of my posture and my body language when I eat. On the street, I acquired a strong animal instinct to protect the food on my plate. Everyone ate with elbows and arms spread around the plate, head down close to the food. One man cautioned me, "Protect the food. It's only yours after you have eaten it."

- Later, when I could afford medical care, I discovered that I had assorted physical maladies resulting from prolonged distress. While my ordeal with court lasted seven years, I was only "on the street" from December 19, 1983, to March 31, 1984. In that time my physical condition had deteriorated to an alarming degree. How do people who are permanently homeless survive— especially those who are not able to find space in a shelter?

- For 10 years I experienced uncomfortable memories when I walked through The Skyway. I would remember all too clearly the weight of former distress on my back and my spirit.

- During Mass at St. Olaf's Church at The Lord's Prayer, I am still deeply aware that I am just another beggar before the Lord and it triggers the internal tape: "Give us this day our daily bread . . . and please don't forget the bread."

✳

BASIC NEEDS

As Abraham H. Maslow was searching for what was normal or well adjusted, he identified a developmental hierarchy which is often represented as a hierarchical pyramid-shaped triangle: "life [often interpreted as meaning 'survival'], safety and security, for belongingness and affection, for respect and self-respect, and for self-actualization."[113]

It is sometimes taught this way:

Self-actualization
Self-esteem
Belonging
Safety
Survival

Maslow himself sometimes refers to this as a hierarchical arrangement.[114]

. . . that the human being has, as part of his[/her] intrinsic construction, not only physiological needs by also truly psychological ones. They may be considered as deficiencies which must be optimally fulfilled by the environment in order to avoid sickness and subjective ill-being. They can be called basic, or biological and likened to the need for salt, or calcium or vitamin D because—

---

[113] Maslow, A. H., *Toward a Psychology of Being*, 2nd edn., New York: Van Nostrand Reinhold, 1968, p. 3.

[114] Maslow, *Toward a Psychology . . .*, pp. 152-153.

(1)   The deprived person yearns for their gratification persistently,

(2)   Their deprivation makes the person sicken and wither,

(3)   Gratifying them is therapeutic, curing the deficiency-illness,

(4)   Steady supplies forestall these illnesses,

(5)   Healthy (gratified) people do not demonstrate these deficiencies.

But these needs or values are related to each other in a hierarchical and developmental way, in an order of strength and of priority. Safety is a more prepotent, or stronger, more pressing, more vital need than love, for instance, and the need for food is usually stronger than either.[115]

I believe he may be in error to present his theory as a hierarchy. In *Toward a Psychology of Being*, in the early part of the book, Maslow indicated the hierarchy was only a supposition based on limited observation and would require further research.[116] He went on to say that the tiers of the pyramid were not necessarily sequential and it was possible to be in two tiers at once or even move back and forth. However, near the end of the book, Maslow, himself, was referring to it as a hierarchy, and college classrooms where I have heard lectures on this theory present the hierarchy as gospel.

My experience, as related in this book, was that while survival was an ever-present need, other needs were greater. The need for safety (in terms of having fear for my own physical safety) never crossed my mind, perhaps because at that time, my personal safety was always at some risk from my ex-husband, so I already took reasonable precautions automatically and didn't dwell on it.

The need to receive love was not a concern either. Having had a bad marriage and worse divorce, I was for twelve years in an "I'll never do that again" mode.

---

[115]   Maslow, *Toward a Psychology. . .*, pp. 152-153.

[116]   Maslow, *Toward a Psychology. . .*, p. 25.

While I felt almost no real belonging, I easily identified with the plight of the other Street People because it was also temporarily my plight. But despite not actually belonging, my self-esteem and concept of self-worth remained intact.

Returning to Maslow's Theory of Basic Needs, under his hypothesis I should have spent all my time on survival skills and seeking belonging, and I would not have reached anything close to self-esteem, spirituality, or self-actualization. Since all Street People were in the survival mode, and excluding the completely deranged, the majority with whom I came in contact were very spiritual people, were more open to discussing religion and spiritual life than people not on the street. They did not seem concerned with belonging anywhere, yet were able to experience humor, were interested in and very aware of politics and political economy. Their sense of well-being was not dependent on physical health so much as it was on having hope that for them things would or could get better. Based on this and my own experience, I believe Maslow's hypothesis, which has been given absolute deference, perhaps needs to be revisited.

> Maslow's research with self-actualized subjects yielded the following characteristics: the capacity to tolerate and even welcome uncertainty in their lives, acceptance of self and others, spontaneity and creativity, a need for privacy and solitude, autonomy, the capacity for deep and intense interpersonal relationship, a genuine caring for others, a sense of humor, inner-directedness, and an open and fresh attitude toward life.[117]

By that standard, many of the Street People had made it to his highest tier, to self-actualization, which is supposed to characterize the epitome of normal.

✳

---

[117] Corey, p. 102.

KNOWING PRIORITIES

While above I listed some of the unpleasant results of my experience on the street, I also came away with an in-depth knowledge of what constitute my core priorities. Obviously my children were my top priority, but apart from them and providing for them, when it got to my core necessities, I came to know my survival priorities. Ranked from the most important to the lesser importance, the list looked and felt like this:

1. **SPIRITUAL SUSTENANCE:** spiritual food and tending my inward spiritual journey was the most important aspect of my life and survival.

2. **JOURNALING, ANALYZING, PROCESSING:** These were the second most important functions. I used them stay clear, to unburden previous adult life's hurts, to gain insight into current situations, to continue my spiritual growth and receptivity, and to come to grips with the absurdities of the system and the situations in which I found myself. Into this category I also place the tools I used to do this: pen, paper, postage stamps and envelopes, and moreover the Time that was required for this personal interior processing.

3. **TOILETS, TOILET PAPER, AND RELATED PRODUCTS:** Tissue for running nose, and toiletries such as toilet paper, sanitary products, bathing soap, and laundry soap.

4. **SHOES AND CLOTHING:** Comfortable shoes and warm, clean, presentable clothing. Weather and wind-proof coat, hat, scarf, gloves, and so forth.

5. **SHELTER:** Warm, safe shelter, preferably with a clean bed and clean bedding.

6. **FLUIDS:** To prevent dehydration, drinking water, fruit and vegetable juices; to lessen fatigue, caffeine-containing tea, coffee, and/or cola.

7. **CLEANLINESS:** A daily shower (but there wasn't opportunity), deodorant soap, deodorant, and a clean towel; as a minimum, a daily P-T-A bath (armpits-twat-and-ass).

8. **BODY FOOD:** Fresh vegetables, wholesome portable food, vitamins, and an availability of fresh, safe, nutritious, appropriate foods to eat (for me, at that time, free of lactose, histamine-triggers, mold, certain chemicals, preservatives, tyramine, and the like).

9. **BOOKS AND OTHER FOOD FOR THE MIND:** Reading as additional food for pondering, materials for mental growth and healing, and to pass time.

10. **POCKET CHANGE:** For the phones, buses, journaling paper, essential toilet articles, and for coffee— not so much to drink the coffee as to buy the right to use a bathroom in a heated area.

11. **ACCESS TO TELEPHONES:** Use of the telephone and privacy during phone communication.

12. **KINDNESS AND RESPECTFULNESS IN INTERACTIONS:** Being treated with decency affirms our humanness and innate dignity.

13. **HUMOR AND APPROPRIATE CONVERSATION:** Someone, preferably of wit and wisdom, to talk to once in a while.

14. **SOME PLACE TO SIT:** Without charge.

15. **BODY MAINTENANCE SERVICES:** Medical, dental, and chiropractic services when absolutely necessary.

Access to over-the-counter cold medicines and pre-scription medicines if needed.

16. **STORAGE AND CONTAINERS:** Daily, temporary and long-term, and secure.

17. **HAIRCUT:** Some sharp implement with which to give myself a haircut and cut nails, as needed. (Important grooming if one is to get and keep work.)

18. **TRANSPORTATION:** When needed.

On my personal priority list spiritual sustenance came first (spirituality, prayer, serenity, meditation, and mental clarity), followed by protective clothing, thick-soled and lined shoes, shelter, something to read, pen and paper, list of phone numbers, food, Kleenex, accessible toilets and toilet articles (soap, certain sanitary products), dental health, physical health, a place to sit inside during the day (without charge), coffee for caffeine and warmth, a Jet Pass for bus transit, and drinking water. Smokers chose cigarettes as a top priority— one's body chemistry doesn't cease demanding when one loses the ability to accommodate it.

✲

Dear Journal,

Time and again through this experience I have hit the glass wall of judgmentalism. Perhaps I dislike it so because my mother is very judgmental (especially of me), whether she is right or not.

I have seen so many people treated like dirt because they are poor or looked poor. Frequently with contempt, poor people, Street People, are pre-judged to be deserving of their fate and attributed addiction or misbehavior on their part which may not actually be in their makeup; when it is the fact that they were seen/observed by someone and perhaps their destitution made that observer uncomfortable, that is the trigger of this contemptuous, defensive look or word.

I have learned from the educated and the ignorant. I have been prayed for and prayed with by the learned and the humble. I have been helped by helping professionals as much as by other recipients. Since every person can give and receive according to their abilities, information, and talents regardless of station in life and regardless of their wealth, education, or lack thereof, it seems to me that the core qualities of humanness come down to paying attention, listening and responding respectfully, helping compassionately when appropriate, taking care how we express our attitude, being appropriately private and self-protective, while at the same time being open to the goodness of spirit in one another. While we cannot always control the circumstances in which we find ourselves, we can be responsible for our attitude, integrity, and behavior. Even evil people have aspects of their person that are good. Even good people have aspects of their person that are evil. While our bodies come in different shapes and forms, we all receive the igniting spark of spirit the same way. We all start as equal in the spirit, and that vital spark of spirit within us which originates with Our Creator and returns to Our Creator, makes us all equal before the Lord. We are all little beggars before Almighty God.

✳

GRADUATE IN THE SKYWAY

A year or two later, I went into the Skyway to pick up the mail from my Post Office box. The Skyways have steel gates in them now, which are locked in the off-hours. On Saturday and Sunday, many of the usual Skyway passages are closed. I had just come from St. Olaf's Church and was dressed up, walking briskly, and looking prosperous. I found three well-dressed, gray-haired ladies anxiously walking up and down the hallways, trapped in the Skyway.

"How did you get in here?" one asked me.

"More important, how do we get out of here?" asked the second.

"We've been trying to get out of here for hours."

"I just stopped in to get my mail," I said. "If you'll follow me, I'll show you the way out." We went through a series of serpentine paths, down hallways, onto elevators, down escalators, up and down stairways, through narrow covered passageways, and through combinations of doorways until we reached the sidewalk on Marquette Avenue, across from the Marquette Hotel.

"We know where we are now. Thanks."

"How did you know your way out like that? We never would have found it."

"I'm a graduate of the National Bag Lady Academy. I studied it here in a past life." They looked at me funny, not knowing what to believe. I took out my wallet and showed them the GUINDON card (that came with my shirt). It was a diploma which read: National Bag Lady Academy Student Identification. Speechless, they handed me back the card, then we said "Good-bye," and I walked back toward my car.

Figure 18. GUINDON Bag Lady Institute Diploma.

THE 7-YEAR TAPESTRY

April 15, 1989

Even in my darkest time, though, I was never wholly abandoned. When I needed money, I prayed for it, and somehow miraculously money always came through. For example, one time I urgently needed $1,500 for car repairs, rent, and utility bills, some merchants in town heard of my plight and brought me a basket of organically grown vegetables and fruit— and in the bottom they had tucked a check for $1,500!

Like Job, I had lost all that was dear to me— my children, my job, my possessions— and I was sorely tested. But God was there for me. Many friends new and old were there for me in a myriad of ways. And through it all, I discovered an interesting thing about faith. That God really can be an active force for good in our life. In my life and the lives of the homeless around me, I saw that when we believe in God and keep our faith life, when we hold onto the belief that our lives can get better, they do get better. And when we lose our faith life, our hope, when we give in to despair and believe our lives can only get worse, they do in fact get worse.

Job's suffering went on for seven years. Today, as I write, I mark the end of my seventh year of trial. I cannot say my troubles are entirely over, but I now have custody of my children; I have my own business and professional standing in the community; I have been recognized by Who's Who of the Women of the World; and I have a faith in God that is stronger than ever. For all they have been through, my children have turned out to be fine human beings of whom I am very proud.

Even times of great tragedy can be woven into the fabric of a life that makes sense. For me, telling my story is part of that weaving. Telling my story and the story of the homeless is one way my personal trials can be turned into my gift.

✳

Figure 19. Max.

PART XI: THAT WAS THEN, THIS IS NOW.

WHERE ARE THEY NOW?

December, 1995

I don't know what happened to most of the Street People I met, but I have seen a few of them from time to time. I think one went on to be a Homeless Advocacy Activist.

Aeneas pulled through the cancer surgery. Five year later, the cancer had not recurred. Was it surgery, ICU nurses, the power of God, prayer? Who knows. Probably all of it. Eventually he broke up with Dolly and left town.

When Max was on the street, the woman he had met in a church in the Southwest learned he had gotten out of prison. I think they had corresponded. I don't think she had ever met him but apparently had the hots for him anyway. Max said, "She quit her job, put her house up for sale, and she says she's gonna move to Minneapolis to marry me." He seemed a little incredulous, so I asked him if he had proposed to her. "Hell no! She's 20 years younger than I am. But she's gonna have money from the sale of her house and she has good job skills. But I'd really rather get a place of my own. Me 'n' some of the guys think if we pool our money, we maybe could, I don't know, come up with a security deposit somewhere. But, Jeeze, I'll marry her if she really wants me to."

Max married the girl. They moved somewhere up north. She bought another house. He got restless and made his way back to Minneapolis. He told me more of this when I ran into him in the Skyway again. "I got an apartment with some of the men I told you about– you know, the guys I met in the shelter" he motioned his arm and three guys emerged from the shadows. "You met'm in the HCMC Canteen one Sunday." Then his face lit up, "But I got her pregnant– because she wanted me too. I'm the papa of a little girl!"

I see Sally around town but I don't think she is on the street. She looks grown up now.

Some of the mentally ill people are in the same circumstances they were in then, only now they are older. But for many, unfortunately, prescribed anti-psychotic medication(s) had terrible side effects. The prescription medication(s) that made it possible for many mentally ill persons to leave the confinement of institutional life were the same drugs that, years later, brought an additional impairment— swelling of the tongue— making it difficult to speak and to prevent drooling. Worse yet, these wonder drugs were found to cause death, when taken over many years at the recommended dosage.

*

WHAT'S HAPPENING NOW?

The League of Women Voters in Minnesota has proposed that all persons, especially the mentally ill, have a right to decent and affordable housing. Another group, Minnesota Initiative to Create Affordable Housing (MICAH), was formed to promote the cause of affordable housing for all by the year 2000. In the late 1980s, I was in business developing affordable housing with several nonprofit organizations, funders, and the City of Minneapolis. We had completed restoration of a duplex apartment house to be sold to low income buyers at a reduced/subsidized sale price.

About that time, Up and Out of Poverty, a radical homeless activist group, was intent on making a political statement by taking over vacant houses owned by HUD and the VA, to have homeless people occupy them as squatters. It so happened that this very house had once been government-owned before we arranged for Project for Pride in Living to purchase it for this renovation project. On the eve of Gorbachev's visit to Minneapolis with then President Bush, Minnesota Up and Out of Poverty took over this house and did substantial damage. When they vacated it a year later, the house had to be re-renovated at substantial cost to the program and taxpayers. While I obviously have empathy for the situation of homeless people, I do not condone the siege mentality of this group and its tactics of malicious destruction in order to secure media exposure.

The House of Charity got some new windows. The Crystal Court no longer has palm trees, has almost no seating, and its restaurants come and go. Many S&L's and restaurants have changed owners and/or folded. The Skyway has barred gates and guards and is usually locked at night. Many of the residence hotels and SROs downtown have been demolished. There is a new Convention Center and a new Hilton where they were. Some social services distribution centers have been combined under the roof of the Centennial Building. There are still lines in front of the House of Charity, The Drake, and some of the Branches. Fewer staff people are involved in the provision of services to many of the shelters and to the Street People.

Fewer people can count themselves as members of the Middle Class. Many employed workers now consider themselves poor and lacking in job security. Unemployment fluctuates with market adjustments. Someone printed handouts for merchants to give out on the law against panhandling.

The Drake was converted from a shelter for men only to a shelter mainly for women accompanied by children. St. Stephen's Shelter is still open and serves good food. The Salvation Army Program at Harbor Lights is still providing services. A shelter for chronic inebriates was constructed. A large facility (Harriet Tubman) for battered women was constructed in south Minneapolis.

Catholic Charities and St. Olaf's Catholic Church initiated the Exodus program to assist Street People to transition from street life into affordable rental housing in a supportive environment.

The Central Housing Trust applied to the Hennepin County Commissioners for a $25,000 grant of operating funds to open a shelter for runaway youth downtown near First Avenue. In the spring of 1995, an employee of The Minneapolis Red Cross told me that "The Red Cross has voted to get out of the homeless shelter thing because they are into temporary disaster relief and *the homeless problem is a permanent [disaster] thing.*" In December, 1995, Our Savior Lutheran Church and shelter were demolished by fire, and the persons then in the shelter transferred to The Drake.

The 1996 federal, county, and city budgets all have cutbacks in funding for shelters and programs connected with them. Twenty shelter staff members in Minneapolis whose salaries are paid by Hennepin County were given notice two weeks before Christmas

1995. As a result, the House of Charity and The Drake were forced to turn away homeless eligible new applicants for shelter at Christmas time [no room in the inn], and there were rumors that the facilities may have to shut down entirely. While this is only one city in one state in the nation, the funding cuts are from national budgets as well, so these measures could be indicative of the national situation.

In December, 1995, when the Work Readiness program was shut down by Congress, the subsidy that permitted certain homeless people to use shelters also terminated. This bitterly cold December found them sleeping on the floor in the Welfare Office. By the first part of 1996, a new shelter called A Safe Place was opened in St. Paul by the Catholic Archdiocese to try to provide indoors a place for these displaced people. January of 1996 was the coldest on record.

The Food Centre now serves a good lunch, with salad, vegetables, and hot dish.[118]

In 1991, a four-room house of approximately 800 square feet was selling for approximately $165,000 in Los Angeles. In Minneapolis, while home purchase prices are still relatively low, redlining of certain neighborhoods by mortgage banks was common in the decades 1960s through 1980s and unnecessarily restrictive qualifications made it difficult for most low-moderate and lower income families to buy a home.

In 1995, the median price of a home nationally was $137,000. To purchase a home, applicants with low- and low-moderate incomes frequently need credit repair, down payment assistance, home ownership training, home repair money as part of the mortgage, and sometimes a buy-down of the sale price. Persons already in their own homes often need temporary help to prevent becoming homeless. Renters need assistance to become home-owners. Some Street People and others of low income frequently are not in a position to undertake home ownership and need supports to get into rental housing, group homes, assisted living, and a variety of other transitional options, depending on their particular need.

---

[118] Minnesotan for "casserole."

The plight of The Homeless, nationally, was just getting better as the newer federal programs had begun to show results at the local level. Now they are all in question as we re-examine our national priorities and face difficult questions of allocation of our national resources.

✳

Dear Journal,

As a consultant, I expect my recommendations to be given consideration. As a Street Person, even simple suggestions are viewed as complaining and ungratefulness.

When I was on the street, I kept trying to think of what would make a difference. Most were very simple things having to do with basic human needs and would benefit the general public as well, and the list has been added to from time to time. Basically what makes a city good for street people's needs makes it a liveable and pleasant place for all citizens, e.g. bathrooms, places to sit, trees, telephones, as well as kindness and compassion. I believe that applies to the nation as well.

SUGGESTIONS FOR CHANGES NEEDED NATIONALLY

- Recognize that a large percentage of Homelessness is a result of national policies and take responsibility for the repercussions of government policies; or better yet, change the policies.

- Increase the minimum wage to become a real living wage so that a person working a full time job 40 hours a week can support a family of four.

- Require every office building, department store, and public building to have free public toilets, maintained in clean condition, and stocked with adequate toilet paper at all times— including some accessible on Sundays.

- Require each public men's, women's, or unisex restrooms to have diaper changing stations. [The

Hennepin County Government Center has now instituted this necessary and beneficial feature.]

- In all public places construct restrooms so that women are provided with as many or more bathroom fixtures as are provided to men.

- As Section 8 Rent Subsidy 15 year contracts are retired, more rental housing is removed from the category of "affordable rental housing." The federal government needs to rethink how it intends to promote/ensure adequate (scattered site) rental housing so that as a nation we do not recreate enormous projects that are fit for demolition on the one hand, or a total absence of affordable rental housing on the other.

- Make it easier for unemployed people seeking work to travel to obtain work. Restructure the federal unemployment compensation claims process to make it faster and easier to achieve prompt transfer of claims among states (e.g., by fax). Allow some unemployment checking-in to be accomplished using touchtone phone, by inserting a plastic card into an automatic teller machine or card-reading payphone, modem, or other such national computerized network, or by sending private e-mail from a computer terminal.

- Create programs with public-private partnerships to employ able-bodied Homeless People in reconstruction of public parks, reforestation, repair of highway potholes, raising food crops for soup-kitchens, as short-order cooks, and using other skills where jobs are available.

- Reinstate summer youth employment opportunity programs which also have a training component.

- Require the Post Office to rent Post Office Boxes to persons whether or not they have a fixed address. Private services, such as Mail Boxes, Etc., are snatching up good customers the USPS had turned away.

- Make it an offense to discriminate against United States citizens because of their state of origin, when they apply in another state for federally funded programs for which they are eligible. If they are present to make an application, they are presenting a need. If necessary, establish some sort of transfer payment among states to keep the burden equitable for states servicing residents of other states. Have a simple computerized database to cross-check with other states, to eliminate double-dipping. Track payments by fingerprints, voiceprint, or plastic identity card. However, I am not in favor of the embedding of computer chips in people's thumbs or foreheads as has been proposed by some and discussed at length by a number of fear-mongering short-wave radio programs.

- Have a coordinated intake system (application) for processing the needs of Homeless People.

- Have enough service personnel to keep lines short.

- Provide (mental health, courtesy, listening) training opportunities at regular and frequent intervals to all government personnel having contact with citizens (customers).

- Establish more Housing Courts.

- Mandate that more funds go directly to nonprofit housing and related service providers to provide direct services and administrative overhead, and fewer funds bottlenecked at the top of a city and/or county bureaucracy, which frequently results in siphoning off federal and other monies to pay for high-salaried micro-managers. Worse yet, it is not unusual for some city agencies to obstruct and compete against the successful front-line service-providing agencies for such admin. dollars.

- Many standard mortgages contain boiler plate language that "should a dispute arise, all parties would submit to *binding* arbitration." After discussions among bankers, borrowers, inspectors, and other housing professionals, many have concluded that *binding* arbitration is not often the best method: in many instances Housing Court is more just and fair to all concerned especially the borrower or renter. Such Housing Courts are set up similar to Small Claims Court with a modest cost to file a complaint (e.g. $18) and use of a lawyer's services is optional. The reasons given for preferring Housing Court to binding artibration is that many times arbitrators are good listeners and good negotiators, but generally not cognizent of housing law, banking law, inspection standards, housing quality standards, housing maintenance standards, etc. While the arbitrator may be a well-meaning person, a good listener, and interested in being fair, a lack of expertise in this particular area makes it difficult to make an informed, just, and fair ruling. When the decision is binding, all other avenues have been cut off. There are about eight other kinds of arbitration, other than being locked into the type that is called binding arbitration, to negotiate a settlement in addition to Housing Court and Civil Court.

- Reinstate/restructure the HUD Foreclosure Prevention Program to have it administered by community-based affordable-housing nonprofit organizations such as the Neighborhood Housing Services, the NeighborWorks network organizations, rather than by conventional lenders, the originators of the FHA-insured mortages being foreclosed upon. Formerly, such conventional lenders were required to notify any mortgagees having trouble meeting mortgage payments that the mortgagee has a right to establish a work-out plan for gettting the mortgage caught up. Because this took more staff time, many conventional lenders did not like to provide this service. Now, they are no longer required to advise the homeowner of this right and may institute foreclosure proceedings without trying to assist the homeowner to make a repayment plan so they can keep their home. In effect, the right was obliterated when the procedure was changed by administrative decree.

- The foreclosure prevention program mentioned above also had a provision to put a moratorium on excess interest charges accumulating while the mortgagee(s) was getting the mortgage caught up under the work-out plan, as long as the plan was being followed, and they had been able to demonstrate that the payment delinquency came about originally by circumstances beyond their control. This provision was also obliterated, making the foreclosure process easier, and the opportunity to catch up on a default much harder. In the early 1990s HUD estimated that it was foreclosing on 35 households a month in Minneapolis alone. They were also foreclosing in the Twin Cities suburbs as well across the nation. Multiply this by the number of urban areas across the country, and it is easy to see that government foreclosure procedures were creating homeless families at a very substantial rate.

  During the years when the foreclosure prevention program was in full force the number of foreclosures dropped by about two-thirds.

- When such a work-out plan is established it should remain in effect for a sufficient period of time for income to be reestablished. Initially the mortgagee pays principle only. Then when a stable income stream has been established, the principle, interest, taxes, and insurance payment is reinstated at the original monthly payment and the accumulated interested and arrearage are added to the last mortgage payment as a balloon payment.

- Have more one-stop shopping for services so that a homeless person could get by with standing in line perhaps part of one day a week instead of every day of every week. This would leave more time for persons able to do temporary or permanent work to do so.

- Allow Street People the dignity of reasonable and negotiated scheduling of appointments.

＊

SUGGESTIONS FOR CHANGES NEEDED WITHIN THE MINNEAPOLIS-HENNEPIN COUNTY SYSTEM

- Set up more places for Street People to be during the day, in proximity to the shelters. Such drop in centers could offer literacy training, life skills training, data entry training, sheltered workshop services as well as being places to be in community.

- Offer English as a Second Language and Adult Basic Literacy within all shelters for those who need and want it.

- Offer computer training and education, in or near shelters.

- Have 12-step groups meet every day and evening in the shelter or nearby.

- Provide clearly designated, easily identifiable access to the Skyway from the city street/sidewalk level.

- Provide an hospitality awareness program for local citizens on how to meet and greet visitors to the Twin Cities so that all visitors are not greeted with hostility and suspicion, and be presumed to be arriving to mooch off the system.

- The Twin Cities is host to millions of persons who spend millions of dollars here annually to make movies, attend sports events, attend conventions, and sightsee. Yet information (for persons of any economic level) to use to get around, to see and to do in the Twin Cities, is almost nonexistent.

- Equally important is public education for local citizens to counter the attitude that bad things are never the result of an action by someone local, but only the result of action by someone who came here from somewhere else.

- Expand the downtown public library schedule to include Sundays.

- Have more shelters be open year-round or at least past the date of last frost.

- Keep some shelters open during the day, with improved access to mail, messages, and to allow recovery of those who are ill. Provide school-type lockers for storage of belongings and equip them with mail slits so that mail and messages could be delivered to the locker.

- Provide programs to help prevent burn-out of social service personnel.

- Have a number to call to listen to a taped message indicating which shelters have bed space available for that evening and which have no vacancy.

- Simplify procedures, especially at HCMC, for obtaining essential antibiotics when needed. It should not be harder to get penicillin and other antibiotics that are non-addictive than to get products containing codeine such as cough medicine and Tylenol with codeine, which are potentially addictive.

- Extend to Street People medical assistance coverage to permit obtaining dentures, eyeglasses, and hearing aids when required. [Some of this has been done.]

- As I write this, there is a crisis in funding of salaries of workers who staff shelters, so I feel compelled to say the obvious: have adequate staff, well-paid, and well-supported (physically and emotionally) for this difficult work they do.

- 70% of Caucausian families in the Twin Cities own homes; 30% of families of color own homes. Caucasian families frequently use home equity loans to finance their children's college education. Therefore, bringing more persons of color into home ownership will provide them more options for finanancing higher education.

- Streamline the City Department of Finance so that invoices and vouchers submitted by service providers move through the system and are paid in a timely manner. Frequently under the present system of delays in reimbursement for services and goods already provided, service-providing agencies must be more concerned about meeting payroll rather than being able to focus on services to their clients.

- Loosen credit so that nonprofits can get low-interest cashflow loans to tide them over while waiting out city, county, or federal reimbursement for approved eligible and/or contracted-for services.

- Minneapolis has a substantial number of vacant and boarded houses. Such unoccupied structures attract gangs. Rather than address the issue of gang activity head-on, the city has frequently used its power of condemnation to destroy the affected housing. Timely and improved policing could preserve more affordable housing.

■ Provide public trash cans on each downtown city block.

■ Continue to restore trees and benches to the downtown area and elsewhere.

■ Make it mandatory to provide a certain number of public places to sit, perhaps spaced every other block at the street level and at the Skyway level. For example, many senior citizens have stopped using the downtown as a place to shop and conduct business, because it is physically difficult for them to navigate without brief intervals of rest. Persons with physical disabilities are not all wheelchair users.

■ Make the city beautiful and hospitable, not just functional. The new riverpark is a good start.

*

SUGGESTIONS FOR CHANGES IN THE HOUSE OF CHARITY PROGRAM AND/OR THE FOOD CENTRE

■ Have the Minneapolis Environmental Health Department certify wholesomeness of donated vending machine food. Hold donated food to the same standard safety as food offered for sale, e.g. don't serve unrefrigerated and outdated chicken, pork, fish or other perishable sandwiches that were discarded from vending machines.

■ Renovate the House of Charity facility to provide a "back door" to the intake rooms so that employees have an emergency exit when needed.

- Increase the number toilets and showers, washing machines and dryers available.[119]

- If not doing so already, supplement the menu with donations of fresh produce through sources such as Second Harvest. Distribute a multiple vitamin daily to guests at the House of Charity, the Food Centre, and other shelters.   Sharing and Caring Hands already does this.

- As much as possible, at the House of Charity, consolidate distribution of goods and services so that an individual admitted for a week can receive things like vouchers, passes, recertification, laundry detergent, Jet Pass, and such, by standing in line only once during the week for all of it, rather than standing in a line for each item on a different day. Provide new arrivals with such a care package on admittance.   Perhaps some items for the care package could be obtained through the same methods that hospitals use, since many items for grooming would be identical.   Streamline the procedure for passing out dinner bags and door keys yet maintain enough flexibility to meet needs as they arise.

---

[119] Substantial renovation has taken place since this list was written. The lobby/living room has been renovated, painted, carpeted. The good old plaster Jesus is no longer there looking out of the window. I do not know whether more toileting and showering facilities have been added or whether the intake rooms have an escape route. The windows have been replaced and upgraded.

- Solicit good used reading material at all reading levels, to keep the bookshelves in the House of Charity waiting rooms stocked.

*

SUGGESTIONS FOR IMPROVEMENTS WITHIN THE VOLUNTEER SECTOR

- Develop training to prepare volunteers for dealing with difficult people, awareness of how their own attitude comes across to recipients, assisting them to "feel safe" in interacting with recipients in respectful casual conversation, training in sensitivity, cross-cultural awareness, confidentiality, and respect or non-judgmental acceptance. Encourage volunteers to interact and converse with recipients, and allow sufficient time for this. Have a back-up in place so that staff and volunteers can have time out for emotional support and personal processing when needed.

- While most volunteers have an agenda of some sort, or a personal motivation for doing volunteer work, it is important that this personal need and need to feel good does not result in either an holier-than-thou attitude, or an implied boasting "See how wonderful I am to help these (despicable) people." Such attitudinal self-aggrandizements, a form of putting stars on one's own forehead, are quickly picked up by recipients, who feel misused despite needing the services being provided. Likewise, recipients also feel misused by people who proffer friendliness, then quickly switch to "You need to be saved. My religion is the one true answer for you, my Brother."

- While it is impossible to regulate motivation, it is appropriate to caution volunteers that sometimes motivation results in behaviors that can be counter-

productive to their own good works. It would be
helpful to include in training time an opportunity
for the volunteer identify and come to self-
knowledge of his/her own helping agenda, and to
think about ways this may assist and ways it may
misfire. This kind of "awareness of self-motivation
for helping" is routine in the training of most
counselors who are to receive pay or fees for their
service, so it is not inappropriate to think that
volunteers would also benefit from such self-
knowledge; especially since their motivation is not
the money, it follows that their personal motivation
to volunteer is an even more significant component.
For many, unveiling this motivation may be
sufficient to temper any potentially inappropriate
behavior and should also bring more satisfaction to
the volunteer for the good that s/he is contributing.

The best training tool I have seen is a video entitled "A Change
of Heart."[120] In it, students were sent out to begin helping others,
then returned to an auditorium to bring back what they learned:

STUDENT: You have to take care of your own
suffering before you can move on to someone else's,
cause if you're not taking care of yourself, then you'll
collapse while you're taking care of someone else. I
think that's almost the . . . key to trying to help others.

DASS: Yeah, the problem with that though is for you
to end your own suffering completely before you help
someone else, they should wait so long, you see. So . . .
what you got to do is end up doing both of them at
once. You got to work on yourself and you've also got
to help others, because the helping others is part of the
way you work on your stuff and yourself. . . ."
But when I was in India. . . . When I said to [my
teacher] 'How can I get enlightened?' He said, 'Serve

_____

[120] "A Change of Heart," 1996, courtesy of Mystic Fire Video, Inc.
800-292-9001.

people.' So I thought something got lost in the translation. So I tried a different tack. I said, 'How can I know God?' And he said, 'Serve people.' . . .[121]

✻

Suggested Improvements at the Individual Level

- Donate along with canned goods, other items such as new underwear, new socks, new shoes, disposable razors, reading material, toothbrushes, toothpaste, combs, gift certificates for haircuts, toilet paper, cloth tote bags, backpacks, hats, sewing kits, folding cups, disposable diapers, female sanitary products, adult diapers, and general clothing.

- Address your own fear, then do something to help.

✻

Quoting from the video "A Change of Heart" on volunteer preparation and service:

> DASS: In this culture there's such a tendency to push away suffering. Put the old folks here and the sick folks there and this suffering there and that suffering there. And we'll abstract and we'll label people and that'll get it out of the way. We'll call them The Homeless, then we don't have to deal with the person that's suffering. But when you push suffering away, you push a part of yourself away. You armor yourself against what is. You're not accepting the way things are, because you're afraid.

> HUERTA: The answers come when you, you know, you go down the path and open the door. . . Take the other path and then another answer will come. But

---

[121] *Ibid.*, p. 5.

none of them [the answers] will come unless you
actually start doing something.

AMY: . . . so I think one of the things is just to
somehow learn to be there and to listen. . . . You don't
necessarily have to say anything, but to just believe what
they're saying is truth. And I think it's hard sometimes
to remember not to be judgmental about what someone
chooses to do and to just try and listen. It's something
I struggle with, 'cause I always want to do something. . .
I don't like pain . . . don't like suffering and I like to fix
things. . . . I mean I'm someone that, in general, tries to
smooth things over and make everything nice and tidy
again. So it's been a challenge. . . .

DASS: It's clear when you look at people like
Mahatma Gandhi, Martin Luther King, and so many
people who were out on the leading edge of action, they
placed considerable stress on their inner work. 'Cause
you understand that if you get so pained, so angry, so
offended, and so crushed, you become debilitated in
your ability to really help other human beings and to
reduce suffering. So you begin to see the pattern that
you work on yourself . . . to become a more effective
instrument for the relief of suffering. . . .

It's like a self-sharpening tool because, as you serve
somebody and you do it in a way that is a process of
working on yourself, you become clearer and quieter,
and more present and able to listen more deeply. And
as you're able to do all that, you're able to serve
better. . . .

NARRATOR: Helping the homeless is one way that
many have put their beliefs into action. . . .[122]

*

---

[122] *Ibid.*, pp. 11, 13, 15-17, 20-21.

RECENT INFORMATION PUBLISHED IN NEWSPAPERS

"The number of homeless adults and families in emergency shelters in Hennepin County, the largest provider of emergency shelter in the state, has increased 1,000 percent in the past 10 years. County officials have estimated they would need to provide a new 150-bed shelter every year for the foreseeable future to meet demand."[123]

The Hennepin County "homeless program (is) serving more than 40,000 a year with a budget of about $10 million. . . . The shelters cost $16.75 per person. . . . The average nightly rate at the motels (is) $53.83. . . Last year (1994), the county (Hennepin) spent $188,000 putting people up in motels."[124]

(County Commissioner) Mark Andrews said he believes government has strong responsibilities toward the homeless and that everyone should share in the responsibility. "It is a fundamental moral obligation of government to assure that a roof is put over a person's head." But others question which government and which taxpayers should pay. Faced with more restrictive policies in Ramsey County and data suggesting that residents of Anoka and Dakota counties may routinely find their way into Hennepin County shelters, a number of Hennepin County officials are interested in changing the system.[125]

✳

---

[123] Brunswick, Mark, "How Far Should Government Go to Help the Homeless?: Debate Stirred Over Policy of Renting Motel Rooms." *Minneapolis Star-Tribune* 5/29/95, p. 01B.

[124] *Ibid.*, p. 01B.

[125] Brunswick, *Ibid.*

Nationally, 300,000 to 500,000 young people are homeless on any given night, according to the National Network for Youth in Washington, D.C. . . . How many homeless children are there in Minnesota? One agency says 500. Another says 800, another 1,000. Whatever the number, . . . the need for more places for homeless young people remains. Counting Project Foundation and facilities for runaways, only about 60 shelter beds are available for older homeless youths in Minneapolis and St. Paul, according to a report from the Minnesota Department of Jobs and Training. (Younger children can be placed in foster care or taken to such places as St. Joseph's Home for Children. . .)[126]

*

Each year about 10,000 Minnesota youths experience at least one night of homelessness.

The average age for young people to become homeless is 14.

Homeless youths ages 10 to 17 are nearly three times more likely to have been sexually or physically abused.[127]

*

"In 1971, surveys in Chicago, Minneapolis, and Philadelphia all reported that about 1/3 of the skid row residents are abstainers, 1/3 are moderate drinkers, . . . and only 1/3 are alcoholics."[128]

---

[126] Hayes Taylor, Kimberly, "These Kids Can't Go Home." *Minneapolis Star-Tribune,* 11/12/95, p. 1B.

[127] *Ibid.*

[128] Rubington, E. "The Changing Skid Row Scene," *Quarterly Journal of Studies on Alcohol 32,* p. 127.

By 1993, the flood of other populations into homelessness had been so significant that "alcoholics now comprise only about 5% or fewer of the Homeless."[129]

✳

> . . . Minnesota's battered women's shelters. . .(350 beds) have been unable to house two-thirds of families that call . . . on any particular day. . . . Shelters in such smaller cities (Mankato, Brainerd, Fergus Falls and St. Cloud) often are filled beyond their licensed capacity and are housing some women and children in living rooms and basements. . . .
>
> "We're getting women who are really in a lot of danger. They absolutely have to leave (home). . . . We have been just jammed," said Louise Seliski, executive director of Mid-Minnesota Women's Center in Brainerd.
>
> Minnesota annually houses more than 10,000 women and children with . . . $5.2 million biennial (legislative) appropriation . . . . there are vast gaps in northern and southwestern Minnesota, and a woman may have to travel 100 miles to get help. . . .
>
> Most counties have a battered women's advocacy program, . . . some . . . gaps are filled through . . . safe houses. . . . Advocates helped more than 32,000 women with legal advocacy in 1994-95 . . . and 88,500 with other needs (crisis intervention, child care, and transportation) . . . . [A new] criminal justice intervention project's . . . object is to get law enforcement, prosecutors and courts working together to solve domestic abuse problems, sometimes by jailing abusers and leaving women at home.[130]

✳

---

[129] Isselbacher, K., ed. *Harrison's Principles of Internal Medicine*, 13th edn. NY: McGraw-Hill, Inc., 1994, p. 2420-2425.

[130] Franklin, Robert, "Domestic Abuse: State Shelters for Battered Women Are in Big Demand and Short Supply." *Minneapolis Star-Tribune*, 10/19/95, p. 3B.

THE MAYOR'S RESPONSE

Radio Broadcast of Minneapolis Mayor Sharon Sayles Belton on Gary
Eichten's Midday Show on KNOW, March 21, 1996.

*CALLER [Pat McDonough]: I heard that Hennepin County has
reported to the City Council that in a ten-year period there has been a
1000% increase in homelessness. In a newsletter from HUD in
August, I saw that $2,000,000 for homeless-assistance was to come to
the City of Minneapolis and more than $7,000,000 to Hennepin
County. But in December, there was a layoff of 20 staff-people in
homeless shelters, and I understand now that some of them have had
to close, some are doubled up, and a lot of it is standing room only.
I was wondering if you could shed some light on that, in terms of
budget, future plans, and just what the situation is?*

MAYOR: First, let me share with you that any money that
the City of Minneapolis gets for homeless sheltering goes
not for direct service, but for the construction of
housing units. Hennepin County has a responsibility for
the operations of the shelters.   We do work
collaboratively with Hennepin County because we know
and understand that most of the Social Service systems
that are needed to support those people who are
homeless and seeking shelter are in Hennepin County.
We have a city-county task-force that helps us to
understand how many shelter-units we need in the City
of Minneapolis, and as well how many low-income
housing-units we need to build so that people who have
limited incomes and who are now homeless can move
into more permanent housing. Through that task-force
we have also devised ways of assisting homeless people in
assessing their skills and in the other problems that they
might have in moving closer to self-sufficiency. We are
in discussion right now with Hennepin County about re-
evaluating the scope of that task-force so that we can be
even more successful than we have been in the past.
    I am aware that some of the shelter-operations are
downsizing, and I don't know what the reasons for that
are; I don't know whether or not there has been less
operating support made available through Hennepin
County because of Federal cuts— I just don't know the

answer to that. I know that it has always worked well for the City of Minneapolis to work in conjunction with Hennepin County on the construction of the housing units and in determining how many of them we need for women and children, how many units we need for families, and how many we need for single individuals. That task-force has been fairly successful.

ANOTHER CALLER: One of the previous callers stated that the homeless rate has reached 1000%. I wonder where these people are coming from and how you can account for that increase?

MAYOR: I don't have any idea where they are coming from, but I will tell you what I do know. A lot of people think that, "Oh, they're coming off the railroad," "They're bussing in from other communities around the country and the Upper Midwest in particular," or that they're coming from other parts of greater Minnesota, coming to the central city looking for jobs and opportunity and in some cases coming to the Twin Cities looking for no good.

I think there's no simple answer to that. I think that what we need to do, to pay attention to, is: Why are people homeless? What are the reasons? Is it mental health? Is it chemical dependency? Is a drug addiction? Is it a lack of a skill? What is it?

I think we need to attack it in a different way. I don't think the answer is just to build another shelter and another shelter and another shelter. I think we need to get pro-active as a community, get at the underlying issues, and then— be responsible. Take some responsible action. I'm personally tired of our answers always being "Let's put a band-aid on the problem."

I am interested in taking the kinds of action that are going to prevent the problem. We intervene effectively and we prevent the problem.

We need also to pay attention to the growing gap in income between people. We've got to think about "What is our strategy to deal with that?" More and more and more people are becoming poorer and poorer and poorer. Now why is that happening and what is the answer? Should we be talking about increasing the minimum wage? Should we be talking about making sure that there is more affordable housing available? Should we be talking about more income tax credits so people can meet their basic needs? What are we talking about here? This is not just the problem of the City of Minneapolis. This is a national problem. I think part of the answer is jobs, more of them everywhere.

*

APPENDICES

APPENDIX I: RULES FOR EMERGENCY HOUSING GUESTS

Room Number *115*
Check Out Date *12/29 8:00 A.M.*
Extension Date *12/28 1:30 P.M.*

Anytime a group of people live together, there must be rules. While it is best to keep the rules to a minimum, it is important to cover everything. In order to avoid misunderstandings, we ask you to read and obey the following rules. They will be strictly followed.

ALCOHOL & DRUGS Individuals staying at the House of Charity are not allowed to use drugs or alcohol. It makes no difference where you use or how much you use. The opinion of the staff member on duty is final. There will be housing restrictions (30 day) for drug usage.

CURFEW If you are not in the building by 9:30 P.M. your bed will be given away. If you have a valid reason (such as a job) to miss curfew, you must clear it with Catholic Charities intake workers or the desk staff before you leave the building. The staff is instructed not to accept any excuses over the phone. The front door is locked at 8:30 P.M. To enter the building after that time, ring the buzzer located at the left of the door.

CHECK OUT Please verify your check out date with the front desk. Remove all your belongings from your room on the morning of your check out date by ~~8:00 A.M.~~ *6:30 A.M.* We know your belongings are important to you but we do not have the space to store them. If clothing and other belongings are left in the rooms, they will be distributed to the Free Stores in the area. Guests are not to be in the building between ~~8:00 A.M.~~ *7:30 A.M.* and 4:00 P.M. except to see Catholic Charities intake workers. Guests who do not follow this rule will be asked to leave. No one is allowed back into their rooms or the building after they leave in the morning.

ACCOUNTABILITY Please check with the desk staff each evening. Let the staff know who you are.

This is the time to ask questions, check your box for messages, or take care of any business you might have with the House of Charity. The people at the desk are busy, so we appreciate it when you do not congregate around the desk. Keep small talk to a minimum.

BEHAVIOR Those who are friendly and cooperative will be treated with warmth and respect. If it becomes necessary to call the police because of your behavior, you will be prosecuted. Violent or threatening behavior will result in permanent restriction from housing.

FRONT DOOR You are to enter and leave the building by the front door only. Please use the emergency exits only in the case of emergencies. Do not let anyone into the building when the door is locked.

PROPERTY Please remember that this is temporary housing— keep your belongings to a minimum. We are not able to store personal belongings. Do not leave your belongings in the room when you check out. If you curfew out, you must come back for your things the next day or they will have [been] distributed to the Free Stores in the area. The House of Charity cannot assume liability for lost or stolen property. House of Charity property is to be left in your room (sheets, towels, washcloths, blankets, etc.)— missing articles will result in restrictions or permanent dismissal.

WEAPONS All guns, knives and other weapons are forbidden.

SMOKING No smoking in bed! This is a city ordinance and a state law.

HYGIENE Please keep yourself and your clothing clean. We provide soap and showers. If you need to wash clothes, tokens and soap are available through Catholic Charities and may also be purchased at the front desk between 8:00 A.M. and 4:00 P.M. If you need a change of clothing, ask at the front desk about the hours of the Free Store.

GUESTS Guests are only allowed in the front lobby. Noisy, disruptive, or disorderly guests are never allowed in the building.

KEYS Keys must be returned to the front desk <u>immediately</u> after you use it to open or lock your room. Keys that are kept will result in housing restrictions.

BUILDING FACILITIES You are welcome to use the lobby for visiting with other guests, the bathrooms on your floor, the vending machine room and the laundry room. Please do not congregate in the other areas of the building. Use only the elevator for traveling to and from your room— not the stairwells. If you are caught wandering around in areas of the building where you do not belong, you will be asked to leave.

HOUSEKEEPING & MAINTENANCE The housemen are responsible for changing linen, sweeping rooms and cleaning sinks. You are responsible for keeping your room <u>neat and clean</u>. Please report any damage or maintenance problems to the desk.

FOOD IN ROOMS There is <u>no food</u> stored in the rooms. Food found in the rooms will be thrown away.

BLUE-SLIPPED If you are blue-slipped into a room (given housing without talking to Catholic Charity intake workers, be sure to see an intake worker on the first week/workday you are at the residence.

BREAKFAST TICKETS Breakfast is available at the <u>Food Centre at 714 Park Ave.</u> Tickets for breakfast must be gotten at the front desk between 7:30-8:00 A.M. A hot lunch is served at the Food Centre Monday through Sunday at 12:00-1:00 P.M. A light supper is given out at the front desk in the evening.

CARDS, ETC. We have found in the past that activities such as card playing tend to get out of hand. Therefore, we request that you use the front lobby for quiet visiting, watching TV, or reading.

CHILDREN Children must have an adult with them at all times— they must not be left alone in the rooms. They must be clothed and are not to be running in the halls.

PHYSICAL CONTACT Any hand-holding, kissing or other physical contact is not allowed by guests while in the building. We have a variety of people staying at the House of Charity and we would like to maintain an atmosphere that is pleasant for everyone. Also, please be dressed while in the halls and laundry room— or while in your room with the door open.

LAUNDRY ROOM The laundry room is open for use by emergency housing guests from 4:00 P.M. to 9:00 P.M. Please do not start washing clothes after 7:30 P.M. as you will not have time to finish by 9:00 P.M.

We ask your cooperation in following the above rules so we may all have a pleasant place to live and work. THANK YOU and we wish you the best of luck and a safe, happy stay at the House of Charity.

*

APPENDIX II: HANDOUT: SUMMARY OF HENNEPIN COUNTY'S "BUS TICKET HOME" POLICY[131]

In a nutshell, the policy requires all applicants to verify a residence address within Hennepin County. If the person can verify their address they are entitled to the usual monthly cash grant. If the person cannot verify, they cannot get a cash grant during their initial 30-day entitlement period. Instead, they will be offered a voucher for food and shelter or a bus ticket.

1. Those Affected:
The policy applies to all applicants for GA [General Assistance] and WR [Work Readiness], effective October 3rd. This includes reapplicants (i.e., those who had been disqualified from WR for 2 months and who reapplied after October 3rd.)

2. Address Verification:
A residence address can be verified in one of two ways:

(a.) by providing a lease, mortgage statement or shelter verification form completed by the landlord/caretaker of an apartment building.

(b.) by providing two items out of a list which includes:

(1.) Minnesota drivers license or permit

---

[131] This handout was given to me sometime later and was dated October 14, 1988. Source unknown.

(2.) Minnesota state ID card

(3.) Postmarked mail (of any kind) addressed to and received by the applicant at the address

(4.) Voter registration card

(5.) A written statement from a roommate verifying that the applicant lives there and the date s/he moved in (the roommate will also need to provide verification that s/he lives at the residence.)

NOTE: Those applicants who had a "30-day slot" in a private shelter (those slots exist at St. Stephen's Shelter, Our Savior's, and Harbor Lights Chapel) can verify a residence address by having the shelter complete a shelter verification form. Those shelter guests who are in these shelters on the "nightly lottery system" are considered NPA [no permanent address].

3. Inability to Verify an Address:
If an applicant is unable to verify a residence address the county is to offer a voucher for 30 days' food and shelter or a bus ticket elsewhere.

(a.) 30 days' food and shelter
If a person chooses this option, the County will give them a shelter voucher on a weekly basis. PSP [People Serving People], Harbor Lights, Pursuit, and the 410 will be the usual board and lodging providers. Other room and board facilities with extra bed space can be used as well. The County will also issue a weekly voucher for personal needs ($1.50 x 30 days = $45.00) to a grocery store, K-Mart, Target, etc.

If an applicant finds an affordable residence address during the initial 30-day period, the County will use the remaining GA grant (applicants are eligible for a cash grant during the initial 30-day period from the date their address is verified) and EGA [emergency general assistance] to help pay the rent and any damage deposit.

<u>The initial month's rent must be vendored to the landlord.</u>

(b.) <u>Bus Tickets</u>
If a person chooses this option they can get a one-way bus ticket to their place of origin <u>or anywhere else</u> as long as the cost of the ticket and meals doesn't exceed $203 (the County can issue a $2.50 per person per meal food voucher with the ticket). The person does not need to verify that they will have a means of support where s/he is going.

The County will try and issue a bus ticket on a same-day basis whenever possible to save on the use of shelter beds.

If a person makes a second request for a bus ticket (it's unclear if this means just within the 30 days or any second request) the County will require verification of a means of support at the destination as well as supervisory approval before another ticket will be given.

WHAT HAPPENS AFTER 30 DAYS? After the initial 30-day entitlement period, applicants are eligible for a cash grant and must be told that by the County. If the applicant is in the Demo Project,* their cash grant will be issued on a weekly basis until a residence address is verified.

*This distinction between Demo Project participants and others may soon become meaningless. Hennepin County has asked DHS to approve expanding the Demo Project to 100% (presently it's 20%) of GA/WR applicants and recipients. If that happens, all applicants and recipients can only be issued weekly cash grants until they verify a residence address.

✳

APPENDIX III: MY SCHEDULE OF ESSENTIAL PHONE CALLS AND APPOINTMENTS

- **Phone and visit younger child.** I went to see my younger child every other afternoon (e.g. the alternate days were his father's visiting time). That meant seven visits in fourteen days for three hours each plus two hours travel time for each visit. I telephoned to my younger child on the days I could not visit. That meant at least seven calls in 14 days. Calls were only put through at certain times of the day, e.g. 2 p.m. and 7 p.m.

- **Phone my older child.** On Tuesdays between 7 p.m. and 8 p.m., the court helped arrange phone visitation for me with my older child. The call was generally intercepted by his father but I continued to attempt to make phone contact with my older child anyway. In-person visits with my older child were sporadic, as the court orders had been less specific and his father was not cooperative.

- **Phone and meet doctor.** At the doctor's request, I called the primary physician and the specialist for progress report, consultation, and set time(s) of next appointment(s). That meant one call and one visit with each doctor per week. Calls were only put through at certain times of day. Even at those times, I was often asked to call back later. That meant a minimum of five calls and five meetings in fourteen days. Meetings lasted ½ to 1 hour and travel time was two hours each.

- **Phone and meet lawyer.** I had to check by phone every weekday morning at 8 a.m. with my Legal Aid attorney and meet with her twice a week at 9 a.m. for up to an hour, resulting in five calls and three meetings every week— sometimes Saturdays, too.

- **Phone county caseworker.** Hennepin County brought suit against my children's father. Usually one call completed every other day, it took three calls to make the contact. Generally there were three meetings per week; average time for meetings was 20 minutes per meeting after one to three hours waiting in the lobby (despite having an appointment) plus 20 minutes travel time.

- **Phone Guardian Ad Litem**. My younger son was granted a Guardian Ad Litem, a trained volunteer advocate, to look out for his rights and his interests in the court process. During this period, I had one phone contact or one meeting per week with the first Guardian Ad Litem.

- **Phone Public Defender**. My younger son's attorney was the Public Defender— technically appointed as an advisor to the Guardian Ad Litem— to assist the Guardian to advocate more effectively. This meant at least one call a week to, and often one meeting with, the Public Defender each week: Total time: about one hour per week.

- **Report to Minnesota Unemployment Office.** I had to check in with Minnesota's Unemployment office every Thursday at 1 p.m., and then return on Friday at 9 a.m., to preserve my claim and keep my right to receive the backlogged checks when I returned to Pennsylvania: average time in line seven hours.

- **Report to caseworker at Brother DePaul's House of Charity for each of the following:**

  □ Renew weekly shelter slot. 1 meeting per week, wait in line every Thursday averages 5½ hours.

  □ Receive extension of curfew to be able to work evenings. One meeting per week, average wait in line two hours on a Monday morning.

  □ Wait to get into main door. Daily usually at 4:30 p.m. The wait in line to be let into the shelter averages 1½ hours.

  □ Borrow key to get into room. The wait in line averages 15 minutes.

  □ Return key after unlocking the door. The wait in line averages 10 minutes.

  □ Line to receive dinner bag. The wait in line for cold dinner of stale vending machine food in a bag averages one hour.

- **Report to Catholic Social Services caseworker for the following:**

  □ Apply for Jet Pass Voucher. One meeting per month to get on the list to apply for a Jet Pass Voucher and one meeting per month to submit the voucher to obtain the pass itself. Each wait in line averages two hours each.

  □ Apply for a haircut voucher. One meeting every six weeks to get a haircut pass. The wait averages two hours.

  □ Apply for Special Need Housing Extension recertification. One meeting a month to get recertified for a special extension on my House of Charity room. Each wait in line averages two hours.

- **Check with Post Office.** I checked twice a week to see if my Post Office box had been approved. The wait in line averaged 15 minutes to get this meeting, and a brisk round-trip walk of ½-hour.

- **Appointments with medical and dental clinics** for myself as indicated in the vignettes. Average time in waiting room was two hours per visit.

- **Report to Manpower, Inc., for work opportunities:**

  □ To request work. I made one telephone call or one in-person visit daily at 8 a.m.

  □ To turn in Timesheet. I made one visit a week.

  □ To pick up check. I made one visit a week. Each wait averaged ½ hour for a ten-minute exchange.

- **Breakfast and lunch at the Food Centre:**

  □ Breakfast: Report to the Food Centre at 8 a.m. The wait in line was 45 minutes to 1 hour.

  □ Lunch: Report at 12 noon precisely. The wait in line averaged 45 minutes.

- **Temporary day job assignment.** I reported to a bank and worked 7:30 a.m. to 5 p.m. as many full days as possible, except every other afternoon was reserved to visit my son.

- **Temporary evening job assignment.** I generally worked 3 evenings each week, reporting to the bank at 5 p.m. and working until 11 pm.

- **Public library** (Optional). I went to the public library when I was not working or otherwise committed, often several times a week, especially Saturdays. The wait for it to open in the morning averaged ½ hour.

- **Daily Mass** (Optional). No wait in line. Daily Masses at St. Olaf's were offered at 7 a.m., 8:10 a.m., 12 noon, and/or 5:10 p.m. I usually attended the 8:10 a.m. as soon as I was finished checking in with Manpower at 7:30 a.m.

Summary: 22 "Productive" hours per week in actual contacts. More than 27¾ non-productive hours per week standing in line. More than 22 hours travel time per week (mostly on foot). Average 18 hours per week part-time temporary day and evening work for wages, over the 2½ month period.

Total hours required per week: 89¾ hr./wk. Add to that the time I spend doing volunteer work (4/wk.) helping with a Food Pantry Volunteers' Manual for Catholic Social Services.

✻

APPENDIX IV: LOSSES I SUSTAINED BEFORE ARRIVAL AT HOUSE OF CHARITY

THE LOSS OF EVERYDAYNESS OF RELATIONSHIP WITH MY CHILDREN
- Loss of unimpeded opportunity to talk with my children
- Loss of my children's presence
- Loss of their childhood

LOSS OF PERSONAL LIBERTY AND FREEDOM
- Loss of geographical home base
- Loss of status and power
- Loss of most control of my personal schedule
- Loss of normal routine

- Loss of income
- Lost of personal safety

LOSS OF SUPPORT SYSTEM
- Loss of some friends, impaired relationship with other friends
- Loss of community
- Loss of most family ties with my family of origin

LOSS OF ALMOST ALL POSSESSIONS (OF A LIFETIME)
- Loss of homestead and mountain land.
- Heirlooms, antiques, jewelry, tools, canoes.

After processing and trying to resolve my feelings about the losses I already was experiencing before I came to the House of Charity, I realize I have had a lot of additional losses as a result of being on the street, but it is hard to separate how much of the diminished vitality was also from the distress of years of court, being subjected to stalking, and harassment.

LOSS OF PERSONAL FREEDOM AND LIBERTY
- Temporary loss of work that was meaningful to me
- Loss of mobility
- Loss of normal routine and familiar activities
- Temporary loss of choices of food
- Increased loss of appropriate control over personal schedule
- Loss of time
- Loss of respect
- Loss of freedom to travel and live outside of Minnesota
- Loss of the opportunity for restorative recreation
- Loss of access to telephones
- Loss of assured access to bathrooms
- Loss of access to places to sit down
- Loss of income
- Loss of uses of money

FURTHER LOSS OF SUPPORT SYSTEM
- Diminishment of some close personal friendships and companionships due to distance and circumstances
- Loss of a home base from which to operate
- Loss of beauty in my immediate environment
- Loss of beautiful restorative pastoral scenery
- Temporary lack of familiar comforts, e.g. a favorite pillow, quilt, etc.

LOSS OF VITALITY FOR SEVERAL YEARS
- Diminished capacity to visualize what the future would be
- Loss of physical well-being and health
- Diminished capacity for joy and delight
- Loss of ease and comfort in normal social interactions
- Lowered energy level

*

APPENDIX V: NORMAL GRIEF REACTIONS[132]

When people are suddenly displaced from home, job, life-style, loved-ones, and other ties, grief occurs spiritually, physically, and mentally in our hearts, minds, and bodies. Most Street People have suffered enormous losses, and these losses take their tole on the individual. Social service workers and volunteers are rarely aware that in addition to the burden of seeking resources and trying to adjust to making a new life, the Street Person often has to work through unresolved grief which may manifest itself in many ways including anger, saddness, depression, exhaustion, despondency, hopelessness, anxiety, compulsive busy-ness, and/or flattened affect (shutting out of emotions, speaking in a monotone).

---

[132] Adapted from a flyer distributed by Ed Holland, Chaplain, Methodist Hospital Pastoral Care Office, St. Louis Park, MN entitled "Loss & Grief." "Loss & Grief: Normal Reactions" *Communications Lifeline* (Minneapolis, MCDONOUGH CONSULTING, July 1988) vol. 2, no. 10.

Here is a partial list common symptoms people experience with any significant loss or grief:

- Feel tightness in the throat or heaviness in the chest.

- Have an empty feeling in the stomach and lose appetite.

- Feel guilty at times, and angry at others.

- Feel restless and look for activity, but find it difficult to concentrate.

- Feel as though the loss isn't real, that it didn't actually happen.

- Sense the loved one's presence, like finding one's self expecting the person to walk in the door at the usual time, hearing their voice, or seeing their face. [I was in pain every time I saw the school bus stop to let kids off.]

- Wander aimlessly and forget and don't finish things they've started to do around the house.

- Have difficulty sleeping, and dream of their loved one frequently.

- Experience an intense preoccupation with the life of the person lost.

- Assume mannerisms or traits of their loved one.

- Feel guilty or angry over things that happened or didn't happen in the relationship with the person lost.

- Feel intensely angry at the loved one for leaving them.

- Feel as though they need to take care of other people who seem uncomfortable around them, by politely not talking about the feelings of loss.

- Need to tell and retell and remember things about the loved one and the experience of their death (loss).

- Feel their mood changes over the slightest things.

- Cry at unexpected times.

All these are natural and normal grief responses.   It is important to cry when you need to, and to talk to supportive people about your loss.

✲

APPENDIX VI: SELF-CARE WHILE IN GRIEF

The following information about dealing with grief was helpful, especially around holidays. It was adapted from a handout *Toward Easing Grief*[133]

1.   Apply cold to your body, if you're feeling helpless, hopeless, lethargic, depressed.

2.   Apply heat to your body if you feel anxious, agitated, tense, hyperactive, or have insomnia.

3.   Engage in a brief period of vigorous exercise every day.

---

[133] Anon., "Toward Easing Grief," *Communications Lifeline* (Minneapolis: MCDONOUGH CONSULTING, March 1, 1989).

4. The skin is the body's largest organ and needs constant nourishment in the form of touch, hugs, cuddles, or massage.

5. Don't isolate yourself, even if you feel like it. Get with people. Find supportive people.

6. Schedule a daily alone-time to "get it all together."

7. Avoid exhaustion, loss of sleep, and overwork.

8. Eat regular, nourishing meals.

9. Avoid remorse.

10. Avoid people who take your energy down or who are "not safe" at this time.

11. Because your short-term memory may be affected, keep yourself organized by making lists of even simple things.

12. Know your new limits and pace yourself accordingly.

13. Accept yourself.

14. Tell others how you want them to comfort you during your feelings of sadness.

15. Choose a time before (any) holidays to implode— to allow all the memories and feelings to come into awareness and wash through your body, mind and spirit.

16. Consider structuring a time for your family to share with you their memories and feelings regarding past holidays.

17. If being with your family is stressful, make plans in advance so that the amount of time you are with them is limited.   Make plans ahead of time to have someplace to go so that before you have "had enough of them" you can excuse yourself to go to your other plans (even if the plan is as simple as to go home and take a nap).

18. Re-evaluate your (family) rituals for any upcoming holiday and make the rituals fit your current needs. Discuss what your needs are to make the coming holiday significant, and what things are too draining to be worthwhile any longer. There will never be new traditions without trying them out the first time.

19. Be gentle with yourself and those around you.

Holidays are often a difficult time for a person experiencing grief. This may be because there is such a disparity between what some holiday messages say "we should feel" versus "what is" the present experience. Past holidays are also times our memory bank can recall with ease, so memories of holidays past flood our present and do not let us deny our real feelings of grief.

Grief is hard work, especially during holidays when there is so much to do. If you take control of how you grieve, you may find it easier to bear. The above suggestions may help you toward a better holiday and a beginning realization that different does not have to mean diminished.

*

APPENDIX VII: TALKING BACK TO BACK PAIN[134]

Many people experience body aches of one kind or another. Often we know the cause of the pain. At other times the pain is real but the cause is non-specific. In dealing with physical pain, psychiatrists at the National Institutes of Health ("NIH"), Bethesda, MD, have confirmed in a new way that words have power. At the NIH psychiatrists there were conducting research in galvanic skin responses to verbal stimuli. They noticed that when certain words came up, people tensed and had galvanic skin responses— such as increases in pulse, tension, skin and body temperature. They noticed that certain words alone produced tension. They called these words *hot words*.

After pondering this for some time, they began to wonder if the opposite might also be true. If there are *hot words*, are there also *cool words*? In a test of 60 people, what they found was that certain phrases were cool, but which cool words caused a response differed by person and by body part.

When pain is located in the front half of the body, 80% got release and the pain disappeared by saying "I can." The other 20% of the persons found release and the pain disappeared when saying: "I can't."

Back pain is viewed as a headache of the body. When pain is located in the lower back, 80% were released from pain by saying the words: "I don't have to," or "I can, but I don't have to."

When pain was being experienced as general overall pain, most found relief by saying: "I don't like it."

Other words and phrases that resulted in release from generalized pain were: "I don't want it" or "I want it."

Generalized tension was released for most by saying: "I don't know what I want and need." Eighty percent found release by

---

[134] "One Way to Release Backpain," Pat McDonough, newsletter *Communications Lifeline*, vol. 4, no. 1, (Minneapolis: MCDONOUGH CONSULTING, August 13, 1990), pp. 1-2. The original article is based on Pat McDonough's notes from a lecture by Sister Mary Sharon Riley at an "Effective Living Seminar" at The Cenacle Retreat House, Wayzata, MN, March 22, 1987.

saying "I don't like it, but I'll do it." Twenty percent found best results from saying "I like it."

When the pain was due to a climate of moods created by and controlled by others, most found release by saying: "I don't want it."

In saying the words, most people experienced the greatest release of tension by taking an affirmative position but not trying to relax. It worked best to focus on the specific area of the body where the tension was most severe, for example, the right side of the back. To determine what phrases are best for you, test the following phrases and be aware of the response. Pause between phrases to observe the response: "I can."

"I can't."

"I like it."

"I don't like it."

"I want it."

"I don't want it."

"I have to."

"I don't have to."

When you identify the phrase which works for you, repeat the phrase until the physical tension has left that spot. If you are in a highly charged environment, such as working in a hospital surgery, a secretarial pool, or an air-traffic control center, you may need to do the exercise several times. This is especially true if your body has accumulated a whole history of stored tension. To do this exercise at work, you may need a quiet place to carry it out, such as the supply closet, or the lavatory.

After completing this exercise, it is also useful to substitute some positive affirmation(s) around this, such as: "I discern and embrace the best course for all concerned. I will be open to discovering another way."

*

APPENDIX VIII: THE CORPORAL WORKS OF MERCY[135]

(1.) Feed the hungry.
(2.) Give drink to the thirsty.
(3.) Clothe the naked.
(4.) Shelter the homeless.
(5.) Comfort the imprisoned.
(6.) Visit the sick.
(7.) Bury the dead.

*

APPENDIX IX: THE SPIRITUAL WORKS OF MERCY[136]

(1.) Admonish sinners.
(2.) Instruct the uninformed.
(3.) Counsel the doubtful.
(4)   Comfort the sorrowful.
(5.) Be patient with those in error.
(6.) Forgive offenses.
(7.) Pray for the living and the dead.

*

---

[135] Listed on the inside front cover of *The Divine Mercy Message and Devotion: with Selected Prayers from the Diary of Blessed Faustina*. Stockbridge, MA: Marian Helpers Press, 1993.)

[136] *Ibid.*

BIBLIOGRAPHY

BOOKS AND PUBLICATIONS

American Psychiatric Association. *Diagnostic and Statistical Manual of Mental Disorders*, 3rd edn. revised, DSM-III-R. Washington, D.C.: American Psychiatric Association, 1987.

_____. *Diagnostic and Statistical Manual of Mental Disorders*, 4th edn., DSM-IV™. Washington, D.C.: American Psychiatric Association, 1994.

Amherst H. Wilder Foundation. *Results of the Twin Cities Survey of Emergency Shelter Residents February 23, 1989*. St. Paul: Wilder Research, 1989.

Author unknown. Quotation appearing on CELESTIAL SEASONINGS™ Tea box #891221/6B

_____. "Differences in Intermediary Metabolism in Mental Illness." *Psychological Reports* 17: 563.582, 1965.

_____. Memo: "Bus Ticket Home" reprinted as "Summary of Hennepin County's Bus Ticket Home' Policy," a handout. October 14, 1988.

_____. The Corporal and Spiritual Works of Mercy, reprinted in *The Divine Mercy Message and Devotion: With Selected Prayers from the Diary of Blessed Faustina*. Stockbridge, MN: Marian Helpers Press, 1933.

_____. *New St. Joseph Weekday Missal Complete Edition, Vol. I: Advent to Pentecost*. New York:Catholic Book Publishing Co., 1975.

The Bible

Binford, Shari M., Siegel, Mark A., and Landes, Alison, eds. *Homeless: Struggling to Survive*. Wylie TX: Information Plus, 1991.

Bossis, Gabrielle. *He & I*. Sherbrooke, Quebec: Editions Paulines, c. 1969.

Brunswick, Mark. "How Far Should Government Go to Help the Homeless?: Debate Stirred Over Policy of Renting Motel Rooms." *Minneapolis Star-Tribune*, May 29, 1995, p. O1B.

Byrns, Ralph T. and Stone, Gerald W. *Economics* 5th edn. New York: Harper Collins Publishers, 1992.

Cameron, Julia. *The Artist's Way: A Spiritual Path to Higher Creativity*. New York: G. P. Putnam & Sons, 1992.

Caruso, Igor A. *Pschonalyse und Syntheses der Existenz*. Vienna: Herder, 1952.

Catholic Book Publishing Company. *New St. Joseph Weekday Missal, Complete Edition: Vol. I—Advent to Pentecost.* New York: Catholic Book Publishing Company, 1975.

Ciszek, Walter J. *He Leadeth Me.* New York: Doubleday, 1973.

_____ with Flaherty, Daniel L. *With God in Russia.* New York: Doubleday Image Books, 1966.

Corey, Gerald. *Theory and Practice of Counseling and Psychotherapy* 3rd ed. Monterey CA: Brooks/Cole Publishing Company, 1986.

Craig, Mary. *Blessings: An Autobiographical Fragment,* 1st US edn. New York: Morrow Publishers, 1979.

Davis, Adelle. *Let's Get Well.* Bergenfield, NJ: New American Library, 1972.

Drews, Toby Rice. *Getting Them Sober: A Guide for Those Who Live With an Alcoholic.* Vol. I. South Plainfield, NJ: Bridge Publishing, 1980.

Edelwich, Jerry, and Brodsky, Archie. *Burn-out: Stages of Disillusionment in the Helping Professions.* New York: Human Sciences Press, 1980.

Egan, Gerard. *The Skilled Helper: Model, Skills, and Methods for Effective Helping* 2nd ed. Monterey CA: Brooks/Cole Publishing Company, 1982.

Fantasia, Rick, and Isserman, Maurice. *Homelessness: A Sourcebook.* New York: Facts on File®, 1994.

Flynn, D., and Bazzell, W., Wagner, Mathew J. (eds.) Psychiatric Aspects of Abnormal Movement Disorders. In: Wagner, Matthew J. (ed.), *Brain Research Bulletin* 2(2): 238, 1983.

Frankl, Viktor E. *Man's Search for Meaning: An Introduction to Logotherapy.* New York: Simon & Schuster Pocket Books, 1982.

Franklin, Robert. "Domestic Abuse: State Shelters for Battered Women are in Big Demand and Short Supply." *Minneapolis Star-Tribune,* 10/19/95, p. 3B.

Friedman, Milton. *Unemployment Versus Inflation?: an Evaluation of the Phillips Curve.* With a British Commentary: The end of demand management, how to reduce unemployment in the late 1970s by David E. W. Laidler (IEA lecture). London: Institute of Economic Affairs, 1975, H11, I47, no. 44

Frost, Robert, "The Death of the Hired Man" (poem), *A Pocketbook of Robert Frost's Poems With An Introduction and Commentary by Louis Untermeyer.* New York: Washington Square Press, 1960.

Griffin, John Harry. *Black Like Me.* New York: Penguin Books USA, 1960.

Grow, Doug. "Finding a Sanctuary of Peace and Strength on Franklin Avenue: Amid Love and Song Lloyd Leeper is Moving on— With a Chorus of Friends by His Side." *Minneapolis Star-Tribune,* November 24, 1995, p. 2B.

Hombs, Mary Ellen. *American HOMELESSNESS: A Reference Handbook, 2nd edn.* Santa Barbara, CA: ABL-CLIO, Inc., 1994.

House of Charity. "Rules for Emergency Housing Guests" 12/22/83.

Issellbacher, K. (ed.) *Harrison's Principles of Internal Medicine (13th edn.)*. NY: McGraw-Hill, Inc., 1994.

Izengar, Smriti, and Rabil, Jamshid: "Role of Serotonin Estrogen-progesterone Induced Lutenizing Hormone Release in Ovarectomized Rats." *Brain Research Bulletin* 10:342, 1983.

Jung, G. "On Criticism" (attributed to).

Keillor, Garrison quotation. "Prairie Home Companion" Minnesota Public Radio series.

Kulman, Jonee, McCormack, Teresa, Grebner, Dennis, and Van Dyne, Judith. *The Search for Shelter: Architects and the Community Working Together to House the Homeless, Design Charrettes 1990-1991* Minneapolis: Minneapolis Chapter of the American Institute of Architects, 1991.

Lair, Jesse *"I Ain't Well, But I Sure Am Better": Mutual Need Therapy.* Garden City, NY: Doubleday & Company, Inc., 1975.

_____. *"I Don't Know Where I'm Going But I Sure Ain't Lost.* New York: Ballantine Books, 1981.

Lawson, Gary W., and Lawson, Ann W. *Alcoholism & Substance Abuses in Special Populations.* Rockville, MD: Aspen Publishers, Inc. 1989.

Lindbergh, Anne Morrow. *Gift from the Sea.* New York: Pantheon Books, 1975.

Maslow, A. H. *Motivation and Personality.* New York: Harper & Brothers, 1954.

_____. *Toward a Psychology of Being*, 2nd edn. New York: Van Nostrand Reinhold, 1968.

McDonough, Patricia A. "Loss and Grief: Normal Reactions" *Communications Lifeline.* Minneapolis: McDONOUGH CONSULTING, 2(10) July, 1988. Adapted from a handout entitled "Loss and Grief" distributed by Ed Holland, Methodist Hospital Pastoral Care Office, St. Louis Park, MN.

_____. "Non-Traditional Sources of Cash," *Ten Neighborhoods Needs Assessments.* St. Paul: Common Profits, Inc., May, 1989.

_____. "Peace of Christ Handshake" *St. Paul Catholic Bulletins*, 74(15) p.3B. 4/12/84

_____. "Pat's Psalm" 1984.

_____. "Our Father of the Street." 1984.

_____. "Talking Back to Back Pain" *Communications Lifeline.* Minneapolis: McDONOUGH CONSULTING 4(1) August, 1990.

_____. "Toward Easing Grief," *Communications Lifeline.* Minneapolis: McDONOUGH CONSULTING, 3(3) March 1, 1989. Adapted from a handout with no source indicated.

Metropolitan Council. *A Target Population Report: Homelessness* December 1986, in Appendix IX-C from Nancy K. Kaufman, "Homelessness: A Continuum of Services" Executive Office of Human Services, Commonwealth of Massachusetts. November, 1985.

Michalenko, Seraphim, and Flynn, Vinny. *The Divine Mercy Message and Devotion: with Selected Prayers from the Diary of Blessed Faustina.* Stockbridge, MA: Marian Helpers, 1993.

Milton, John. Sonnet XIX, *The Poems of John Milton*, 2nd edn. New York: The Ronald Press Co., 1953.

Minnesota Act Up and Out of Poverty. "Facts on Homeless Youth in Minnesota," 7/10/91.

Minnesota Coalition for the Homeless. "State Survey" 8/30/88.

Minnesota State Planning Agency. *Homelessness in Minnesota.* St. Paul, 2/1988.

Mitchell, John Hanson. *Ceremonial Time: Fifteen Thousand Years on One Square Mile.* New York: Warner Books, 1984.

Newman, B. M., & Newman, P. R. *Development Through Life: A Psychosocial Approach* rev. ed. Homewood, IL: Dorsey Press. 1979.

Nietzsche, Friedrich. *The Portable Nietzsche: Selected and Translated, with an Introduction, Prefaces, and Notes by Walter Kaufmann.* New York: Viking Penguin, Inc. 1982.

Peers, E. Allison. "Introduction by Thomas Merton to Counsels of Light and Love by St. John of the Cross," in *THE COMPLETE WORKS OF ST JOHN OF THE CROSS.* New York: Paulist Press, 1978.

Pheiffer, Carl C., and the Publications Committee of the Brain-Bio Center. "Mental and Elemental Nutrients," *A Physicians Guide to Nutrition and Health Care.* New Canaan, CT: Keats Publishing, Inc., 1975.

Rubin, Theodore J. with Eleanor Rubin. *Compassion & Self Hate: An Alternative to Despair.* New York: David McKay Co., Inc., 1975.

Rubington, E., "The Changing Skid Row Scene," *Quarterly Journal of Studies on Alcohol* 32, p. 127.

Ryan, Patricia M. "Pockets." *IMAGES: Women in Transition* compiled by Janice Grana. Winona, MN: St. Mary's College Press, 1977.

St. Teresa of Avila (attributed source).

Shapiro, Isaac, and Greensteen, Robert. "Holes in the Safety Nets: Poverty Programs and Policies" *The States: Minnesota, a State Analysis.* Washington, D.C.: Center on Budget and Policy Priorities. Spring, 1988.

Sheehy, Gail. *Spirit of Survival.* New York: William Morrow & Co., Inc., 1986.

Taylor, Kimberly Hayes. "These Kids Can't Go Home." *Minneapolis Star-Tribune,* November 23, 1995, p. 1B.

ten Boom, Corrie, with John & Elizabeth Sherrill. *The Hiding Place.* Old Tappan, NJ: Fleming H. Revell Company, 1971.

Tournier, Paul. *The Meaning of Persons.* New York: Harper & Row, 1973.

Two hospital studies on Sprouting and Nutrition in India. Seattle: University of Washington, c. 1984.

U.S. Conference of Mayors (attributed source), "Profile of U.S. Homeless." *St. Paul Pioneer Press,* 12/20/90 A10.

USDA. *Agricultural Handbook #8 and Garden Bulletin #72*. Washington, D.C.: USDA, 1963.

U.S. General Accounting Office. *Homelessness: Too Early to Tell What Kinds of Prevention Assistance Work Best*. Washington, DC: Government Printing Office, 1990. GAO/RCED-90-89.

Vine, Phyllis. *Families in Pain: Children, Siblings, Spouses, and Parents of Mentally Ill Speak Out*, New York: Random House, 1982.

Wadell, Helen. *Vitae Patrum. The Desert Fathers: Translations from the Latin*. Ann Arbor: University of Michigan Press, 1957.

Watson, George. "Psychochemical Test" *Nutrition and Your Mind*. New York: Harper & Row, Inc., 1972.

OTHER MEDIA

Sharon Sayles Belton (Mayor of Minneapolis), guest on "Gary Eichten's Midday Show" (KNOW), March 21, 1996, audio transcript of call-in and interview.

Richard Guindon. "STUDENT IDENTIFICATION" card for the National Bag Lady Academy.

Kris Kristopherson, "Me and Bobby McGee." Combine Music Corp., EMI Music Publishing, 810 7th Av, NY, NY 10019.

John Newton. "Amazing Grace" (ascribed to Sir John Ries).

U S WEST Direct Map of the Minneapolis Skyway System, *Yellow Pages*, Minneapolis, 1990.

Video transcript "Change of Heart," 1996, courtesy of Mystic Fire Video, Inc. (800) 292-9001

Tom Wilson, Ziggy Cartoon: *In case of emergency. . .* which appeared in a desktop calendar. Reprinted by permission of Universal Press Syndicate.

Rick Young, "The Crystal Court, IDS Center, Minneapolis, MN" Photograph reproduced as a Postcard published by NMN, Inc, Crosslake, MN.

PERMISSIONS ACKNOWLEDGEMENTS

Sharon Sayles Belton, text from transcript of radio call-in show on KNOW March 21, 1996. Reprinted courtesy of Mayor Sharon Sayles Belton.

Shari M. Binford, Mark A. Siegel, and Alsion Landes, eds. *Homeless: Struggling to Survive*, pp. 6. 10-11. Copyright © 1991 by Information Plus, Wylie TX. Reprinted by permission of the publisher.

Brunswick, Mark. "How Far Should Government Go to Help the Homeless?: Debate Stirred Over Policy of Renting Motel Rooms." *Minneapolis Star-Tribune*. Reprinted by permission of the Minneapolis Star-Tribune.

From the House of Charity, Minneapolis, MN— Winter 1983-84. Reprinted by permission of Catholic Charities of Minneapolis.

From *Theory and Practice of Counseling and Psychotherapy* by Gerald Corey. Copyright © 1991, 1986, 1982, 1977 Brooks/Cole Publishing Company, Pacific Grove CA 93950, a division of International Thomson Publishing Inc. By permission of the publisher.

Jerry Edelwich and Archie Brodsky, *Burn-out: Stages of Disillusionment in the Helping Professions*. Copyright © 1980 by Human Sciences Press. Reprinted by permission of Plenum Publishing.

Gerard Egan, *The Skilled Helper: Model, Skills, and Methods for Effective Helping* 2nd ed. Copyright © 1982 by Brooks/Cole Publishing Company.

Franklin, Robert. "Domestic Abuse: State Shelters for Battered Women are in Big Demand and Short Supply." *Minneapolis Star-Tribune*. Reprinted by permission of the Minneapolis Star-Tribune.

Richard Guindon. "STUDENT IDENTIFICATION" card for the National Bag Lady Academy. Copyright © 1985 by Richard Guindon and reprinted with his permission.

Jonee Kulman, Teresa McCormack, Dennis Grebner, and Judith Van Dyne, *The Search for Shelter: Architects and the Community Working Together to House the Homeless, Design Charrettes 1990-1991*. Copyright © 1991 by the publisher the Minneapolis Chapter of the American Institute of Architects, and reprinted by permission of the publisher.

Carl C. Pheiffer and the Publications Committee of the Brain-Bio Center. Copyright © 1968 by Keats Publishing, Inc., pp. 163-164. Reprinted by permission of the publisher.

Patricia M. Ryan, "Pockets". Copyright © 1977 by St. Mary's College Press, Winona, MN. Reprinted by permission of St. Mary's College Press.

Taylor, Kimberly Hayes. "These Kids Can't Go Home." *Minneapolis Star-Tribune*. Reprinted by permission of the Minneapolis Star-Tribune.

INDEX

ABOUT THE ARTIST

The original art for *Without Keys* was created by R. Padre Johnson. The cover is an etching-in-oil technique providing a rare pastel-oil image. The 14 drawings in the body of the book were created with pencil and charcoal. Padre Johnson's distinctive talent is to skillfully capture not only the features of an individual, but also depict the spirit and emotion that makes up the totality of the person or character. Each face incorporates more than an individual, it speaks to an entire range of people that occupy this particular cultural ground.

Recently during the International Year of the Human Family, Padre was honored by the United Nations and the Canadian government for the contributions his work has made to understanding of the world human family. He uses portrait art as an instrument of interpretation.

In his most famous book *Journeys with the Global Family*, renders his global philosophical insights in art and prose. To complete that particular project, over a 15-year period he lived with the people who occupied the family and cultural space within the territories of 159 nations. For the *Journeys* book, he painted 500 faces on 25 different canvases representing the racial, ethnic and national origins of the entire world human family by country and continent.

Initially he began his successful and distinguished art career as painter of Western Art and Wildlife Art. He has had the good fortune of receiving many international awards for his art.

ORDERING INFORMATION

For additional copies of this book, contact your local bookseller, or the publisher at the address below. Other inquiries about the book, art, or availability of the author to Pat McDonough c/o the publisher.

TERRA SANCTA PRESS, INC.   612-988-6999
P. O. Box 576   fax 612-938-5154
Hopkins, MN 55343-0576

ORDERED BY:
Name: Phone _____
Title: Fax _____
Organization:
Street Address:
City/State/ZIP:

SHIP TO:
Name: Phone _____
Title: Fax _____
Organization:
Street Address:
City/State/ZIP:

Please send me the following:

Quantity		Unit Price	Total
__	*Without Keys*		
	0-9653467-0-6 Perfect bound	$24	$
__	*Without Keys*		
	0-9653467-1-4 Hardbound	$42	$
	Subtotal		$
	MN Sales Tax at 6.5%		
	Shipping $4.50 each		_____
	Total		$

MN orders please add 6.5% sales tax.
For quantity orders, call about specific pricing.
Make checks payable to Terra Sancta Press, Inc.